143 Mallard Street, Suite E
Saint Rose, Louisiana 70087
www.kaplanfinancial.com

At press time, this edition contains the most complete and accurate information currently available. Owing to the nature of certification examinations, however, information may have been added recently to the actual test that does not appear in this edition. Please contact the publisher to verify that you have the most current edition.

This publication is designed to provide accurate and authoritative information in regard to the subject matter covered. It is sold with the understanding that the publisher is not engaged in rendering legal, accounting, or other professional services. If legal advice or other expert assistance is required, the services of a competent professional should be sought.

We value your input and suggestions. If you found imperfections in this product, please let us know by sending an email to errata@kaplan.com. Please include the title, edition, and PPN (reorder number) of the material.

KAPLAN REVIEW FOR THE CFP® CERTIFICATION EXAMINATION, VOLUME VI: ESTATE PLANNING, 11TH EDITION ©2007 DF Institute, Inc. All rights reserved.

Published by DF Institute, Inc.

Printed in the United States of America.

ISBN: 1-4195-9950-X

PPN: 4302-4702

07	08	10	9	8	7	6	5	4	3	2	1
J	F	**M**	A	M	J	J	A	S	O	N	D

If found, please notify the following:

Name of CFP® Candidate:_____

Address:_____

City, State, ZIP:_____

Phone:_____

Email: _____

Additional information on review materials and live
instructional review courses near you is available at:

www.kaplanfinancial.com

Please visit our Website regularly
for updates to this and other products.

For answers to your technical questions on the contents of this text, please contact us at:

fpstudent@kaplan.com

PRODUCTS AND SERVICES FOR THE CFP® CERTIFICATION EXAMINATION

KAPLAN FINANCIAL REVIEW COURSES FOR THE CFP® CERTIFICATION EXAMINATION

Kaplan Financial offers several options to meet the diverse needs of candidates—the Live Review Course, which offers both traditional and virtual classrooms, and the Online Review Course.

THE LIVE REVIEW COURSE

Traditional Classroom Program

Kaplan Financial offers the Traditional Classroom Program in over 30 classes in more than 19 states across the country. The Five-Day Review is an intensive program consisting of 38 hours of instruction conducted Wednesdays through Sundays. The Six-Day Review consists of 48 hours of instruction conducted over two (nonconsecutive) weekends, Friday through Sunday. Instruction consists mainly of teaching substantive material and mastering both knowledge and application. The course includes working problems to ensure that the substantive materials taught can be applied to the examlike questions, as well as actual exam-management techniques.

The Virtual Classroom Program

Kaplan Financial's Virtual Review is an instructor-led, Web-based program that provides all the benefits of a classroom review from the convenience of the learner's home or office. This program format is a great option for those who have access to the Web and prefer not to incur the expense of travel. This course is an intensive program consisting of 48 hours of instruction conducted over 17 three-hour sessions held on Mondays, Wednesdays, and Thursdays. Learners receive real-time interaction with the instructor and students and access to a recorded playback option. Playbacks remain active until the first day of the CFP® Certification Examination.

THE ONLINE REVIEW COURSE

For students who have completed the Kaplan University Certificate in Financial Planning, this course provides an extensive review of the concepts covered in our six-course program. The Online Review proceeds through the topics listed by CFP Board, beginning with a detailed outline of each topic to highlight key aspects of the material and concluding with review questions that will help you assess your mastery of each topic. The course also includes a 300-item simulation that can be used by prospective CFP® certificants to prepare for the exam.

VOLUMES I–VI

Volumes I–VI contain complete reference outlines that give detailed coverage of the six tested areas of the CFP® Certification Examination. Each volume contains examples, illustrations, and an index. Combined, the six volumes offer over 1,500 multiple-choice problems to prepare you for the exam. The answers and explanations for each multiple-choice problem are also provided. The answers to the multiple-choice problems are identified by topical categories to assist you in focusing your study efforts. The introduction to each volume presents helpful tips on what to expect when taking the exam, tips for studying, sample study plans, and tips for solving both straight and combination-type multiple-choice problems. The introduction also forecasts the number of questions expected in each area of the exam. Each volume has been updated to reflect law and inflation adjustments through January 2007.

VOLUME VII—CASE BOOK

Volume VII—Case Book provides the exam candidate with 16 comprehensive cases, 40 item sets (minicases), and Cognitive Connection questions. The answers and explanations for each multiple-choice question are provided, and the text has been updated to reflect law and inflation adjustments through January 2007. This text prepares you for the three comprehensive cases given on the exam. Your preparation in this area is extremely important because case questions are weighted more heavily than the general multiple-choice questions. Our students who have used the *Case Book* have said that this book is a must if you want to be prepared for the exam.

VOLUME VIII—MOCK EXAM AND SOLUTIONS

Volume VIII—Mock Exam and Solutions simulates the 10-hour comprehensive CFP® exam. The text is broken up into three mock exams, each containing multiple-choice questions, item sets, and a comprehensive case. This text can serve as a diagnostic tool useful in identifying the areas of strength and weakness in a study plan and can be used to create a unique study program to meet your individual needs. This text is also updated to reflect law and inflation adjustments through January 2007.

UNDERSTANDING YOUR FINANCIAL CALCULATOR

Understanding Your Financial Calculator is designed to assist you in gaining proficiency in using and understanding your financial calculator. In addition to helping master the keystrokes for the financial calculator, it is also designed to assist students with the underlying financial theory problems given on the exam. Being familiar with the financial calculations is critical, because mastering these problems is an important step to passing the exam.

All calculations are worked out step by step, showing keystrokes and displays for five of the most popular financial calculators. These include the HP-17bII, HP-12c, HP-10bII, TI-BAII PLUS, and Sharp EL-733A.

Understanding Your Financial Calculator covers the basic operations of the calculators, basic time value of money calculations, fundamental problems (such as mortgages, education needs analysis, and retirement needs analysis), investment planning concepts, calculations (such as IRR, YTM, YTC, Sharpe, Treynor, Jensen, and standard deviation), and more. This text also includes a student workbook with over 200 basic, intermediate, and advanced practice problems and calculations. This text is a great reference for the exam and for practitioners.

FINANCIAL PLANNING FLASHCARDS

Kaplan Financial's Financial Planning Flashcards were created as a study supplement to *Volumes I–VI* study materials. The Flashcards include over 1,000 cards covering topics in each of the areas on the exam and can help you learn basic concepts and definitions. Flashcards provide an excellent way to learn the material by prompting you to recall facts and information quickly. Their portability makes them a valuable study tool for those on the go.

DRILL & PRACTICE SOFTWARE

Our computerized test bank is an interactive software product including over 1,700 questions taken from *Volumes I-VI*, *Released Cases and Questions*, and additional practice questions written by our authors. The software will allow you to keep score, track your time and progress, and break down your score by sections.

FROM THE PUBLISHER

This text is intended as the basis for preparation for the CFP® Certification Examination (the exam), either as self-study or as part of a review course. The material is organized according to the six functional areas tested on the exam and is presented in an outline format that includes examples with questions and illustrations to help candidates quickly comprehend the material.

We have structured the material into six manageable study units:

- Volume I—*Fundamentals*
- Volume II—*Insurance Planning*
- Volume III—*Investments*
- Volume IV—*Income Tax Planning*
- Volume V—*Retirement Planning*
- Volume VI—*Estate Planning*

The multiple-choice problems and item sets within each volume have been grouped into primary categories that correspond to the major topic headings in the outlines. In addition, the answers also identify more specific topical categories within each study unit.

We are indebted to Certified Financial Planner Board of Standards, Inc. for permission to reproduce and adapt their publications and other materials.

We welcome any comments concerning materials contained in or omitted from this text. Please send your written comments to Kaplan Financial, 143 Mallard Street, Suite E, St. Rose, Louisiana 70087, or fax your comments to us at (504) 461-9860.

Wishing you success on the exam,

Kaplan Financial

ACKNOWLEDGMENTS AND SPECIAL THANKS

We are most appreciative of the tremendous support and encouragement we have received from everyone throughout this project. We are extremely grateful to the users of out texts who were gracious enough to provide us with valuable comments.

We very much appreciate the continued support of the many registered programs who have adopted our Review Materials. We understand that our success is a direct result of that support.

We greatly appreciate the assistance of the following individuals, who reviewed the outlines and problems and solutions for technical accuracy:

- Kathy L. Berlin
- Cindy R. Hart, CLU, ChFC, CFP®
- Lisa Treece Keleher, MS, CFA
- Bobby M. Kosh, AAMS, CFP®
- James J. Pasztor, MS, CFP®
- Joyce Osche Schnur, MBA, CFP®
- Scott A. Wasserman, CPA/PFS, ChFC, RFC, CFP®

We have received so much help from so many people, it is possible that we inadvertently overlooked thanking someone. If so, it is our shortcoming, and we apologize in advance. Please let us know if you are that someone, and we will correct it in our next printing.

We deeply appreciate the cooperation of CFP Board for granting us permission to reproduce and adapt their publications and other materials. CFP Board's Standards of Professional Conduct, copyrighted by CFP Board, is reprinted (or adapted) with permission.

Thanks to John J. Dardis for granting us permission to use material from "Estate & Benefit Planning Symposium" in *Volume VI—Estate Planning*.

INTRODUCTION

Introduction

Volumes I–VI serve as the basis for preparation for the CFP® Certification Examination (the exam) either as self-study materials or as part of a review course. These volumes are organized by the six topic areas tested on the exam. Each volume presents its core content in outline format using examples, questions, and exhibits to help candidates quickly comprehend the material. The core content is followed by multiple-choice questions with answers and rationales provided to test candidates' mastery of the material.

Volumes I–VI cover the following topics:

- Volume I—Fundamentals
- Volume II—Insurance Planning
- Volume III—Investments
- Volume VI—Income Tax Planning
- Volume V—Retirement Planning
- Volume VI—Estate Planning

ABOUT THE CFP® CERTIFICATION EXAMINATION (THE EXAM)

EXAMINATION PROCEDURES

Read carefully the procedures outlined in the *Guide to CFP® Certification*. The section entitled "CFP® Certification Examination" covers:

- dates of examinations;
- alternate test dates and test facilities;
- fees for the examination;
- scheduling confirmations;
- withdrawal from the exam;
- medical emergencies;
- items to bring to the examination;
- examination misconduct;
- examination scoring;
- score reports;
- pass score;
- reexamination procedures; and
- review and appeals.

A copy of the *Guide to CFP® Certification* may be obtained from CFP Board, at the following address:

Certified Financial Planner Board of Standards, Inc.
1670 Broadway, Suite 600
Denver, CO 80202-4809
Telephone: 1-800-487-1497
            1-303-830-7500
Fax: 1-303-860-7388
Website: www.cfp.net
Email: mail@CFPBoard.org

DATE GIVEN

The exam is generally given on the third Friday and Saturday of March, July, and November each year.

Friday (1 session—afternoon)	4 hours
Saturday (2 sessions)	6 hours
Total	**10 hours**

It is the student's responsibility to verify the exam and registration dates, as well as register for the exam.

For updates and information regarding the CFP® Certification Examination, your exam registration, exam application deadlines, and so forth, please refer to CFP Board's Website at **www.cfp.net**.

For updates to Kaplan Financial study materials (e.g., errata, legislative changes, and inflation-adjusted tax rate summaries), please refer to our updates page at **www.bisyseducation.com/products/fp/exam_review/ material_updates.aspx**.

QUESTION TYPES

The examination consists of approximately 285 multiple-choice questions. The majority of these are stand-alone questions that contain all relevant information within the body of a problem. Also included are item set questions where one fact pattern will be used to answer several questions. A portion of the exam is in the form of case analysis. Each session of the exam contains one case with 15–20 questions. The information needed to answer these questions is generally found within the body of the case. These cases can be several pages long, making it difficult to efficiently organize the information to answer the questions.

The stand-alone questions, item sets, and case questions may test only one particular area of financial planning, such as investments. Many of the questions, however, are integrated questions, meaning that more than one topic is covered in the question. For example, a question might integrate investments and taxation. These integrated questions are designed to test your ability to analyze fact situations involving many planning considerations.

DISTRIBUTION OF TOPICS

The topics on the exam are targeted as follows:

Topic Covered	Percentage of the Exam
Fundamentals	11%
Insurance	14%
Investments	19%
Income tax	14%
Employee benefits*	8%
Retirement	19%
Estates	15%
Total	**100%**

* The majority of topics within the employee benefits section are discussed in the retirement section. The remaining topics in employee benefits are discussed in the tax and insurance sections. For an in-depth breakdown of all topics, please refer to the updated topic lists found later in this introduction.

Cognitive Levels Tested (Target)	Percentage of the Exam
Knowledge level	5%
Comprehension/application	35%
Analysis/synthesis/evaluation	60%
Total	**100%**

Scoring Method	Point Value per Question	Approximate Number	Points	Percentage
Stand-alone questions and item sets	2 points	235	470	76%
Case questions	3 points	50	150	24%
Total		**285**	**620**	**100%**

The examination division of CFP Board assigns the value weights to questions according to type, cognitive level, and level of difficulty.

TIME AND TIME ANALYSIS

There are 10 hours of examination time:

- Friday (4 hours)—1 case, item sets, and multiple choice

- Saturday (morning session, 3 hours)—1 case, item sets, and multiple choice

- Saturday (afternoon session, 3 hours)—1 case, item sets, and multiple choice

- Approximately 285 questions overall

- Case questions, 15–20 per case

	Time (minutes)	Approximate Number of Multiple-Choice Questions	Average Time
Average indicated time per stand-alone and item set question	400	235	1.5–1.7 minutes each (Friday and Saturday)
Average indicated time per case question	200	50	4.0 minutes each (Friday and Saturday)
Average indicated time per question	600	285	2.1 minutes each (overall)

You should strive to average 1.5 minutes per question throughout your study of *Volumes I–VI*. The cases and case analyses presented in *Volume VII: Case Book* should provide you with a realistic approximation of exam conditions regarding cases. The case multiple-choice questions should take about 75–90 minutes per set, including reading the case.

PASS RATES

The pass rates have ranged from 42% to 66% on recent exams. This exam is a pass/fail professional exam with no partial credit. Therefore, it is vitally important that you be thoroughly prepared for all the topics covered on this examination.

KAPLAN FINANCIAL'S PASS RATES

The Kaplan Financial Live Instructional Reviews have consistently averaged a 70% to 80% first-time pass rate, which is 20% higher than the national average.

TOPIC LISTS FOR THE CFP® CERTIFICATION EXAMINATION

TOPIC LIST FOR CFP® CERTIFICATION EXAMINATION

The following topics, based on the 2004 Job Analysis Study, are the basis for the CFP® Certification Examinations. Each exam question will be linked to one of the following topics, in the approximate percentages indicated following the general headings. Questions will pertain to all levels in Bloom's taxonomy with an emphasis on the higher cognitive levels. Questions often will be asked in the context of the financial planning process and presented in an integrative format.

In addition to being used for the CFP® Certification Examination, this list indicates topic coverage requirements to fulfill the pre-certification educational requirement. Continuing education (CE) programs and materials that address these topics will be eligible for CFP Board CE credit.

(References to sections (§) in this list refer to sections of the Internal Revenue Code)

First Test Date: November 2006

GENERAL PRINCIPLES OF FINANCIAL PLANNING (11%)

1. Financial planning process
   A. Purpose, benefits, and components
   B. Steps
      1) Establishing client-planner relationships
      2) Gathering client data and determining goals and expectations
      3) Determining the client's financial status by analyzing and evaluating general financial status, special needs, insurance and risk management, investments, taxation, employee benefits, retirement, and/or estate planning
      4) Developing and presenting the financial plan
      5) Implementing the financial plan
      6) Monitoring the financial plan
   C. Responsibilities
      1) Financial planner
      2) Client
      3) Other advisors

2. CFP Board's *Code of Ethics and Professional Responsibility* and *Disciplinary Rules and Procedures*
   A. *Code of Ethics and Professional Responsibility*
      1) Preamble and applicability
      2) Composition and scope
      3) Compliance
      4) Terminology
      5) Principles
         a) Principle 1 – Integrity
         b) Principle 2 – Objectivity
         c) Principle 3 – Competence
         d) Principle 4 – Fairness
         e) Principle 5 – Confidentiality
         f) Principle 6 – Professionalism
         g) Principle 7 – Diligence
      6) Rules
   B) *Disciplinary Rules and Procedures*

3. CFP Board's *Financial Planning Practice Standards*
   A) Purpose and applicability
   B) Content of each series (use most current *Practice Standards*, as posted on CFP Board's Web site at www.CFP.net)
   C. Enforcement through *Disciplinary Rules and Procedures*

4. Financial statements
   A. Personal
      1) Statement of financial position
      2) Statement of cash flow
   B. Business
      1) Balance sheet
      2) Income statement
      3) Statement of cash flows
      4) *Pro forma* statements

5. Cash flow management
   A. Budgeting
   B. Emergency fund planning
   C. Debt management ratios
      1) Consumer debt
      2) Housing costs
      3) Total debt
   D. Savings strategies

6. Financing strategies
   A. Long-term vs. short-term debt
   B. Secured vs. unsecured debt
   C. Buy vs. lease/rent
   D. Mortgage financing
      1) Conventional vs. adjustable-rate mortgage (ARM)
      2) Home equity loan and line of credit
      3) Refinancing cost-benefit analysis
      4) Reverse mortgage

7. Function, purpose, and regulation of financial institutions
   A. Banks
   B. Credit unions
   C. Brokerage companies
   D. Insurance companies
   E. Mutual fund companies
   F. Trust companies

8. Education planning
   A. Funding
      1) Needs analysis
      2) Tax credits/adjustments/ deductions
      3) Funding strategies
      4) Ownership of assets
      5) Vehicles
         a) Qualified tuition programs (§529 plans)
         b) Coverdell Education Savings Accounts
         c) Uniform Transfers to Minors Act (UTMA) and Uniform Gifts to Minors Act (UGMA) accounts
         d) Savings bonds
   B. Financial aid

 CERTIFIED FINANCIAL PLANNER™ | CFP®

9. Financial planning for special circumstances
   A. Divorce
   B. Disability
   C. Terminal illness
   D. Non-traditional families
   E. Job change and job loss
   F. Dependents with special needs
   G. Monetary windfalls

10. Economic concepts
    A. Supply and demand
    B. Fiscal policy
    C. Monetary policy
    D. Economic indicators
    E. Business cycles
    F. Inflation, deflation, and stagflation
    G. Yield curve

11. Time value of money concepts and calculations
    A. Present value
    B. Future value
    C. Ordinary annuity and annuity due
    D. Net present value (NPV)
    E. Internal rate of return (IRR)
    F. Uneven cash flows
    G. Serial payments

12. Financial services regulations and requirements
    A. Registration and licensing
    B. Reporting
    C. Compliance
    D. State securities and insurance laws

13. Business law
    A. Contracts
    B. Agency
    C. Fiduciary liability

14. Consumer protection laws
    A. Bankruptcy
    B. Fair credit reporting laws
    C. Privacy policies
    D. Identity theft protection

INSURANCE PLANNING AND RISK MANAGEMENT (14%)

15. Principles of risk and insurance
    A. Definitions
    B. Concepts
       1) Peril
       2) Hazard
       3) Law of large numbers
       4) Adverse selection
       5) Insurable risks
       6) Self-insurance
    C. Risk management process

   D. Response to risk
      1) Risk control
         a) Risk avoidance
         b) Risk diversification
         c) Risk reduction
      2) Risk financing
         a) Risk retention
         b) Risk transfer
   E. Legal aspects of insurance
      1) Principle of indemnity
      2) Insurable interest
      3) Contract requirements
      4) Contract characteristics
      5) Policy ownership
      6) Designation of beneficiary

16. Analysis and evaluation of risk exposures
    A. Personal
       1) Death
       2) Disability
       3) Poor health
       4) Unemployment
       5) Superannuation
    B. Property
       1) Real
       2) Personal
       3) Auto
    C. Liability
       1) Negligence
       2) Intentional torts
       3) Strict liability
    D. Business-related

17. Property, casualty and liability insurance
    A. Individual
       1) Homeowners insurance
       2) Auto insurance
       3) Umbrella liability insurance
    B. Business
       1) Commercial property insurance
       2) Commercial liability insurance
          a) Auto liability
          b) Umbrella liability
          c) Professional liability
          d) Directors and officers liability
          e) Workers' compensation and employers liability

18. Health insurance and health care cost management (individual)
    A. Hospital, surgical, and physicians' expense insurance
    B. Major medical insurance and calculation of benefits
    C. Continuance and portability
    D. Medicare
    E. Taxation of premiums and benefits

19. Disability income insurance (individual)
    A. Definitions of disability
    B. Benefit period

   C. Elimination period
   D. Benefit amount
   E. Provisions
   F. Taxation of premiums and benefits

20. Long-term care insurance (individual)
    A. Eligibility
    B. Services covered
    C. Medicare limitations
    D. Benefit period
    E. Elimination period
    F. Benefit amount
    G. Provisions
    H. Taxation of premiums and benefits

21. Life insurance (individual)
    A. Concepts and personal uses
    B. Policy types
    C. Contractual provisions
    D. Dividend options
    E. Nonforfeiture options
    F. Settlement options
    G. Illustrations
    H. Policy replacement
    I. Viatical and life settlements

22. Income taxation of life insurance
    A. Dividends
    B. Withdrawals and loans
    C. Death benefits
    D. Modified endowment contracts (MECs)
    E. Transfer-for-value
    F. §1035 exchanges

23. Business uses of insurance
    A. Buy-sell agreements
    B. Key employee life insurance
    C. Split-dollar life insurance
    D. Business overhead expense insurance

24. Insurance needs analysis
    A. Life insurance
    B. Disability income insurance
    C. Long-term care insurance
    D. Health insurance
    E. Property insurance
    F. Liability insurance

25. Insurance policy and company selection
    A. Purpose of coverage
    B. Duration of coverage
    C. Participating or non-participating
    D. Cost-benefit analysis
    E. Company selection
       1) Industry ratings
       2) Underwriting

2

26. Annuities
    A. Types
    B. Uses
    C. Taxation

EMPLOYEE BENEFITS PLANNING (8%)

27. Group life insurance
    A. Types and basic provisions
        1) Group term
        2) Group permanent
        3) Dependent coverage
    B. Income tax implications
    C. Employee benefit analysis and application
    D. Conversion analysis
    E. Carve-out plans

28. Group disability insurance
    A. Types and basic provisions
        1) Short-term coverage
        2) Long-term coverage
    B. Definitions of disability
    C. Income tax implications
    D. Employee benefit analysis and application
    E. Integration with other income

29. Group medical insurance
    A. Types and basic provisions
        1) Traditional indemnity
        2) Managed care plans
            a) Preferred provider organization (PPO)
            b) Health maintenance organization (HMO)
            c) Point-of-service (POS)
    B. Income tax implications
    C. Employee benefit analysis and application
    D. COBRA/HIPAA provisions
    E. Continuation
    F. Savings accounts
        1) Health savings account (HSA)
        2) Archer medical savings account (MSA)
        3) Health reimbursement arrangement (HRA)

30. Other employee benefits
    A. §125 cafeteria plans and flexible spending accounts (FSAs)
    B. Fringe benefits
    C. Voluntary employees' beneficiary association (VEBA)
    D. Prepaid legal services
    E. Group long-term care insurance
    F. Dental insurance
    G. Vision insurance

31) Employee stock options
    A. Basic provisions
        1) Company restrictions
        2) Transferability
        3) Exercise price
        4) Vesting
        5) Expiration
        6) Cashless exercise
    B. Incentive stock options (ISOs)
        1) Income tax implications (regular, AMT, basis)
            a) Upon grant
            b) Upon exercise
            c) Upon sale
        2) Holding period requirements
        3) Disqualifying dispositions
        4) Planning opportunities and strategies
    C. Non-qualified stock options (NSOs)
        1) Income tax implications (regular, AMT, basis)
            a) Upon grant
            b) Upon exercise
            c) Upon sale
        2) Gifting opportunities
            a) Unvested/vested
            b) Exercised/unexercised
            c) Gift tax valuation
            d) Payment of gift tax
        3) Planning opportunities and strategies
        4) Employee benefits analysis and application
    D. Planning strategies for employees with both incentive stock options and non-qualified stock options
    E. Election to include in gross income in the year of transfer (§83(b) election)

32. Stock plans
    A. Types and basic provisions
        1) Restricted stock
        2) Phantom stock
        3) Stock appreciation rights (SARs)
        4) Employee stock purchase plan (ESPP)
    B. Income tax implications
    C. Employee benefit analysis and application
    D. Election to include in gross income in the year of transfer (§83(b) election)

33. Non-qualified deferred compensation
    A. Basic provisions and differences from qualified plans
    B. Types of plans and applications
        1) Salary reduction plans
        2) Salary continuation plans
        3) Rabbi trusts
        4) Secular trusts
    C. Income tax implications
        1) Constructive receipt
        2) Substantial risk of forfeiture
        3) Economic benefit doctrine
    D. Funding methods
    E. Strategies

INVESTMENT PLANNING (19%)

34. Characteristics, uses and taxation of investment vehicles
    A. Cash and equivalents
        1) Certificates of deposit
        2) Money market funds
        3) Treasury bills
        4) Commercial paper
        5) Banker's acceptances
        6) Eurodollars
    B. Individual bonds
        1) U.S. Government bonds and agency securities
            a) Treasury notes and bonds
            b) Treasury STRIPS
            c) Treasury inflation-protection securities (TIPS)
            d) Series EE, HH, and I bonds
            e) Mortgage-backed securities
        2) Zero-coupon bonds
        3) Municipal bonds
            a) General obligation
            b) Revenue
        4) Corporate bonds
            a) Mortgage bond
            b) Debenture
            c) Investment grade
            d) High-yield
            e) Convertible
            f) Callable
        5) Foreign bonds
    C. Promissory notes
    D. Individual stocks
        1) Common
        2) Preferred
        3) American depositary receipts (ADRs)
    E. Pooled and managed investments
        1) Exchange-traded funds (ETFs)
        2) Unit investment trusts
        3) Mutual funds
        4) Closed-end investment companies

3

5) Index securities
6) Hedge funds
7) Limited partnerships
8) Privately managed accounts
9) Separately managed accounts

F. Guaranteed investment contracts (GICs)

G. Real Estate
1) Investor-managed
2) Real estate investment trusts (REITs)
3) Real estate limited partnerships (RELPs)
4) Real estate mortgage investment conduits (REMICs)

H. Alternative investments
1) Derivatives
   a) Puts
   b) Calls
   c) Long-term Equity AnticiPation Securities (LEAPS®)
   d) Futures
   e) Warrants and rights
2) Tangible assets
   a) Collectibles
   b) Natural resources
   c) Precious metals

35. Types of investment risk
A. Systematic/market/nondiversifiable
B. Purchasing power
C. Interest rate
D. Unsystematic/nonmarket/diversifiable
E. Business
F. Financial
G. Liquidity and marketability
H. Reinvestment
I. Political (sovereign)
J. Exchange rate
K. Tax
L. Investment manager

36. Quantitative investment concepts
A. Distribution of returns
1) Normal distribution
2) Lognormal distribution
3) Skewness
4) Kurtosis
B. Correlation coefficient
C. Coefficient of determination (R^2)
D. Coefficient of variation
E. Standard deviation
F. Beta
G. Covariance
H. Semivariance

37. Measures of investment returns
A. Simple vs. compound return

B. Geometric average vs. arithmetic average return
C. Time-weighted vs. dollar-weighted return
D. Real (inflation-adjusted) vs. nominal return
E. Total return
F. Risk-adjusted return
G. Holding period return
H. Internal rate of return (IRR)
I. Yield-to-maturity
J. Yield-to-call
K. Current yield
L. Taxable equivalent yield (TEY)

38. Bond and stock valuation concepts
A. Bond duration and convexity
B. Capitalized earnings
C. Dividend growth models
D. Ratio analysis
1) Price/earnings
2) Price/free cash flow
3) Price/sales
4) Price/earnings ÷ growth (PEG)
E. Book value

39. Investment theory
A. Modern portfolio theory (MPT)
1) Capital market line (CML)
   a) Mean-variance optimization
   b) Efficient frontier
2) Security market line (SML)
B. Efficient market hypothesis (EMH)
1) Strong form
2) Semi-strong form
3) Weak form
4) Anomalies
C. Behavioral finance

40. Portfolio development and analysis
A. Fundamental analysis
1) Top-down analysis
2) Bottom-up analysis
3) Ratio analysis
   a) Liquidity ratios
   b) Activity ratios
   c) Profitability ratios
   d) Debt ratios
B. Technical analysis
1) Charting
2) Sentiment indicators
3) Flow of funds indicators
4) Market structure indicators
C. Investment policy statements
D. Appropriate benchmarks
E. Probability analysis, including Monte Carlo
F. Tax efficiency
1) Turnover
2) Timing of capital gains and losses

3) Wash sale rule
4) Qualified dividends
5) Tax-free income
G. Performance measures
1) Sharpe ratio
2) Treynor ratio
3) Jensen ratio
4) Information ratio

41. Investment strategies
A. Market timing
B. Passive investing (indexing)
C. Buy and hold
D. Portfolio immunization
E. Swaps and collars
F. Formula investing
1) Dollar cost averaging
2) Dividend reinvestment plans (DRIPs)
3) Bond ladders, bullets, and barbells
G. Use of leverage (margin)
H. Short selling
I. Hedging and option strategies

42. Asset allocation and portfolio diversification
A. Strategic asset allocation
1) Application of client lifecycle analysis
2) Client risk tolerance measurement and application
3) Asset class definition and correlation
B. Rebalancing
C. Tactical asset allocation
D. Control of volatility
E. Strategies for dealing with concentrated portfolios

43. Asset pricing models
A. Capital asset pricing model (CAPM)
B. Arbitrage pricing theory (APT)
C. Black-Scholes option valuation model
D. Binomial option pricing

INCOME TAX PLANNING
(14%)

44. Income tax law fundamentals
A. Types of authority
1) Primary
2) Secondary
B. Research sources

4

45. Tax compliance
    A. Filing requirements
    B. Audits
    C. Penalties

46. Income tax fundamentals and calculations
    A. Filing status
    B. Gross income
        1) Inclusions
        2) Exclusions
        3) Imputed income
    C. Adjustments
    D. Standard/Itemized deductions
        1) Types
        2) Limitations
    E. Personal and dependency exemptions
    F. Taxable income
    G. Tax liability
        1) Rate schedule
        2) Kiddie tax
        3) Self-employment tax
    H. Tax credits
    I. Payment of tax
        1) Withholding
        2) Estimated payments

47. Tax accounting
    A. Accounting periods
    B. Accounting methods
        1) Cash receipts and disbursements
        2) Accrual method
        3) Hybrid method
        4) Change in accounting method
    C. Long-term contracts
    D. Installment sales
    E. Inventory valuation and flow methods
    F. Net operating losses

48. Characteristics and income taxation of business entities
    A. Entity types
        1) Sole proprietorship
        2) Partnerships
        3) Limited liability company (LLC)
        4) Corporations
        5) Trust
        6) Association
    B. Taxation at entity and owner level
        1) Formation
        2) Flow through of income and losses
        3) Special taxes
        4) Distributions
        5) Dissolution
        6) Disposition

49. Income taxation of trusts and estates
    A. General issues
        1) Filing requirements
        2) Deadlines
        3) Choice of taxable year
        4) Tax treatment of distributions to beneficiaries
        5) Rate structure
    B. Grantor/Nongrantor trusts
    C. Simple/Complex trusts
    D. Revocable/Irrevocable trusts
    E. Trust income
        1) Trust accounting income
        2) Trust taxable income
        3) Distributable net income (DNI)
    F. Estate income tax

50. Basis
    A. Original basis
    B. Adjusted basis
    C. Amortization and accretion
    D. Basis of property received by gift and in nontaxable transactions
    E. Basis of inherited property (community and non-community property)

51. Depreciation/cost-recovery concepts
    A. Modified Accelerated Cost Recovery System (MACRS)
    B. Expensing policy
    C. §179 deduction
    D. Amortization
    E. Depletion

52. Tax consequences of like-kind exchanges
    A. Reporting requirements
    B. Qualifying transactions
    C. Liabilities
    D. Boot
    E. Related party transactions

53. Tax consequences of the disposition of property
    A. Capital assets (§1221)
    B. Holding period
    C. Sale of residence
    D. Depreciation recapture
    E. Related parties
    F. Wash sales
    G. Bargain sales
    H. Section 1244 stock (small business stock election)
    I. Installment sales
    J. Involuntary conversions

54. Alternative minimum tax (AMT)
    A. Mechanics
    B. Preferences and adjustments
    C. Exclusion items vs. deferral items

D. Credit: creation, usage, and limitations
E. Application to businesses and trusts
F. Planning strategies

55. Tax reduction/management techniques
    A. Tax credits
    B. Accelerated deductions
    C. Deferral of income
    D. Intra-family transfers

56. Passive activity and at-risk rules
    A. Definitions
    B. Computations
    C. Treatment of disallowed losses
    D. Disposition of passive activities
    E. Real estate exceptions

57. Tax implications of special circumstances
    A. Married/widowed
        1) Filing status
        2) Children
        3) Community and non-community property
    B. Divorce
        1) Alimony
        2) Child support
        3) Property division

58. Charitable contributions and deductions
    A. Qualified entities
        1) Public charities
        2) Private charities
    B. Deduction limitations
    C. Carryover periods
    D. Appreciated property
    E. Non-deductible contributions
    F. Appraisals
    G. Substantiation requirements
    H. Charitable contributions by business entities

RETIREMENT PLANNING
(19%)

59. Retirement needs analysis
    A. Assumptions for retirement planning
        1) Inflation
        2) Retirement period and life expectancy
        3) Lifestyle
        4) Total return
    B. Income sources
    C. Financial needs
        1) Living costs

5

2) Charitable and beneficiary gifting objectives
3) Medical costs, including long-term care needs analysis
4) Other (trust and foundation funding, education funding, etc.)
D. Straight-line returns vs. probability analysis
E. Pure annuity vs. capital preservation
F. Alternatives to compensate for projected cash-flow shortfalls

60. Social Security (Old Age, Survivor, and Disability Insurance, OASDI)
A. Paying into the system
B. Eligibility and benefit
1) Retirement
2) Disability
3) Survivor
4) Family limitations
C. How benefits are calculated
D. Working after retirement
E. Taxation of benefits

61. Types of retirement plans
A. Characteristics
1) Qualified plans
2) Non-qualified plans
B. Types and basic provisions of qualified plans
1) Defined contribution
a) Money purchase
b) Target benefit
c) Profit sharing
1) 401(k) plan
2) Safe harbor 401(k) plan
3) Age-based plan
4) Stock bonus plan
5) Employee stock ownership plan (ESOP)
6) New comparability plan
7) Thrift plan
2) Defined benefit
a) Traditional
b) Cash balance
c) 412(i) plan

62. Qualified plan rules and options
A. Nondiscrimination and eligibility requirements
1) Age and service requirements
2) Coverage requirements
3) Minimum participation
4) Highly compensated employee (HCE)
5) Permitted vesting schedules
6) ADP/ACP testing
7) Controlled group

B. Integration with Social Security/disparity limits
1) Defined benefit plans
2) Defined contribution plans
C. Factors affecting contributions or benefits
1) Deduction limit (§404(c))
2) Defined contribution limits
3) Defined benefit limit
4) Annual compensation limit
5) Definition of compensation
6) Multiple plans
7) Special rules for self-employed (non-corporations)
D. Top-heavy plans
1) Definition
2) Key employee
3) Vesting
4) Effects on contributions or benefits
E. Loans from qualified plans

63. Other tax-advantaged retirement plans
A. Types and basic provisions
1) Traditional IRA
2) Roth IRA, including conversion analysis
3) SEP
4) SIMPLE
5) §403(b) plans
6) §457 plans
7) Keogh (HR-10) plans

64. Regulatory considerations
A. Employee Retirement Income Security Act (ERISA)
B. Department of Labor (DOL) regulations
C. Fiduciary liability issues
D. Prohibited transactions
E. Reporting requirements

65. Key factors affecting plan selection for businesses
A. Owner's personal objectives
1) Tax considerations
2) Capital needs at retirement
3) Capital needs at death
B. Business' objectives
1) Tax considerations
2) Administrative cost
3) Cash flow situation and outlook
4) Employee demographics
5) Comparison of defined contribution and defined benefit plan alternatives

66. Investment considerations for retirement plans
A. Suitability

B. Time horizon
C. Diversification
D. Fiduciary considerations
E. Unrelated business taxable income (UBTI)
F. Life insurance
G. Appropriate assets for tax-advantaged vs. taxable accounts

67. Distribution rules, alternatives, and taxation
A. Premature distributions
1) Penalties
2) Exceptions to penalties
3) Substantially equal payments (§72(t))
B. Election of distribution options
1) Lump sum distributions
2) Annuity options
3) Rollover
4) Direct transfer
C. Required minimum distributions
1) Rules
2) Calculations
3) Penalties
D. Beneficiary considerations/Stretch IRAs
E. Qualified domestic relations order (QDRO)
F. Taxation of distributions
1) Tax management techniques
2) Net unrealized appreciation (NUA)

ESTATE PLANNING (15%)

68. Characteristics and consequences of property titling
A. Community property vs. non-community property
B. Sole ownership
C. Joint tenancy with right of survivorship (JTWROS)
D. Tenancy by the entirety
E. Tenancy in common
F. Trust ownership

69. Methods of property transfer at death
A. Transfers through the probate process
1) Testamentary distribution
2) Intestate succession
3) Advantages and disadvantages of probate
4) Assets subject to probate estate
5) Probate avoidance strategies

6

7

CERTIFIED FINANCIAL PLANNER™ | CFP®

84. Intra-family and other business transfer techniques
   A. Characteristics
   B. Techniques
      1) Buy-sell agreement
      2) Installment note
      3) Self-canceling installment note (SCIN)
      4) Private annuity
      5) Transfers in trust
      6) Intra-family loan
      7) Bargain sale
      8) Gift or sale leaseback
      9) Intentionally defective grantor trust
      10) Family limited partnership (FLP) or limited liability company (LLC)
   C. Federal income, gift, estate, and generation-skipping transfer tax implications

85) Generation-skipping transfer tax (GSTT)
   A. Identify transfers subject to the GSTT
      1) Direct skips
      2) Taxable distributions
      3) Taxable terminations
   B. Exemptions and exclusions from the GSTT
      1) The GSTT exemption
      2) Qualifying annual exclusion gifts and direct transfers

86. Fiduciaries
   A. Types of fiduciaries
      1) Executor/Personal representative
      2) Trustee
      3) Guardian
   B. Duties of fiduciaries
   C. Breach of fiduciary duties

87. Income in respect of a decedent (IRD)
   A. Assets qualifying as IRD
   B. Calculation for IRD deduction
   C. Income tax treatment

88. Postmortem estate planning techniques
   A. Alternate valuation date
   B. Qualified disclaimer
   C. Deferral of estate tax (§6166)
   D. Corporate stock redemption (§303)
   E. Special use valuation (§2032A)

89. Estate planning for non-traditional relationships
   A. Children of another relationship
   B. Cohabitation
   C. Adoption
   D. Same-sex relationships

ADDENDUM

The following topics are an addendum to the *Topic List for CFP® Certification Examination*. Although individuals taking the CFP® Certification Examination will not be tested directly over these topics, CFP Board registered programs are strongly encouraged to teach them in their curricula) Continuing education (CE) programs and materials that address these topics will be eligible for CFP Board CE credit.

1. Client and planner attitudes, values, biases and behavioral characteristics and the impact on financial planning
   A. Cultural
   B. Family (e.g. biological; non-traditional)
   C. Emotional
   D. Life cycle and age
   E. Client's level of knowledge, experience, and expertise
   F. Risk tolerance
   G. Values-driven planning

2. Principles of communication and counseling
   A. Types of structured communication
      1) Interviewing
      2) Counseling
      3) Advising
   B. Essentials in financial counseling
      1) Establishing structure
      2) Creating rapport
      3) Recognizing resistance
   C. Characteristics of effective counselors
      1) Unconditional positive regard
      2) Accurate empathy
      3) Genuineness and self-awareness
   D. Nonverbal behaviors
      1) Body positions, movements, and gestures
      2) Facial expressions and eye contact
      3) Voice tone and pitch
      4) Interpreting the meaning of nonverbal behaviors
   E. Attending and listening skills
      1) Physical attending
      2) Active listening
      3) Responding during active listening; leading responses
   F. Effective use of questions
      1) Appropriate types of questions
      2) Ineffective and counterproductive questioning techniques

8

PLAN YOUR STUDY TIME

TIME MANAGEMENT

- After you determine your areas of strength and weakness, you should be able to estimate the number of hours you will need to study to pass the exam. At this point, you should take out your calendar and count the number of weeks you have remaining to study before the exam. Divide the number of hours you need to study by the number of weeks until the exam. This will allow you to determine the number of hours you must study per week. This figure can then be further refined into hours to study per weekday and per weekend, and so forth.

- For example, Paul is taking the exam in November. It is now the middle of July, and he has just received his Kaplan Financial materials. He purchased *Volumes I–VIII, Understanding Your Financial Calculator,* the *Financial Planning Flashcards,* and the *Test Bank.* He has registered for and plans to attend a Kaplan Financial Live Instructional Review. He has 17 weeks until the exam and has decided that he needs to study a full 350 hours to pass. On the basis of this information, he will need to study 20 hours per week. To accomplish this goal, Paul decided to study 2 hours each weekday and 10 hours on the weekend (except for the weeks he attends the Live Review). He will always carry at least one section of the flashcards with him so that he can make the best use of any downtime he encounters. Using this information (along with Paul's knowledge of his own areas of strength and weakness), Paul decided the following schedule would be appropriate.

Week	Topics to Cover	Hours
1	*Understanding Your Financial Calculator*	20
2	*Vol. I—Fundamentals of Financial Planning*—text (all) and questions (half)	20
3	*Vol. I—Fundamentals of Financial Planning*—questions (half) and *Vol. II—Insurance Planning* text (all)	20
4	*Vol. II—Insurance Planning* questions (all) and *Vol. III—Investments Planning* text (half)	20
5	*Vol. III—Investment Planning* text (half) and questions (all)	20
6	*Vol. VI—Estate Planning* text (all) and questions (half)	20
7	*Vol. VI—Estate Planning* questions (half) and *Vol. V—Retirement Planning* text (all)	20
8	*Vol. V—Retirement Planning* questions (all) and *Vol. IV—Income Tax Planning* text (half)	20
9	*Vol. IV—Income Tax Planning* text (half) and questions (all)	20
10	*Volume VII—Case Book*—Item Sets, Cognitive Connections, and catch-up	20
11	*Test Bank* and attend Live Review	34
12	*Test Bank* and attend Live Review	34
13	*Vol. VII—Case Book* (half)	20
14	*Vol. VII—Case Book* (half)	20
15	*Vol. VIII—Mock Exam and Solutions* and review	12
16	Review weak topics and catch-up	20
17	Review weak topics	10

MONTHLY CALENDAR

- You might find it beneficial to invest in a large monthly calendar and hang it where you will see it every day. Be sure to mark all of your upcoming commitments with regard to work, family, outside activities, and so forth, on your calendar. This will help you plan and anticipate any time constraints that may lead to obstacles in your study program. For example, during Week 3 of Paul's schedule, he knows that he must attend an out-of-town wedding and will only have time to study the two hours he is on the airplane. Even though he will make good use of his flashcards during that time, he still must adjust his schedule to spend more time studying during Weekend 2 and on the weekdays during Weeks 2 and 3 in order to compensate for the fluctuation in his study program. You may find that you will need to cancel commitments or turn down new commitments you would otherwise accept in order to maintain your focus. Remember, your study time for the CFP® Certification Examination is limited and must be one of your top priorities.

- You will also want to indicate on your calendar the subject areas on which you plan to focus your study time each week. This will help you plan which commitments you will and will not be able to accept as weeks go by. For example, in Week 8 Paul's brother calls and wants to schedule dinner for Week 9. Paul knows that he will be studying Income Tax Planning (his hardest subject) and that this area might require more study time than other areas. Thus, Paul decides that he should not schedule any additional events for Week 9, and declines.

- Make the most of your travel time to and from the Live Review. For example, because Paul will be traveling to and from the Live Review by train, he can study the remaining sections of his flashcards.

WEEKLY CALENDAR

- Before you begin your first week of study, list all of the activities in which you participate. Determine how long each activity takes to complete and whether this activity is performed at a specific time each day, week, or month.

- Make sure to include your work hours, drive time, family time, meals, sleep, and any other miscellaneous activities you might do that take up your time. You may want to use the sample schedule at the end of this section to track your activities.

- Once you have logged your activities in your weekly and monthly calendars, review your schedule, and decide which time slots are full and which are open. Using this information, you should be able to develop a realistic study plan for each day. If you find that your current activities do not leave you enough free time to study, you will need to eliminate enough activities so that you will have adequate study time to prepare for the exam. If you discover that you do not have the appropriate amount of time for exam preparation, it would be to your benefit to postpone taking the exam until it is a higher priority or until you have fewer commitments. Before each week begins, review your weekly schedule and update it for any new commitments. Although you will need to be flexible with your scheduled study time, it is important to stick with your scheduled study time as much as possible. Try to anticipate missed study time and be sure to reschedule the missed time for another day.

MAKE A DAILY TO-DO LIST

- Before you begin each study session, make a tentative list of what you want to accomplish during your study time. You may also want to keep a spiral notebook or binder so you will be able to continuously evaluate and reevaluate your progress. Write down the number of pages that you plan to read or the number of problems that you plan to work during your study session or both. Be realistic when you write this list and work very hard to stick to your study plan.

PREPARE TO STUDY

There are many ways you can maximize the benefits of your study time. The following are some of our suggestions to most efficiently and effectively study.

CREATE A SUITABLE STUDY ENVIRONMENT

The most important thing you can do to help facilitate your studying is to create a suitable study environment.

- Your study area should be quiet. You want to find a place that is free from all extraneous noise (including the television and disruptive people).

- Your study area should be away from distractions. Stay away from areas where there are a lot of distractions. For example, try not to study close to a telephone, since you might be tempted to answer it and talk. You might also want to try to avoid studying at work or at home if coworkers or family members will interrupt you.

- Study in a well lit location. You will want to study in an area where you will be able to see the information as well as stay awake and alert.

- Be comfortable, but not too comfortable. You want to be relaxed so that you see studying as a beneficial activity and not a punishment. You should not, however, let yourself get so comfortable that you will be tempted to fall asleep.

- Have all of your materials readily available. Gather everything you will need during your study session beforehand. This includes pencils, pens, books, highlighters, a calculator, and paper. Try to sit at a desk or table so that you have a firm writing surface and room for all of your materials.

USE THE MULTIPLE-CHOICE QUESTIONS TO DIRECT YOUR STUDY

- Keep in mind that you should not spend the majority of your study time on material you've already learned. There is a natural tendency to do so, because it is a lot more fun and certainly more comforting but, unfortunately, counter-productive. The subject in which you scored the lowest should be studied the most. The multiple-choice questions can be used as a monitoring tool if you keep thorough records. We recommend that you study the multiple-choice questions and the outlines as needed.

BECOME THOROUGHLY KNOWLEDGEABLE ABOUT THE MATERIAL

- The exam is professionally rigorous and tests across Bloom's taxonomy of cognitive learning. You can expect a small percentage of problems to test at the knowledge level and a much larger percentage to test at the application, synthesis, and evaluation levels.

- The difference in passing and failing is the difference between being thoroughly prepared and proactive, versus being casually acquainted and reactive. For example, when you think of IRAs, your mind should create a picture of the following topics that relate to IRAs:
  - Eligibility
  - Deductible/nondeductible
  - Allocation between spouses
  - Transferability
  - Rollover
  - Assignment/pledging
  - Investments

- Penalties
- Distribution before age 70½
- Minimum distributions
- Roth IRAs and Coverdell Education Savings Accounts
- Death
- Inclusion in gross estate
- QDRO
- Active participation in a pension plan
- Joint life distribution

- You should be immediately prepared and ready to answer any question about any subtopic in IRAs. If the mentioning of IRAs does not bring anything to mind, or if only a few of the listed topics come to mind, you are not thoroughly knowledgeable.

- The problem with being only casually acquainted with the material is twofold: (1) you take too much time thinking of an answer, and (2) you let the exam lead you to incorrect answers. You must discipline yourself to aggressively answer the questions and you must monitor the time it takes you to answer the average multiple-choice question. Remember, when you are thoroughly knowledgeable, the questions are fairly easy. When you are only casually acquainted, the questions are much harder and take longer to answer.

TEXTBOOK PREVIEWING

As you are reviewing all of the texts, there are two things you should do.

- Be sure to study the title of each section. Not only will this preview what you are about to read, it will also help you to narrow your scope of study.

- Look for relationships. This is extremely important. By looking for relationships between current information and subjects you have read about previously, you can learn to group concepts together and increase memory retention. Most of the questions on the CFP Exam tie many topics and subjects together into one question, so it is important to look for relationships.

THINGS TO MARK

- **Definitions.** Often knowing a word's definition can help you to distinguish terms that might otherwise prove confusing. On the exam, knowing the definition of key words and concepts can often help you eliminate possible answers on multiple-choice questions.

- **Signal words.** Such words as *and*, *or*, *except*, *not*, and *also* indicate the relationships between concepts.

- **Key words and phrases.** Key words are words or phrases that should instantly bring to mind a number of questions, issues, or ideas relating to the topics identified by the key words or phrases. For example, the phrase *substantial and reoccurring* is a key phrase that relates to the funding of profit-sharing plans. Keywords and phrases are the foundation on which you should build your basis of knowledge.

NOTE-TAKING METHODS

- **Flashcards or note cards.** Notes taken on note cards can also be used as valuable tools for review. You can use them as flashcards, which are much more portable than textbooks or notebooks, and force memory recall, which is a requirement of the exam. You can create your own flashcards or use Kaplan Financial's more than 1,000 Financial Planning Flashcards to enhance your studying when you're on the go.

- **Study notes.** Traditional study notes allow you to trigger key concepts that you have read about. This is crucial for review purposes. Study notes should be rewritten within 48 hours of taking them to clarify any areas that seem ambiguous.

STUDY METHODS

SQ3R Study System

- **Survey.** Glance through material and get a general idea about the key information within the text.

- **Question.** Think about questions that could be asked about the material. If the section title is "Key Concepts of Estate Planning," a possible question might be, "*What are the key concepts of estate planning?*"

- **Read.** Read through the material carefully, marking the text and taking notes as you go.

- **Recite.** After each section, pretend that you are lecturing to a friend or colleague on the material. Are you able to retain the information?

- **Review.** Be sure to go over each section and review information about which you might be confused.

SOAR Study Formula

- **Survey the book.** Skim over the outline topics. Review the table of contents to see the major categories of information. Review the index for important topics and keywords. Also look at each individual section and review the topics, major points, and information contained within each section.

- **Organize.** Organize the information that you have read and taken notes on. Some ways to facilitate this are to:

  – underline books; and

  – make notes for books (e.g., charts and note cards).

- **Anticipate.** Anticipate the information that you think will be tested. Formulate possible test questions, and evaluate your ability to answer these questions correctly in a testing environment.

- **Recite and review.** Just as with the SQ3R method, the SOAR method places final emphasis on being able to recite information as if lecturing on its key points and reviewing any areas where you have deficiencies.

MNEMONICS

- *Mnemonics* literally translates as, "to help the memory." These are techniques that can be incorporated into your study plan to increase your retention of information. The most common use of mnemonics is to create an acronym or a sentence with the first letter of each keyword. For instance, PRIME is an acronym used to help students remember systematic risks. The letters *P*, *R*, *I*, *M*, and *E* stand for purchasing power risk, reinvestment rate risk, interest rate risk, market risk, and exchange rate risk.

KAPLAN'S FINAL TIPS

- **Avoid whining.** Avoid whining about your having to know or learn some area of financial planning that is technical and that most planners have to look up. One purpose of the exam is to serve as gatekeeper to the profession; another is to help you develop a healthy sense of professional humility about what you know. Also, clients will expect you to know everything.

- **Study what you don't know.** Your lowest-scoring subject should be the subject you study the most.

- **Think positively.** It will help you pass.

- **Find a way to make it fun.** Don't fight the problem.

STUDY PLAN

Date	No. Attempted	No. Correct	Correct, %	Average Time per Question	Study Outline	Total Time	Notes

WEEKLY ACTIVITIES/COMMITMENTS

Time	Monday	Tuesday	Wednesday	Thursday	Friday	Saturday	Sunday
12 am							
1							
2							
3							
4							
5							
6							
7							
8							
9							
10							
11							
12 pm							
1							
2							
3							
4							
5							
6							
7							
8							
9							
10							
11							

SOLVING MULTIPLE-CHOICE QUESTIONS

- **Read the last line (the requirement) first.** The last line will generally be the question part of the problem and will identify the types of important information that will be needed to answer the question. See Example 1 on the following page (How many personal and dependency exemptions can Mike and Pam claim on their 2007 income tax return?). This last sentence identifies the type of information needed from the body of the problem. You can now look for key information while reading through the body of the problem.

- **Read the question carefully.** Underline the concepts, words, and data, and make important notes of data or relevant rules to help formulate your answer.

- **Formulate your answer.** Do not look at the answer choices presented on the exam until you have formulated your answer. Looking at the answer choices may have a tendency to distract you or change your thinking.

- **Select your answer if it is presented.** Write your answer or circle it directly on the examination. Watch the clock and enter answers on the answer sheet as you go, or all at once at the end. If at the end, be sure you have enough time. Be consistent.

- **Review other answer choices.** Was your answer sufficiently precise? Was your answer complete?

- **If your answer is not presented**, you know you are incorrect. For alternative answers, reread question and requirements, evaluate answers presented, guess, or skip the question and come back to it later. Note: You are not penalized for guessing, so if time is running out, be sure to fill in all of the open questions.

SOLVING A-TYPE QUESTIONS

STRAIGHT MULTIPLE-CHOICE QUESTIONS

Example 1

Mike and Pam, ages 67 and 65, respectively, filed a joint tax return for 2007. They provided all of the support for their 19-year-old son, who had $2,200 of gross income. Their 23-year-old daughter, a full-time student until her graduation on June 25, 2007, earned $2,700, which was 40% of her total support during the year. Her parents provided the remaining support. Mike and Pam also provided total support for Pam's father, who is a citizen and lifelong resident of Colombia. How many personal and dependency exemptions can Mike and Pam claim on their 2007 income tax return?

Example 1 Analysis

Step 1	Read last line and identify the topic: personal and dependency exemptions.
Step 2	Read question and make notes:

- Mike and Pam ⇒ 2 personal exemptions

- 19-year-old son ⇒ 1 dependency exemption (because gross income test is met)

- 23-year-old daughter ⇒ 1 dependency exemption (because full-time student for 5 months)

- Pam's father ⇒ None because he is not a citizen (note: he could qualify if he were a citizen of Mexico or Canada)

Step 3	Count exemptions (4) and select Choice c.

a. 2

b. 3

c. 4

d. 5

e. None of the above

Answer: c

Exemptions are allowed for Mike, Pam, their son, and their daughter. They are not entitled to an exemption for Pam's father because he was not a citizen or resident of the United States or other qualifying country. Their son qualifies as a dependent because his gross income was less than the exemption amount ($3,400 in 2007). The gross income test is waived for their daughter, who was a full-time student for at least 5 months during the year.

Example 2

George, whose wife died in November 2006, filed a joint tax return for 2006. He did not remarry and has continued to maintain his home for his two dependent children. In the preparation of his tax return for 2007, what is George's filing status?

Example 2 Analysis

Step 1	Read last line and identify the topic: filing status for George for 2007.
Step 2	Read question and make notes:

- Wife died November 2006

- Joint return filed for 2006

- Unmarried with 2 dependents

Step 3	With these facts and notes, you should immediately recall that the surviving spouse's filing status can be used for the 2 years following the year of death of the first spouse if there is a dependent child.
Step 4	Delete the clearly wrong answers by striking through them (e.g., delete answer d because he is not married). This will help you to focus on the viable alternatives.
Step 5	Select Choice b.

a.   Single

b.   Qualified widow/widower

c.   Head of household

d.   Married filing separately

e.   None of the above

Answer: b

George correctly filed a joint return in 2006. He will file as a qualified widower for 2007.

Example 3

Brenda, an employee of Duff Corporation, died December 25, 2007. During December, Duff Corporation made employee death payments of $10,000 to her widower and $10,000 to her 17-year-old son. What amounts can be excluded from gross income by the widower and son in their respective tax returns for 2007?

Example 3 Analysis

Step 1	Read last line and identify the topic: amounts excluded from gross income for 2007.
Step 2	Read question and make notes:

- Brenda died during 2007

- Employee death payments of $10,000 to widow and $10,000 to son

Step 3	With these facts and notes, you should recall that the law allowing an exclusion for death benefits was repealed.
Step 4	Analysis:

- Total amount excludable = $0

- Total death benefits = $20,000

Step 5	Select Choice a.

	Widower	Son
a.	$0	$0
b.	$2,500	$2,500
c.	$5,000	$5,000
d.	$7,500	$7,500
e.	$10,000	$10,000

Answer: a

No death proceeds are excludable.

Example 4

Clark wants to retire in 9 years. He needs an additional $300,000 (today's dollars) in 9 years to have sufficient funds to finance this objective. He assumes inflation will average 5% over the long run, and he can earn a 4% compound annual after-tax return on investments. What will be Clark's payment at the end of the second year?

Example 4 Analysis

Step 1	Read last line and identify the topic: TVM serial payment second year-end.
Step 2	Read question and make notes:

- Needs $300,000 in today's dollars in 9 years

- Inflation rate = 5%; earnings rate = 4%

Step 3	Analysis:

FV	=	$300,000	
i	=	−0.95238, or $[(1.04 \div 1.05) - 1] \times 100$	
n	=	9	
PV	=	0	
PMT	=	$34,623.42	Payment at the beginning of the year 1
		× 1.05 = $36,354.60	Payment at the end of year 1
		× 1.05 = $38,172.33	Payment at the end of year 2

Step 4	Select Choice b.

    a. $38,244.62

    b. $38,172.33

    c. $36,354.60

    d. $34,623.42

    e. None of the above

Answer: b

$36,354.60 × 1.05 = $38,172.33. This is an example of a serial payment. A serial payment is not an annuity due or ordinary annuity level payment. A serial payment increases annually at the rate of inflation.

Example 5

A taxpayer gives her son property with a basis to donor of $35,000 and a fair market value of $30,000. No gift tax is paid. The son subsequently sells the property for $33,000. What is his recognized gain (or loss)?

Example 5 Analysis

Step 1	Read last line and identify the topic: gain or loss on sale of donated property. Note: This topic should bring to mind the important points for this area, such as basis and sales price.
Step 2	Read question and make notes: • FMV < basis • FMV < sales price < basis • If an asset is sold between the gain basis and the loss basis, there will be no gain or loss.
Step 3	Select Choice a.

    a. No gain or loss

    b. Loss

    c. Gain

    d. None of the above

Answer: a

The son's basis is $35,000 for gains. His loss basis is $30,000. Because his selling price of $33,000 is between the gain and the loss basis, there is no recognized gain or loss.

CALCULATION QUESTIONS

Example 6

Helen, a single taxpayer, purchases an airplane for $130,000. To obtain financing for the purchase, Helen issues a lien on her personal residence in the amount of $130,000. At the time, the residence had a fair market value of $400,000 and a first mortgage of $320,000. For the plane loan, Helen may claim as qualified residence interest the interest on what amount?

Example 6 Analysis

Step 1	Read last line and identify the topic: qualified residence interest/home equity limit.
Step 2	Read question and make notes:

- QRI limit to $1,000,000 debt or fair market value, whichever is less
- Home equity line limited to the lesser of equity or $100,000

Step 3	Analysis:

FMV	$400,000
First Mortgage	– 320,000
	$80,000 Equity limit

Step 4	Answer $80,000. Select Choice b.

    a. $30,000

    b. $80,000

    c. $100,000

    d. $130,000

    e. None of the above

Answer: b

Home equity loans are limited to the lesser of:

- the fair market value of the residence, reduced by acquisition indebtedness; or
- $100,000.

Thus, $400,000 (fair market value) minus $320,000 (first mortgage) provides a limit of $80,000. Interest on the remaining $50,000 of the loan will be treated under the consumer interest rules (i.e., not deductible).

Example 7

Connie wants to withdraw $1,200 at the beginning of each month for the next 5 years. She expects to earn 10% compounded monthly on her investments. What lump sum should Connie deposit today?

Example 7 Analysis

Step 1	Read last line and identify the topic: analysis of PMT (AD).
Step 2	Read question and make notes: PV problem.
Step 3	Analysis:

- PV
- n
- i
- PMT
- FV

Step 3	Fill out information and identify objective.

$$PV \quad = \quad ?$$

$$n \quad = \quad 60$$

$$i \quad = \quad 10\% \div 12$$

$$PMT \quad = \quad \$1,200 \text{ (annuity due)}$$

$$FV \quad = \quad \text{Not applicable (put 0 in cell to eliminate any numbers)}$$

Step 4   Calculate PV_{AD} = $56,949.10. Answer: b.

If your result was $56,478.44, you calculated an ordinary annuity (payments at the end of the period) instead of an annuity due.

Make sure that your calculator is in "begin" mode.

a. $56,478.44

b. $56,949.10

c. $58,630.51

d. $59,119.10

e. None of the above

Answer: b

$$PMT_B \quad = \quad \$1,200$$

$$i \quad = \quad 0.8333 \ (10 \div 12)$$

$$n \quad = \quad 60 \ (5 \times 12)$$

$$PVAD \quad = \quad \$56,949.10$$

Example 8

Gary has received an inheritance of $200,000. He wants to withdraw equal periodic payments at the beginning of each month for the next 5 years. He expects to earn 12% compounded monthly on his investments. How much can he receive each month?

Example 8 Analysis

Step 1	Read last line and identify the topic: analysis of PMT (AD).
Step 2	Analysis:

- PV
- n
- i
- PMT
- FV

Step 3   Fill out information and identify objective.

PV	=	$200,000
n	=	60
i	=	$12 \div 12$
Objective $\Rightarrow$ PMT$_{AD}$	=	$4,404.84 (therefore Choice a)
FV	=	Not applicable

Note closeness of Choice b; make sure you have the annuity due, ordinary annuity issue correct. Does Choice c or Choice d make any sense? No, 60 payments at those levels would be $2–3 million.

Step 4   Select Choice a.

a. $4,404.84

b. $4,448.89

c. $49,537.45

d. $55,481.95

e. None of the above

Answer: a

PV	=	$200,000
i	=	1.00 ($12 \div 12$)
n	=	60 (5×12)
PMT$_{AD}$	=	$4,404.84

<u>EVALUATE ANSWERS</u>

Example 9

On January 1, Mike loaned his daughter Allison $90,000 to purchase a new personal residence. There were no other loans outstanding between Mike and Allison. Allison's only income was $30,000 salary and $4,000 interest income. Mike had investment income of $200,000. Mike did not charge Allison interest. The relevant federal rate was 9%. Which of the following statements regarding the transaction is CORRECT?

   a.   Allison must recognize $8,100 (0.09 × $90,000) imputed interest income on the loan.

   b.   Mike must recognize imputed interest income of $4,000.

   c.   Mike must recognize imputed interest income of $8,100.

   d.   Allison is allowed a deduction for imputed interest of $8,100.

   e.   None of the above.

Example 9 Analysis

To answer this type of question, you must evaluate each presented option.

Step 1	Read each option and identify the topic(s): lender's imputed interest.
Step 2	Read question and make notes:
	• No interest on loans < $10,000
	• No interest on loans < $100,000 if no income
Step 3	Analysis of answer choices:
	a. No, it is not Allison who would impute interest information.
	b. Looks correct; Mike's inputed interest is equal to lesser of Allison's interest income or federal rate.
	c. Is federal rate; therefore, wrong.
	d. Allison is wrong person.
	e. Choices b and c are both possible.
Step 4	Select Choice b.

Answer: b

The $100,000 exemption applies, and thus Mike's imputed interest income is limited to Allison's net investment income.

Example 10

Judy estimates her opportunity cost on investments at 12%, compounded annually. Which of the following is the best investment alternative?

    a.   To receive $50,000 today

    b.   To receive $250,000 at the end of 14 years

    c.   To receive $40,000 at the end of four years and $120,000 8 years later

    d.   To receive $5,000 at the beginning of each 6-month period for 9 years, compounded semiannually

    e.   To receive $60,000 at the end of 3 years

Example 10 Analysis

Step 1   Read each option and identify the topic(s): present value.

Step 2   Read question.

Step 3   Analysis of answer choices:

	a	b	c	d	e
FV		$250,000.00	$120,000.00		$60,000.00
n		14	12	18	3
i		12	12	6	12
PMT				$5,000 AD	
Objective $\Rightarrow$ PV	$50,000.00	$51,154.95	$30,801.01	$57,386.30	$42,706.81
FV			$40,000.00		
n			4		
i			12		
PV			$25,420.72		
Total			$56,221.73		

Step 4   Select Choice d.

Answer: d

PMT   = $5,000

i =   6 (12 ÷ 2)

n =   18 (9 × 2)

PV_{AD} = $57,386.30

SOLVING K-TYPE QUESTIONS

<u>EVALUATE EACH K-TYPE STATEMENT</u>

Example 11

Which of the following transactions is(are) permissible regarding an IRA?

1. A nonspouse IRA beneficiary must distribute the balance of an IRA, where distribution had begun, over a period not exceeding 5 years.

2. A nonspouse IRA beneficiary may distribute the balance of an IRA, where distribution had not begun, over the life expectancy of the beneficiary.

3. A beneficiary spouse of a deceased owner of an IRA can delay any distribution of such IRA until April 1 following the year in which such heir or beneficiary is 70½.

4. A spouse beneficiary of a deceased owner IRA can roll such IRA balance into her own IRA, even if distributions had begun to the owner prior to death.

Example 11 Analysis

Step 1	Read last line and identify the topic. Note: positive/are or negative/are not. IRA/Distributions.
Step 2	Read question.
Step 3	Analysis of statements:
	1. False
	2. True
	3. True
	4. True
Step 3	Read answers.
Step 4	Select Choice d.

      a. 1 and 2

      b. 2 and 3

      c. 1, 2, and 3

      d. 2, 3, and 4

      e. 1, 2, 3, and 4

Answer: d

Statement 1 is incorrect. The option is to pay at least as fast as the original payment schedule. For K-type questions, anchor yourself in certainty. Include the answers that are certainly correct and exclude any answer with a statement that is certainly incorrect.

Example 12

Which of the following is(are) deductible for adjusted gross income?

1. Alimony paid to the taxpayer's former spouse

2. Capital losses

3. Ordinary and necessary expenses incurred in a business

4. A deductible individual retirement account (IRA) contribution

Example 12 Analysis

Step 1	Read last line and identify the topic: Note: is/are versus are not/AGI.
Step 2	Read question.
Step 3	Analysis of statements:

    1. True

    2. Let's suppose I don't know

    3. Let's suppose I don't know

    4. True

Step 4	Evaluate answers.

    a. 1 only (definitely incorrect)

    b. 4 only (definitely incorrect)

    c. 1 and 4 (possible answer)

    d. 1, 3, and 4 (possible answer)

    e. 1, 2, 3, and 4 (possible answer)

Step 5	Evaluate statements 2 and 3 above.
Step 4	Select Choice e.

    a. 1 only

    b. 4 only

    c. 1 and 4

    d. 1, 3, and 4

    e. 1, 2, 3, and 4

Answer: e

All are deductible for adjusted gross income.

Example 13

Which of the following would best describe the action of a fiscal policy economist?

1. Increase in government spending

2. Decrease in the money supply

3. Decrease in income taxes

4. Increase in the inflation rate

Example 13 Analysis

Step 1	Read last line and identify the topic: fiscal policy.
Step 2	Read question and make notes:
	• Fiscal is taxation and spending; monetary is interest rates.
Step 3	Analysis of statements:
	1. Yes, fiscal
	2. Do not know
	3. Yes, fiscal
	4. Do not know
Step 4	Evaluate answers.
	a. Possible answer
	b. Possible answer
	c. No
	d. No
	e. No
Step 5	Reevaluate statements: statement 4 is incorrect, therefore Choice a is incorrect.
Step 4	Select Choice b.

a. 1, 2, 3, and 4

b. 1 and 3

c. 2 only

d. 2 and 4

e. 1 only

Answer: b

Fiscal policy economists believe that the economy can be controlled through the use of government spending and income tax adjustments. Choice c is the answer to describe economists who believe that economic activity is controlled through the use of the money supply. Choice a is incorrect since that answer describes all the choices that include both fiscal policy as well as monetary policy economists. Choice d is incorrect because inflation is determined by market factors. Choice e partially describes the actions of a fiscal policy economist.

YOUR COMMENTS FOR VOLUMES I–VI

Our goal is to provide a high-quality product to you and other CFP® candidates. With this goal in mind, we hope to significantly improve our texts with each new edition. We welcome your written suggestions, corrections, and other general comments. Please be as detailed as possible and send your written comments to:

Kaplan Financial
143 Mallard Street, Suite E
St. Rose, Louisiana 70087
(504) 461-9860 Fax

	Volume	Page	Question	Comments (please be as specific as possible)
1.				
2.				
3.				
4.				
5.				
6.				
7.				
8.				
9.				
10.				
11.				
12.				
13.				
14.				
15.				

Name

Address

Phone _____ (Work) _____ (Home) _____ (Fax)

Email _____ Do you require a response? _____ YES _____ NO

TABLE OF CONTENTS

Solutions

TABLE OF EXHIBITS

TABLE OF APPENDIXES

ESTATE PLANNING

Outline

Estate Planning

I. BASIC CONCEPTS

A. WHAT IS ESTATE PLANNING?

1. Estate planning is the process of accumulation, management, conservation, and transfer of wealth, considering legal, tax, and personal objectives. In short, it is financial planning for death.

2. Estate planning choices are not always clear cut because emotional issues such as control and affection must be considered

3. Estate planning objectives should include the efficient transfer of assets (minimize costs)

   a. Costs include opportunity costs, costs of transfer taxes, costs of documents, and costs of probate

4. Estate planning objectives should include the effective transfer of assets (the assets go to the desired beneficiary)

   a. Eliminate conflicts between the will and property titled with survivorship rights

   b. Eliminate conflicts between the will and named beneficiaries in contracts

B. WHO NEEDS ESTATE PLANNING?

Persons who have:

1. Spouses

2. Minor children

3. Dependents (parents, handicapped individuals, and children)

4. Substantial assets

5. Specific items of personal property that they want to go to someone in particular (e.g., jewelry, antiques, and art)

6. Charitable objectives

7. Issues that need to be dealt with after their death, including:

   a. Unrelated persons who need to be provided for (e.g., life partners)

   b. Pets

   c. Businesses

   d. Problem or special need family members (e.g., those who may contest the will or who cannot handle money)

C. BENEFITS FROM ESTATE PLANNING (OBJECTIVES)

1. The client can reduce or eliminate the estate tax. This is relatively simple for estate of less than $2–4 million.

2. The client can make effective transfers during life and at death. Gifts of assets may include assets that are expected to appreciate greatly in the future.

3. Allows the client to arrange for efficient business succession

4. A plan can be designed for health care decisions that may need to be made in the event the client is unable to do so

5. Allows the estate to avoid the probate process including costs and delays (in certain instances)

6. Enables the client to pass property to the individuals of the client's choice

7. Affords the client peace of mind

D. COSTS AND RISKS ASSOCIATED WITH FAILING TO EFFECTIVELY PLAN FOR ESTATE TRANSFERS

1. Assets are not transferred to the desired heir (intestacy)

2. Costs and delays associated with probate are incurred as a result of the failure to optimize the use of techniques that allow assets to pass outside of probate (e.g., joint property with survivorship features, contracts with named beneficiaries, and trusts)

3. Unnecessary estate taxes may be incurred. Heirs receive a smaller portion of the estate than they would with estate planning (see Common Estate Planning Mistakes on page 109)

E. COLLECTING CLIENT INFORMATION AND DEFINING TRANSFER OBJECTIVES

1. Information to be collected:

   a. Family information (e.g., parents, children, ages, and health)

   b. Detailed list of assets, ownership, and liabilities

   c. Medical and disability insurance

   d. Life insurance in force, ownership, insured, and beneficiaries

   e. Annuities

   f. Wills, trusts, or gifts previously made

   g. Powers of appointment held by the client

   h. Value of assets at fair market value and an estimate of the expected growth rate

   i. Tax returns and mortgage information

2. Determine transfer objectives

   a. Minimize estate and transfer taxes (this will maximize the assets received by heirs)

   b. Avoiding probate

   c. Using lifetime transfers—applicable exclusion amount (credit equivalent)

   d. Meeting liquidity needs

   e. Planning for children from all marriages of the client

   f. Planning for possible incapacity

   g. Providing for the needs of the surviving spouse

   h. Fulfilling charitable intentions

F. THE ESTATE PLANNING PROCESS

1. Gather client information

   a. Net worth statement (list all assets, including FMV, basis, date acquired, how title is held)

   b. Cash flow statement

   c. Family information

2. Establish client objectives

3. Define problem areas, which may include:

   a. Disposition of assets

   b. Liquidity issues

   c. Excessive taxes or costs

   d. Other situational needs (e.g., disability)

4. Determine liquidity needs now and at every five-year interval for remaining life expectancy including estate transfer costs

5. Establish priorities for objectives

6. Develop a comprehensive plan with all information and objectives

7. Implement the plan

8. Review the plan periodically and update when necessary

G. THE ESTATE PLANNING TEAM

1. May consist of a number of professionals

   a. Attorney

   b. Accountant

   c. Life insurance agent

   d. Financial planner

   e. Trust officers

2. The financial planner helps to integrate the work of the team in developing the plan

3. The financial planner must avoid the unauthorized practice of law, as defined in the state in which she practices

---

Example

Although a financial planner would usually ask a client for a current cash flow statement, recommend a specified type of disability policy, and discuss tax-planning opportunities with the client's accountant, he cannot draft a will or trust document, or any other legal document, unless he is also a practicing attorney.

II. BASIC DOCUMENTS INCLUDED IN AN ESTATE PLAN

A. WILL

1. A will is a legal document that enables the testator (maker) to transfer the property at the testator's death in the manner the testator desires.

2. Advantages of a will

   a. Executor can be named

   b. Can transfer property to anyone desired

   c. Ensures the maximum marital deduction if decedent wants property to pass to spouse

   d. Can specify how estate taxes are apportioned

   e. Can designate guardians for minors

   f. Can contain provisions to establish trusts

   g. Charitable beneficiaries can be named

3. Intestacy

   a. To die *intestate* is to die without a valid will

      1.) The probate court directs how the decedent's property will be distributed according to the state's intestacy laws

      2.) The intestacy laws are not likely to distribute property the way the decedent would have if he had written his own will

   b. There are some possible adverse consequences of intestacy

      1.) In some states, a spouse's share of the decedent's estate will be equal to a child's share. For example, the surviving spouse's share with one child would be one-half of the total estate; with nine children, it would be one-tenth of the total estate.

      2.) Some states provide that a spouse's share is only a life estate with the true owner being the children

      3.) The surviving spouse may share with the deceased spouse's parents or brothers and sisters when there are no children from the marriage

      4.) Children may be treated equally, but not necessarily equitably. Each child's needs may be quite different.

      5.) Intestacy may require the administrator to furnish a surety bond and obtain probate court approval of the administrator's actions, thereby increasing the cost of administration

      6.) The court will select the administrator of the estate

      7.) Assets cannot be left to charity

4. General rules for making a valid will

   a. The will-maker must be 18 years old (unless emancipated minor)

   b. The will-maker must be of sound mind (testamentary capacity). The sound mind rules are not as stringent as those that are required for a contract.

      1.) Must understand the nature of the act

2.) Must understand the general nature of the property

3.) Must have the ability to remember and understand the nature of the relationship to the persons affected

c. Absence of undue influence—undue influence is present when the testator's free will has been substituted by someone else's free will

---

Example

A university official visits a dying alum and convinces the alum that building a new business school will give the alum immortality. This is considered undue influence.

---

d. Absence of fraud

1.) Fraud is the intentional misstatement of fact with the intent of deceiving the testator, which results in amending the will

2.) Must ask if fraud was the sole motive of the bequest

5. Types of wills

a. Holographic (handwritten) will

1.) Allowed by about half of the states

2.) Material provisions are in the testator's handwriting

3.) Must be signed and dated by the testator

4.) Need not be witnessed

b. Nuncupative (oral) will—dying declaration before sufficient witnesses

1.) Recognized by less than half of all states

2.) May only be able to pass personal property (and not real) in some states

3.) Use is fairly restricted

c. Statutory (formal) will

1.) Should be drawn by an attorney

2.) Must comply with the laws of the domiciliary state

3.) Usually signed in the presence of two witnesses (beneficiary usually can't be a witness)

6. The general provisions of a will

a. An introductory clause to identify the testator

b. Establishment of the domicile is important because each jurisdiction has its own probate rules. Any property outside the domicile will be subject to ancillary probate.

c. A declaration that this is the last will and testament

d. A revocation of all prior wills and codicils

e. Identification of executor/executrix and successor executor/executrix

f. A payments of debts clause

g. A payments of taxes clause

h. A disposition of tangible personal property clause

i. A disposition of real estate clause (residence)

j. Specific bequests of intangibles and cash

k. A residuary clause (the transfer of the balance of any other assets to someone or something)

> **Note:** Failure to have a residuary clause results in the risk of having intestate assets (e.g., from assets being accumulated after the will was prepared) that will pass through probate. Also, taxes generally will be paid from the residuary unless specifically directed otherwise.

l. An appointment and powers clause that names fiduciaries, guardians, tutors, and so forth

m. A testator's signature clause

n. An attestation clause (witness clause)

7. Other clauses in a will

a. Simultaneous death clause—in the event that both spouses die simultaneously, it creates the presumption that the testator died after the other spouse

b. Survivorship clause—a beneficiary must survive a specified period beyond the testator's death in order to receive the inheritance or bequest

1.) Such a clause will prevent property from being included in two estates in rapid succession

2.) To qualify for the marital deduction, the will cannot require the spouse to survive for more than six months to receive the bequest

c. Spendthrift clause—bars transfer of beneficiary's interest to a third party and stipulates that the interest is not subject to claims of beneficiary's creditors. The spendthrift clause is not usually effective in a will.

d. Clauses regarding disclaimers—while unnecessary to include, a disclaimer clause reminds the reader that disclaiming may be an effective tool in estate planning (see item 6, Disclaimer on page 37 for more information on disclaimers)

e. No contest clause—discourages heirs from contesting the will by substantially decreasing or eliminating their bequest if they file a formal contest

f. A codicil—a separate document that amends a will

8. Ways property can be distributed in a will

a. Per stirpes distribution

1.) *Per stirpes* means by the roots

2.) With a per stirpes distribution, members of a designated class inherit property as members of the class

a.) This election usually is used by the courts in the absence of a selection in the will

---

Example

Stephen has three children (Jay, Tawnee, and Laura). Tawnee is deceased and is survived by two children (Paul and Damien). Laura is alive and has one child (Marie). If Stephen had a $300,000 asset, and his will had a per stirpes distribution:

- Jay would receive $100,000 (1/3);

- Paul and Damien would each receive $50,000 (half of Tawnee's 1/3);

- Laura would receive $100,000 (1/3); and

- Marie would receive nothing since her mother was alive at the time of Stephen's death.

---

    b. Per capita distribution

        1.) *Per capita* means by the head

        2.) Members of a class, including heirs of a deceased member, share in the inheritance as individuals

---

Example

Stephen has three children (Jay, Tawnee, and Laura). Tawnee is deceased and is survived by two children (Paul and Damien). Laura is alive and has one child (Marie). If Stephen had a $300,000 asset, and his will had a per capita distribution:

- Jay would receive $75,000 (1/4);

- Paul would receive $75,000 (1/4);

- Damien would receive $75,000 (1/4); and

- Laura would receive $75,000 (1/4).

Most people want to transfer an equal portion to each of their children, and barring abnormal circumstances, will leave grandchildren the portion the deceased child would have received. Notice the difference in distributions received by each child/grandchild. Close attention must be used in referring to this type of distribution as it will greatly affect the wealth transfer to each beneficiary.

B. PRENUPTIAL AGREEMENT

    1. A prenuptial agreement is a legally binding agreement between two future spouses

        a. Also referred to as an antenuptial agreement

        b. Can be very useful if the forthcoming marriage is not the first marriage for one or both of the individuals

        c. Similar to trusts, a prenuptial agreement can provide full protection of one's estate for his intended heirs

    2. The agreement provides for restrictions on transfers of property between the two individuals in exchange for a relinquishment of their marital rights to each other's property

---

3. The spouse who agrees to a prenuptial agreement will receive the property agreed to upon the death of the decedent instead of a statutory share that is usually the right of a surviving spouse

4. Other purposes of a prenuptial agreement

   a. May provide for appropriate division of property upon subsequent divorce of the individuals

   b. May provide for certain transfers from one party to another before the marriage

   c. May substitute for statutory elections and other inheritance rights of a spouse upon the other spouse's death

   d. May provide for the receipt of a fixed estate by the surviving spouse

C. LIVING WILLS AND MEDICAL DIRECTIVES (ADVANCED MEDICAL DIRECTIVES)

1. A living will establishes the medical situations in which the testator no longer wants life-sustaining treatment

   a. Must generally meet the requirements of a formally drafted state statute. A durable power of attorney for health care may or may not substitute (usually not).

   b. Only covers a narrow range of situations, usually applies only to terminal patients

   c. Does not appoint a surrogate decision maker

   d. May create problems that arise from vagueness or ambiguities in drafting

D. A DURABLE POWER OF ATTORNEY FOR HEALTH CARE

1. Appoints person to make health care decisions for the principal

2. Always springs (becomes effective) on incapacity

3. Recognized in most states

4. May not be used to terminate life support in some states

E. DURABLE POWER OF ATTORNEY FOR PROPERTY

1. A written document enabling one individual (principal) to designate another person or persons to act as his attorney-in-fact (agent) is termed a durable power of attorney. When executed, the principal:

   a. Must be 18

   b. Must be competent

2. The power survives disability and/or incapacity, but not death (a nondurable power of attorney does not survive client's incapacity)

3. The power may be limited (e.g., to pay any bills) or unlimited (e.g., all of the legal powers I have myself)

   a. A limited power is a special power

      1.) Held to an ascertainable standard (health/education/maintenance/support)

      2.) May be almost as broad as a general power except no appointing to one's self, one's creditors, one's estate, or one's estate creditors

   b. An unlimited power is a general power that gives the appointee the power to do anything the principal could do

1.) The unlimited power to appoint to oneself, one's creditors, one's estate, or one's estate creditors may result in gift tax or inclusion in the estate of the one who has the power

> **Note:** A person possessing an unlimited durable power of attorney, in most cases, is not permitted to make gifts to himself or other family members (usually in conjunction with estate planning). If the power to gift is a desirable feature of the power of attorney, it should be separately and explicitly stated.

4. Such a device may negate the necessity to petition a local court to appoint a guardian ad litem or conservator

5. Such a device provides for continuity in the management of affairs in the event of disability and/or incapacity

6. The power may be springing or immediately effective (nonspringing). Generally, if springing, the device must indicate that the power springs upon disability or incapacity and is not affected by subsequent disability or incapacity (not authorized by all states).

7. The power is revocable by the principal

8. Usually less expensive to set up and administer than a living trust or conservatorship

9. Durable powers of attorney can be abused. Therefore, the principal should give serious consideration to naming the attorney-in-fact.

Example

Sam, a small business owner in poor health, is concerned about who will make not only business decisions should he become incapacitated, but also who would manage his personal affairs. Sam could execute two durable springing powers, each naming an attorney-in-fact to make decisions. A relative could be named to manage personal affairs, while a business associate could be named to manage the business. The powers would only spring upon Sam's incapacity.

---

10. Durable powers of attorney are particularly important for nontraditional couples (heterosexual couples who have decided not to marry or same-sex couples). Without this document in place (for both property and health care), the ability to make crucial decisions may fall to family members rather than a partner in the relationship.

F. A SIDE OR PERSONAL INSTRUCTION LETTER

1. Details and wishes regarding tangible possessions of nominal pecuniary value and disposition of the remains of decedent, including funeral arrangements and so forth

2. Avoids cluttering the will with small details

G. TESTAMENTARY TRUSTS

1. A testamentary trust is a type of trust that is created after an individual's death

   a. Created within a will

   b. Effective at the time of testator's death

   c. Irrevocable at the time of the testator's death

2. Because the trust is established at the time of death, the assets transferred to the trust through the decedent's will are subject to probate

   a. May cause delays in the creation of the trust

   b. Assets will be subject to public scrutiny

3. Testamentary trusts must contain the same elements of a living trust

   a. Beneficiaries can be determined

   b. Testator must have intended to create the trust

   c. Trustee manages property after the trust is created

   d. Trustee holds legal title to the property after the trust is created

4. Advantages of testamentary trusts

   a. Can be revoked by the testator anytime before death

   b. Can provide flexibility in income and corpus distributions that would not be possible with a direct bequest by will

   c. Can contain power of appointment provisions, allowing one or more beneficiaries (holders) to control trust property to some extent

   d. Trust assets can be managed by a professional trustee, rather than beneficiaries

   e. Can provide life income and security to beneficiaries after the testator's death

5. Disadvantages of testamentary trusts

   a. Subject to probate because the assets pass through the will first

   b. No income tax or estate tax savings during the testator's lifetime

      1.) Assets will be included in the testator's gross estate upon death

      2.) Because assets are owned by testator during his or her lifetime, income from the assets will be taxed to the testator

   c. Depending on the provisions of the trust, the beneficiary may have no control over when the trust corpus is received

   d. Trust may be associated with large costs, such as annual trustee fees

III. OWNERSHIP OF PROPERTY AND HOW IT IS TRANSFERRED

A. PROPERTY INTERESTS (TITLE AND OWNERSHIP)

1. Types

    a. Fee simple—complete ownership with all rights (e.g., sell, gift, alienate, or convey). Property will pass through probate process (fee simple absolute). Fee simple property is also referred to as sole ownership property.

    b. Life estate—the holder of the life estate has an exclusive right to the use and enjoyment of the property for life. The interest terminates upon the life estate holder's death.

    c. Interest for term—similar to life estate except that the interest is for a definite term as opposed to a life term

    d. Remainders and revision—the future interest in the property that goes to a person after the termination of either a life estate or interest term. If the future interest goes to someone other than the grantor, it is called a remainder. If it goes back to the original grantor, it is called a revision.

2. Forms of joint ownership

    a. Tenancy in common—two or more persons holding an undivided interest in the whole property (relative ownership percentage may differ)

        1.) The property is treated as owned outright and one's interest can be sold, donated, willed, or pass through intestate succession

        2.) When one tenant in common dies, the remaining tenants in common do not automatically receive the decedent's interest

        3.) The property usually passes through probate

        4.) There is a right of partition

Example

Richard and Robert own a piece of land in southern Alabama. Richard is a two-thirds owner and Robert owns one-third. Because the percent interests differ, the property must be held as tenants in common. Joint tenants must be equal owners.

---

    b. Joint tenancy—two or more persons holding the same fractional interest (equal owners)

        1.) Normally implied is the right of survivorship (JTWROS)

        2.) Joint tenants have right to sever interest in property without the consent of the joint tenant (and destroy the survivorship right)

        3.) Property held JTWROS passes to the surviving owners outside of probate according to operation of law

        4.) Nonspousal JTWROS property

            a.) Gift tax ramifications

- If two or more unmarried individuals purchase property as JTWROS, there are no gift tax consequences if each individual contributed the same amount toward the purchase price

- If the unmarried tenants contributed unequal amounts toward the purchase price, the tenant contributing the majority of the purchase price has made a gift to the other tenant(s)

   — Gift is eligible for the annual exclusion, because it is a present interest gift

   — Gift is equal to the difference between an equal contribution amount and the actual amount contributed by the tenant contributing the lesser amount

---

Example

Steve and Sandy are siblings who purchased a $100,000 vacation home in Florida and titled the home as JTWROS. Because Sandy was short of funds, Steve agreed to provide $80,000 of the purchase price. Sandy provided the other $20,000 toward the purchase price.

Because Steve contributed more to the purchase price than Sandy, he has given her a gift for gift-tax purposes. The amount of the gift is $30,000 ($50,000 amount Sandy would have provided had she made an equal contribution less $20,000 of funds actually provided by Sandy.

The gift is considered a present interest gift, eligible for the annual exclusion ($12,000 for 2007) for gift-tax purposes. Therefore, Steve has given Sandy an $18,000 ($30,000 gross gift less $12,000 annual exclusion) taxable gift.

Example

Joey owns a piece of real estate he purchased outright several years ago. When the value of the real estate increased to $300,000, he added his daughter's name to the title as a JTWROS.

Joey has made a gift to his daughter in the amount of $150,000, one-half of the value of the real estate. The gift will be eligible for the gift-tax annual exclusion.

---

    b.) Estate tax ramifications

- JTWROS property will avoid probate because the decedent's share of the property will pass to the surviving tenant(s) automatically by operation of law

- The percentage-of-contribution rule determines what portion of the property will be included in the decedent's gross estate

   — The portion of the property included in the decedent's gross estate is based on his relative contribution toward the purchase price of the property

   — If the surviving tenant contributed the entire purchase price, the deceased tenant is not required to include the property in his gross estate

   — The burden of proof to demonstrate that the surviving tenant made some contribution lies with the decedent's estate or the surviving tenant

---

Example

Joey owns a piece of real estate he purchased outright several years ago. When the value of the real estate increased to $300,000, he added his daughter's name to the title as a JTWROS.

If Joey predeceases his daughter, the entire date of death value of the real estate will be included in his gross estate, because he contributed 100% of the purchase price.

If Joey's daughter predeceases Joey, none of the value of the property will be included in her gross estate, because she contributed nothing toward the purchase price; however, the daughter's estate or Joey must be able to sufficiently prove that the entire purchase price was provided by Joey.

---

    c.) Income tax ramifications

- There are no income tax ramifications when individuals purchase property as JTWROS

  — Even if one tenant contributes more than the other tenant(s), there are no income tax ramifications

  — At the time a tenant is added to the title of property as a joint tenant, there are no income tax ramifications

- A tenant's basis in the JTWROS property is equal to the amount the tenant contributed to the purchase of the property

  — If a tenant receives a gift of JTWROS property, the recipient's basis will be the carryover basis of the donor

  — When a tenant dies, the portion of the JTWROS property included in the tenant's gross estate will receive a step-up in basis

---

Example

Joey and his daughter purchased a piece of real estate several years ago for $300,000. Joey and his daughter each paid one-half of the purchase price for the real estate.

Joey died when the value of the real estate was $1 million. Because Joey provided one-half of the purchase price, one-half of the date of death value of the real estate ($500,000) will be included in his gross estate.

His daughter will receive his half of the property by operation of law, meaning she will now be the outright owner of the real estate. Her basis in the property will be $650,000 ($150,000 original basis, plus Joey's $500,000 stepped-up basis.

---

    c. Tenancy by the entirety—a JTWROS between husband and wife

       1.) One spouse will not be able to sever interest without the consent of the other spouse

    2.) This form of ownership is recognized only in certain states and gives greater creditor protection than a regular JTWROS

  d. Community property

    1.) In general

      a.) With community property, married individuals own an equal undivided interest in all wealth accumulated during the marriage

      b.) Community property states are Arizona, California, Idaho, Louisiana, Nevada, New Mexico, Texas, Washington, and Wisconsin

      c.) Property acquired by a married couple in a community property state will be held as community property

    2.) Characteristics

      a.) Generally, there is no automatic right of survivorship for ownership of community property

      b.) One-half of the value of all community property is included in the gross estate of the first spouse to die

      c.) There is a step-up in basis to fair market value in both halves of community property at the death of the first spouse

      d.) Quasi-community property—property acquired by residents of noncommunity property states that would be considered community property if acquired in a community property state

EXHIBIT 1: KEY PROPERTY INTEREST

	Gross Estate Inclusion	Inclusion in Probate Estate	Rights of Survivorship	Unlimited Marital Deduction	Partitionable Without Consent
Fee Simple (outright ownership)	100%	Yes	No	If spouse	N/A
Tenants in Common (two or more holding nonproportional interests)	Percentage ownership	Yes	No	If spouse	Yes
Joint Tenancy (WROS)	Nonspouses— rule of contribution; spouses—50%	No	Yes	If spouse	Yes
Tenancy by Entirety (between spouses)	50%	No	Yes	Yes	No
Community Property (between spouses)	50%	Yes	No	Yes	No

    3.) Exceptions to community property (separate property)

      a.) Property acquired prior to marriage

      b.) Property acquired by gift by one spouse during marriage

c.) Property inherited by one spouse during marriage

d.) Property acquired by court award during marriage compensating for physical injury

e.) It is possible to create separate property out of community property by donating one spouse's interest to the other spouse (and vice versa). Individuals in community property states can usually opt out of the community property scheme by filing a declaration with the state (partition of community property).

4.) Migratory couples

a.) Moving from a community property state to a common law (separate property) state

- In general, the character of property is not changed and, therefore, will remain community property

- The spouses may choose to divide the property upon arrival in a common law state. If the property is divided, when one spouse dies, the benefits of a stepped-up basis of both halves of the property will be lost.

b.) Moving from a common law state to a community property state

- In general, separate property owned while in a common law state remains separate property after a move to a community property state

- Upon death, a surviving spouse typically has no claim against the separate property. However, several states have elective share statutes that prevent a spouse from being disinherited.

B. TYPES OF INTERESTS TRANSFERRED

1. Outright—transferee receives both legal title and beneficial (economic) ownership

2. Legal—transferee receives only legal title (e.g., trustee of a trust)

3. Beneficial—transferee receives economic or beneficial ownership but not legal title (beneficiary of a trust)

C. TRANSFERS DURING LIFE

1. Arms-length transactions

   a. Sales and exchanges

   b. Installment sales

2. Transfers to loved ones

   a. Sales/exchanges include:

      1.) Sales and installment sales

      2.) Private annuities

      3.) Self-canceling installment notes (SCINs)

   b. Partial gift/sales

      1.) Grantor retained trusts (i.e., GRATs and GRUTs)

      2.) Qualified personal residence trust (QPRT)

   c. Transfers not subject to gift tax

      1.) Legal support

      2.) Qualified transfer (tuition and medical expenses paid directly to institutions)

      3.) Gifts to spouses who are US citizens (initially subject to tax and part of the taxable gifts, but unlimited marital deduction usually eliminates any tax). Gifts to noncitizen spouses qualify for a larger annual exclusion.

      4.) Annual exclusion

      5.) Gift loans

      6.) Disclaimers

   d. Transfer subject to gift tax

      1.) Use of gift tax applicable lifetime exclusion amount ($1 million for 2007) will reduce transfers subject to tax

      2.) Gifts above applicable exclusion amount will create a gift-tax liability

   e. Common order of transfers to loved ones (precise order depends on facts and circumstances)

      1.) Legal support

      2.) Annual exclusion gifts ($12,000 per year per donee)

      3.) Gift loans

      4.) Qualified transfers (tuition and medical payments made directly to the provider)

      5.) Gifts to spouses

      6.) Use of applicable credit amount

      7.) Taxable gifts

      8.) Private annuities

      9.) Use of disclaimers

3. Transfers to charities

   a. Completed gifts

   b. Direct gifts

   c. Partial gifts/exchanges

   d. Charitable gift annuity

   e. Pooled income fund

   f. Charitable remainder trusts (CRATs and CRUTs)

   g. Charitable lead trusts (CLATs and CLUTs)

4. Advantage of lifetime gifts

   a. Qualified transfers (tuition and medical payments made directly to the provider) reduce gross estate

   b. Using the annual exclusion reduces the gross estate

   c. Can give unlimited gifts to spouse without transfer tax consequences (provided spouse is a US citizen)

d. Can give up to $1 million (for 2007) without incurring gift tax

e. After completion of the gift, appreciation on the gifted property is not subject to transfer tax

f. Gift tax paid on gifts prior to three years before death is not subject to estate tax

g. Income shifting on gifts can be accomplished

D. TRANSFERS AT DEATH

1. By will

2. By laws of intestacy

3. By operation of law (e.g., jointly held property—JTWROS)

4. By contract (named beneficiary—other than estate), such as:

    a. Insurance policies

    b. IRAs

    c. Retirement plan assets (e.g., 401(k) plans)

    d. Marriage contracts

    e. Annuities

    f. Pay on death (PODs) account—bank account that has a named beneficiary and passes outside of probate (similar to Totten Trust)

    g. Transfer on death (TODs) account—investment account that has a named beneficiary and passes outside of probate

5. By trust

    a. Revocable trusts (revocable prior to death, irrevocable at death)

    b. Irrevocable trusts (usually treated as a gift during life)

E. CONSEQUENCES OF TRANSFERS

    a. Loss of control if sale or gift

    b. Taxes may have to be paid. Gift taxes may be due for inter vivos (lifetime) transfers and are paid by the donor (unless net gift).

> **Note:** Gifts of a future interest generally do not qualify for the annual exclusion. A remainder interest in a trust is an example of a future interest gift.

    c. Costs and delays may occur in probate for assets transferred by will or intestacy (see Duties of an Executor or Administrator on page 23)

F. NONTRADITIONAL RELATIONSHIPS

1. In general

    a. Nontraditional relationships include same-sex relationships, communal relationships, and cohabitation

    b. Nontraditional relationships can have many gift and estate tax disadvantages

  c. Certain planning opportunities available to married couples are not available to unmarried couples

 2. Disadvantages

  a. No gift tax marital deduction is available to unmarried couples

   1.) In some cases, a common law husband and wife may be eligible for the marital deduction

   2.) An unmarried donor will only be able to use the annual exclusion to reduce the amount of the taxable gift. (In addition, gift splitting is not available.)

  b. No estate tax marital deduction is available to unmarried couples

   1.) The estate of an unmarried person is more likely to pay federal estate tax than the estate of a married individual

  c. Surviving cohabitants have no intestacy rights to the decedent's property

   1.) If decedent dies without a will, the intestacy laws determine who will receive the decedent's property

   2.) Unmarried couples should generally have a will, use legal titling, or create trusts to prevent undesired consequences

 3. Planning for nontraditional relationships (generally avoid probate)

  a. Create a will leaving specific bequests to the partner—although effective, not necessarily the best choice because of potential for will contests

  b. Make lifetime gifts to partner

  c. Convert property owned outright into Joint Tenancy With Right of Survivorship (JTWROS) or Tenancy in Common.

   1.) JTWROS property will avoid probate, but the entire date-of-death value must be included in the gross estate of the decedent who purchased the property initially

   2.) Tenancy in Common property will not avoid probate, but only the decedent's share of the property will be included in his estate at death

  d. Name the other cohabitant as the beneficiary of qualified plans and IRAs

  e. Obtain a life insurance policy with the other cohabitant as beneficiary

  f. Use POD and TOD beneficiary designations for bank and investment accounts

IV. THE PROBATE PROCESS

A. OVERVIEW OF PROBATE

1. Purposes of the probate process:

   a. Enables title of property to be transferred from a decedent to the rightful beneficiary

   b. Proves the validity of a will

   c. Verifies the orderly distribution of assets to the heirs

2. Advantages of the probate process:

   a. Protects creditors by ensuring that debts of the estate are paid

   b. Implements disposition objectives of testator of valid will

   c. Provides clean title to heirs or legatees

   d. Increases the chance that all parties in interest have notice of proceedings and, therefore, a right to be heard

   e. Provides for an orderly administration of decedent's assets

3. Disadvantages of the probate process:

   a. Can be costly and complex

      1.) Real property located in a state outside the testator's domicile may trigger a separate probate in that state

      2.) Probate costs are frequently calculated on the basis of a percentage of the assets in the probate estate

   b. Can create delays in transferring assets to heirs

   c. Process is open to public scrutiny

B. TRANSFER OF ASSETS AT DEATH

1. The method by which property is transferred to heirs at death will determine whether the property will pass through probate

2. Methods in which property may be transferred at death:

   a. By will (testate)—passes through the probate process

      1.) If a decedent dies with a valid will, the decedent is said to have died testate

      2.) Property transferred through the decedent's will passes through the probate process

      3.) Types of property passing by will:

         a.) Assets owned outright by the decedent at death (fee simple titling)

         b.) Decedent's share of property owned as tenancy in common or community property

   b. By law of intestacy—passes through the probate process

      1.) Property not passing by will, contract, or operation of law passes under the laws of intestate succession

         a.) A person who dies without a valid will is said to die intestate b.) Partial intestacy occurs when a testator has a valid will but fails to dispose of all of his or her property through the will

2.) State law determines the distribution of all property located within that state

a.) Each state has a prescribed order for disposition to the heirs of the decedent

b.) Typically, the decedent's surviving spouse is given primary consideration under the intestacy laws

c.) If the decedent does not have a surviving spouse, the decedent's children may inherit the decedent's estate in equal shares

d.) If there are no living relatives, the decedent's property passes to the state

3.) Intestacy law does not provide for the distribution of assets to the decedent's friends, business associates, or charity

---

Example

Billy dies intestate, leaving $1.5 million worth of assets. In Billy's state of domicile, the laws of intestacy leave one-half of a decedent's assets to the surviving spouse, with the remaining estate divided equally among the decedent's surviving children.

Billy has a surviving spouse and three surviving children. Under the intestacy laws, his surviving spouse will receive $750,000, and each of his three surviving children will receive $250,000. No assets will pass to Billy's friends, business associates, other relatives, or charity.

---

c. By contract—avoids probate

1.) If assets pass to an heir by contract, the assets will avoid the probate process

2.) Assets passing by contract

a.) Life insurance proceeds with a named beneficiary

b.) All retirement plans with named beneficiaries

c.) All annuities with named joint annuitants

d. By operation of law—avoids probate

1.) If assets pass to an heir by operation of law, the assets will avoid the probate process

2.) Assets passing by operation of law

a.) Property titled as joint tenants with rights of survivorship (JTWROS)

b.) Property titled as tenants by the entirety

c.) Trust property—both revocable and irrevocable trusts avoid probate

EXHIBIT 2: ASSET PASSING THROUGH AND AROUND THE PROBATE PROCESS

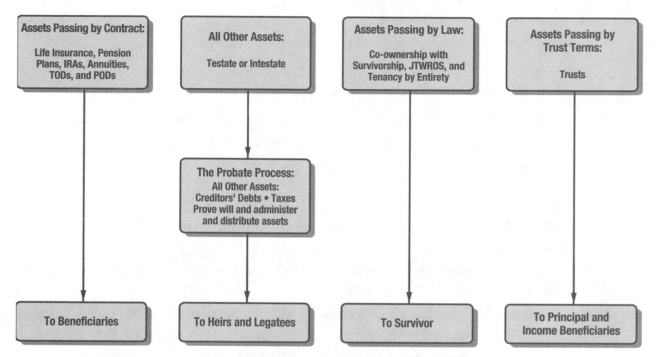

C. DUTIES OF AN EXECUTOR OR ADMINISTRATOR

1. Executor—an executor is the personal representative of an estate that is named specifically in a decedent's will

   a. Executor locates and proves will

   b. Locates witnesses to will

   c. Receives letters testamentary from court

2. Administrator—an administrator is a personal representative of an estate appointed by a court, if the decedent died without a valid will (intestate) or failed to name an executor in his will

   a. Petitions court for his or her own appointment

   b. Receives letters of administration

   c. Posts required bond

3. Personal representative—many states no longer make a distinction between an executor and an administrator, but merely refer to such person as the personal representative of the Estate

4. Duties of executors and administrators:

    a. Locate and assemble property

    b. Safeguard, manage, and invest property

    c. Advertise in newspapers

    d. Locate and communicate with potential beneficiaries

    e. Pay expenses of decedent

    f. Pay debts and taxes (files tax returns, such as Forms 1040, 1041, and 706)

    g. Distribute assets to beneficiaries according to will or laws of intestacy

D. ABATEMENT

1. Occasionally, an individual dies with assets that are not sufficient to pay all bequests and pay all creditors

2. The process of abatement reduces or eliminates bequests so that all debts and administrative expenses are paid in full

    a. In states that follow the Uniform Probate Code, the beneficiaries shares abate in the following order:

        1.) Probate property not disposed of in the decedent's will

        2.) Residuary bequests

        3.) General bequests

        4.) Specific bequests

    b. Some states abate gifts to a spouse only after abatement of bequests to individuals unrelated to the decedent

---

Example

Scott dies in a state that follows the Uniform Probate Code. His will leaves his car to his daughter, Mary; $30,000 in cash to his cousin, Chris; and the residue of his estate to his wife, Stacy.

At the time of his death, Scott's estate consisted of the car and $35,000 in cash. He also had debts of $7,000. The state will require the $7,000 debt to be paid, leaving $28,000 in cash. The Uniform Probate Code abatement would result in Chris receiving the $28,000 remaining cash balance. Mary would receive the car, and Stacy would receive nothing.

V. FEDERAL GIFT AND ESTATE TAXATION

A. HISTORY

1. Prior to the Tax Reform Act of 1976, A separate federal estate tax and a separate federal gift tax existed. The gift tax rates were lower than those applicable to the federal estate tax. For gifts in excess of the annual exclusion, a specific lifetime exemption of $30,000 was allowed per donor.

2. The Tax Reform Act of 1976 made sweeping changes to the existing structure of the federal gift and estate taxes. For transfers after 1976:

    a. The separate sets of gift and estate tax rates were replaced with a unified transfer tax rate schedule, progressive in nature

    b. Both gift and estate tax exemptions were replaced by a unified tax credit. The unified credit is now referred to as the applicable credit amount. For 2007, the applicable credit amount is $345,800 for lifetime gifts and $780,800 for transfers at death. These amounts can effectively shelter up to $1 million of assets from gift tax and $2 million from estate tax.

    c. Taxable gifts made after December 31, 1976, must be added to the taxable estate in arriving at the tax base for applying the estate tax at death

3. The Economic Growth and Tax Relief Reconciliation Act of 2001 (EGTRRA 2001) created different gift and estate applicable exclusion amounts and applicable credit amounts (See following table.)

    a. Estate tax—the estate tax applicable exclusion amount is increased in future years, and the highest estate tax rate will be decreased on the basis of the following schedule. The estate tax is repealed completely after 2009.

    b. Gift tax—the gift tax applicable exclusion amount is $1 million ($345,800 gift tax applicable credit amount) for 2007. This applicable exclusion amount will remain at $1 million for all future years. The gift tax is not repealed after 2009.

    c. Generation-skipping transfer taxes are repealed after 2009

    d. Sunset provisions—under the new law, the estate and transfer tax provisions provided for in EGTRRA 2001 will sunset in 2010. Thus, rates, laws, and exclusions will return to 2001 rates after 2010.

Year of Death	Maximum Gift Tax Rate	Gift Tax Applicable Exclusion Amount	Gift Tax Applicable Credit Amount	Maximum Estate Tax Rate	Estate Tax Applicable Exclusion Amount	Estate Tax Applicable Credit Amount
2007	45%	$1,000,000	$345,800	45%	$2,000,000	$780,800
2008	45%	$1,000,000	$345,800	45%	$2,000,000	$780,800
2009	45%	$1,000,000	$345,800	45%	$3,500,000	$1,455,800
2010	35%	$1,000,000	$330,800	Repealed	Repealed	Repealed

B. TRANSFER TAXES—OVERVIEW

1. The unified transfer tax, which is an excise tax, covers all taxable gratuitous transfers after December 31, 1976

    a. The gift tax is a tax on transfers during the donor's lifetime (including gifts prior to 1977 and after 1976)

    b. The estate tax is a tax on transfers at or after death

2. Persons subject to the tax

    a. The gift tax applies to all completed transfers of property during the donor's lifetime, wherever situated, by individuals who, at the time of the gift, are citizens or residents of the United States. For those who are neither residents nor citizens of the United States, the federal gift tax is applicable to only those gifts of property located within the United States.

    b. The federal estate tax applies to US citizens, residents, and nonresidents owning US property. However, the application may be different in cases involving nonresident property owners, depending on individual treaties.

3. Tax formula (See Exhibit 4: Gift Tax Formula on page 48).

   a. The computation of the federal gift tax is as follows:

	Current Transfers/Gifts
–	Split gifts
–	Annual exclusion
=	Taxable transfer
–	Marital deduction
	Charitable deduction
=	Taxable gifts made in current year
+	Adjusted taxable gifts from prior years (post 1976)
=	Total taxable gifts
	Unified transfer tax on total taxable gifts
–	Tax paid or deemed paid on prior taxable gifts*
–	The applicable credit amount
=	**Tax due on gifts made in current year**

   b. The federal estate tax is computed as follows (See Exhibit 6: Estate Tax Formula on page 58).

	Gross estate
–	Funeral expenses
	Administrative costs
	Debts
	Unpaid taxes (including any state death taxes)
	Losses
=	Adjusted gross estate
–	Marital deduction
	Charitable deduction
=	Taxable estate
+	Adjusted taxable gifts from prior years (post 1976)
=	Tax base
	Tentative tax on total transfers
–	Tax paid or deemed paid on prior taxable gifts*
–	Tax credits (including applicable credit amount)
=	Federal estate tax due

Credit on prior gifts is calculated at current unified transfer tax rates (See Section Deemed Paid Adjustment on page 39).

4. The fair market value of property on the date transferred generally determines the amount subject to gift or estate tax. An estate may elect the alternate valuation date. (See Alternate Valuation Date on page 107.)

EXHIBIT 3: 2007 UNIFIED TAX RATE SCHEDULE (FOR GIFTS AND ESTATES)

Over $0 but not over $10,000	18% of such amount
Over $10,000 but not over $20,000	$1,800 plus 20% of the excess of such amount over $10,000
Over $20,000 but not over $40,000	$3,800 plus 22% of the excess of such amount over $20,000
Over $40,000 but not over $60,000	$8,200 plus 24% of the excess of such amount over $40,000
Over $60,000 but not over $80,000	$13,000 plus 26% of the excess of such amount over $60,000
Over $80,000 but not over $100,000	$18,200 plus 28% of the excess of such amount over $80,000
Over $100,000 but not over $150,000	$23,800 plus 30% of the excess of such amount over $100,000
Over $150,000 but not over $250,000	$38,800 plus 32% of the excess of such amount over $150,000
Over $250,000 but not over $500,000	$70,800 plus 34% of the excess of such amount over $250,000
Over $500,000 but not over $750,000	$155,800 plus 37% of the excess of such amount over $500,000
Over $750,000 but not over $1,000,000	$248,300 plus 39% of the excess of such amount over $750,000
Over $1,000,000 but not over $1,250,000	$345,800 plus 41% of the excess of such amount over $1,000,000
Over $1,250,000 but not over $1,500,000	$448,300 plus 43% of the excess of such amount over $1,250,000
Over $1,500,000	$555,800 plus 45% of the excess of such amount over $1,500,000

VI. THE FEDERAL GIFT TAX

A. INTRODUCTION

1. A gift is a completed transfer of an interest in property by an individual in exchange for less than full and adequate consideration

   a. Gifts, for gift tax purposes, generally fall under the category of love and affection

   b. Gifts by businesses are generally not considered to be for love and affection and, subject to de minimis exceptions, may be included in the income of the recipient

2. Gift tax applies to completed lifetime (inter vivos) gifts

3. Gifts effective at death are not gifts, but testamentary transfers, and are subject to federal estate tax

B. COMPLETED INTER VIVOS TRANSFERS (COMPLETED LIFETIME GIFTS)

1. Under state law, for a gift to be complete, all of the following conditions must be present:

   a. The donor must be competent to make the gift

   b. There must be donative intent on behalf of the donor

   c. There must be actual or constructive delivery of the property (gift) to the donee or to the donee's representative

   d. There must be valid cceptance of the gift by the donee

   > **Note:** As with bequests, the donee may refuse to accept the gift.

2. Completed gifts are subject to gift tax unless de minimis or a particular exclusion applies

3. For federal gift tax purposes, donative intent is not required to fall within the statutes but is presumptive evidence that a gift has occurred

4. Outright transfers where the donor has completely given up dominion and control over the property are completed. Donations in trust may be complete, partially complete, or totally incomplete. Recalls (contingent gifts) and gifts that are incomplete are not subject to gift tax until they become complete.

Example

Pedro gave his girlfriend an antique box that he paid $15 for at a flea market. When the girlfriend opened the present, she was so excited that she dropped the box and a diamond rolled out of a secret compartment. The diamond was appraised for $15,000. Pedro made a gift of $15. There was no donative intent on the diamond because he didn't know it existed; therefore, there was no gift of the diamond.

C. PERSONS SUBJECT TO GIFT TAX

1. The federal gift tax applies to all individual US citizens or residents, regardless of where the property is located and whether the transfer is direct or indirect, tangible or intangible, personal or real property

2. The federal gift tax also applies to nonresident aliens with regard to transfers of real and tangible personal property located within the United States

D. INCOMPLETE TRANSFERS

1. The federal gift tax oes not apply to incomplete transfers

2. Examples of incomplete transfers include those where the donor retained a right to reclaim the interest donated, or where the donor had not completely given up dominion and control over the property (revocable trusts)

3. An incomplete transfer may subsequently become complete and would, at that time, be subject to gift tax (i.e., when a revocable trust becomes irrevocable)

4. The creation of a joint bank account does not result in a gift until the noncontributing party withdraws funds for her own benefit

---

Example

Patrick created a joint bank account for himself and his friend Kristie. There is no gift until Kristie (the donee) draws on the account for her own benefit.

E. THE ANNUAL EXCLUSION AND GIFT SPLITTING

1. A donor may exclude from taxable gifts the first $12,000 (for 2007) of gifts each year to each donee

   a. The gifts must be of a present interest, meaning that the donee has the immediate right to the use and enjoyment of the transferred property

   b. Gifts of a future interest, such as a remainder interest where the donee's interest is vested at a future time or on the basis of some contingency, are not eligible for the annual exclusion

   c. For gifts in trust that contain a Crummey power, the annual exclusion applies to each beneficiary or contingent beneficiary of the trust

---

Example

Jennifer, who is single, gave an outright gift of $60,000 to a friend, Tiffany, who needed the money to pay her medical expenses. The gift is outright to Tiffany and, therefore, qualifies for the annual exclusion. This is not a qualified transfer for educational or medical purposes because the payee is not an institution.

---

2. The annual exclusion can be doubled to $24,000 (for 2007) per donee by electing gift splitting with a spouse

   a. The gift is made by the donor, but the spouse must consent to gift splitting

   b. A gift tax return (Form 709) must be filed when gift splitting is elected, and both spouses must sign the return

   c. Gifts of community property do not require gift splitting because, by nature, each spouse is deemed to own one-half of the community property

    d.   Gift splitting was enacted as a way to equalize community and noncommunity property states

> **Note:** If an election to split gifts is made, it applies to all gifts made during that year. In addition, a gift may only be split with a spouse, and the donor must have been married at the time of the gift.

Example

Kelly (single) made the following gifts in the current year:

Gift	Donee	Value
Cash	Nephew	$13,000
6-month CD	Niece	8,000
Antique rifle	Friend	20,000
Bonds in irrevocable trust: Life estate to:	Father	60,000
Remainder to:	Niece	18,000

Kelly's total taxable gifts for the current year are $75,000.

Donee	FMV	Annual Exclusion	Taxable Gifts
Nephew	$13,000	$12,000	$1,000
Niece	8,000	8,000	0
Friend	20,000	12,000	8,000
Father	60,000	12,000	48,000
Niece	18,000	—	18,000
Total	$119,000	$44,000	$75,000

Possible mistakes:

1.   Not knowing the difference between gross gifts and taxable gifts

2.   Not knowing remainder interest does not qualify for gift of present interest (niece's interest in irrevocable trust)

3.   Believing that five donees × $12,000 = $60,000 in total exclusions

---

Example

John and Mary made the following present interest gifts during the current year:

	From John	From Mary	Total
To son, Paul	$40,000	$16,000	$56,000
To daughter, Virginia	40,000	6,000	46,000
To granddaughter, Terry	20,000	4,000	24,000
	$100,000	$26,000	$126,000

John and Mary's taxable gifts with and without gift splitting:

Gift Splitting Elected (Must split all gifts made during year)

	From John	From Mary	Total
To Paul	$28,000	$28,000	$56,000
To Virginia	23,000	23,000	46,000
To Terry	12,000	12,000	24,000
Total Gross Gifts	$63,000	$63,000	$126,000
Less Exclusions			
For Paul	$12,000	$12,000	$24,000
For Virginia	$12,000	$12,000	$24,000
For Terry	$12,000	$12,000	$24,000
Total Exclusions	$36,000	$36,000	$72,000
Current Taxable Gifts	$27,000	$27,000	$54,000

No Gift Splitting

	From John	From Mary	Total
To Paul	$40,000	$16,000	$56,000
To Virginia	40,000	6,000	46,000
To Terry	20,000	4,000	24,000
Total Gross Gifts	$100,000	$26,000	$126,000
Less Annual Exclusions			
For Paul	$12,000	$12,000	$24,000
For Virginia	$12,000	$6,000	$18,000
For Terry	$12,000	$4,000	$16,000
Total Exclusions	$36,000	$22,000	$58,000
Current Taxable Gifts	$64,000	$4,000	$68,000

The gift-splitting election decreased the current taxable gifts from $68,000 to $54,000.

F. EXCEPTION TO THE FUTURE INTEREST RULE

1. An exception to the future interest rule concerns gifts to minors. Provided the following conditions are met, the gift will be considered a gift of a present interest (2503(c) trust):

   a. Both the property and the income from the property may be expended by or for the benefit of the minor donee before he attains the age of 21

   b. If the property is not expended, it will pass to the minor upon the attainment of age 21

   c. If the donee dies before reaching the age of 21, the property will pass to his estate or to another entity as he may appoint under a general power of appointment

G. EXCLUSION VERSUS EXEMPTION

1. Exclusion—the annual exclusion of $12,000 per donee or $24,000 per donee if gift splitting is elected. If a gift is $12,000 or less and the annual exclusion applies, then there is no taxable gift.

2. Exemption—the gift tax applicable credit amount of $345,800 (for 2007–2010) is the equivalent of $1 million of gifts and must be utilized prior to paying gift tax. In other words, for gifts over and above the annual exclusion, an individual can make another $1 million in aggregate taxable gifts to all donees before she has to pay any gift tax.

H. OTHER TRANSFERS THAT MAY BE SUBJECT TO THE GIFT TAX

1. Creation of joint ownership (joint tenancy)

   a. Generally, when an individual transfers a partial interest in property, a gift has been made

---

Example

Mom buys a condo at the beach for $200,000 and takes title in her name and the names of her three daughters equally. Mom has made a gift of $50,000 to each of the three daughters ($200,000 ÷ 4 owners = $50,000/owner). For the annual exclusion, $12,000 of each gift is eligible.

---

   b. Exceptions—there are two exceptions to the general rule

      1.) Joint tenancy bank account—gift not made until funds are withdrawn by donee

      2.) Joint tenancy savings bond—gift not made until redeemed by donee

2. Transfers of life insurance policies

   a. Transfer of ownership during life will trigger a gift in the amount of cash value of the policy plus any unexpired premiums

      1.) Not a completed gift unless all incidents of ownership are relinquished

      2.) Premium payment on a policy owned by someone else is considered a gift to the owner of the policy

---

Example

Rue transfers ownership of her $100,000 life insurance policy to her niece, Carol. The cash value of the policy on the date of the gift was $12,000. In addition, Rue intends to continue paying the $800 annual premium each year. Rue has made a gift of $12,000 and will make a gift each year of $800 when she pays the premium.

---

    b.   Gift tax can arise at death of insured if a noninsured owner and beneficiary of the policy are different. For example, wife buys policy on husband and names her boyfriend as beneficiary. When husband dies, she has made a gift to her boyfriend for the amount of proceeds.

  3. Exercise of a general power of appointment

    a.   Power of appointment—the power to name someone to receive a beneficial interest in property

    b.   Events that trigger gift tax to holder of power of appointment:

       1.) Holder exercises general power of appointment

       2.) Holder releases general power of appointment

       3.) Lapse of holder's right to exercise (See Section Crummey Powers on page 45 for discussion of Crummey Powers.)

Example

Jim transfers property into a irrevocable trust, with the income benefiting his wife, Carol, for her life. Jim has made a gift to Carol. Carol also has the power to direct the principal or income to anyone she wishes either during life or at death. If Carol does not direct the remainder in her will, the principal goes to Jim's personal secretary, Sue. Carol has been given a general power of appointment.

• If Carol directs any part of the assets to someone else during her life, she has exercised her power of appointment and has made a gift.

• If Carol dies and leaves the trust assets to her children, the assets are included in her gross estate.

• If Carol dies and fails to exercise her power of appointment, the assets are still included in Carol's estate and the assets pass to Sue.

---

  4. Gift loans (between family or related parties)

    a.   Imputed interest on gift loans will be considered a gift from the lender to the borrower (See page 35, Section I.3, Interest on Gift Loans, for exceptions to the below-market rate loan rule.)

I. TRANSFERS NOT SUBJECT TO GIFT TAX

1. Qualified transfers—medical payments and tuition paid directly to the provider

   a. A transfer of any amount (unlimited) to a qualified educational institution for the payment of tuition is not subject to gift tax

   b. A payment of any amount to a provider of qualified medical care is not subject to gift tax

   c. The payment must be made directly to the educational institution or medical provider to qualify for this exclusion

2. Property settlements between divorcing spouses—as part of a written divorce agreement are deemed to be for full and adequate consideration and, therefore, not subject to gift tax. Applies to transfers up to three years after divorce.

3. Interest on gift loans

   a. Gift loans $10,000 or less are not subject to gift tax unless the loan proceeds are used by the donee to purchase income-producing property (in which case, apply the rules of point *b* below)

   b. Gift loans of $100,000 or less, where the donee's net investment investment income does not exceed $1,000, are not subject to gift tax

      1.) Net investment income is gross income from all investments less related expenses

   c. If the loan is less than or equal to $100,000 and the unearned income of the borrower is greater than $1,000, the imputed interest is the difference between the interest at the federal rate less the interest charged, not to exceed the borrower's net investment income

   d. If there is no imputed interest, there is no gift. If there is imputed interest, then the lender is deemed to have given a gift of the imputed interest and the borrower as having received a gift of the imputed interest.

   e. These limitations for loans of $100,000 or less do not apply if the principal purpose of a loan is tax avoidance

   f. On below-market interest rate loans between employer and employee, the imputed interest is deemed to be compensation. On loans between corporation and shareholder, the imputed interest is characterized as a dividend. No gift has been made.

Example

In the current year, Marilyn, who is single, made the following gifts:

- Paid $16,000 in medical bills for her friend, Lisa. The payments were paid directly to her friend's hospital.

- $18,000 to her mother to pay for her apartment rent, utilities, and food.

- $14,000 to her nephew, Skip, to get him started in business.

- Made a $30,000 interest-free demand loan to her nephew, Skip, during the previous year. The loan is still outstanding at the end of the current year. The applicable federal interest rate during the year remained constant at 8%. Skip had no investment income.

Marilyn's taxable gifts in the current year are $8,000:

Payment directly to hospital is a qualified transfer, not a gift	$0
$18,000 to mother is reduced by $12,000, therefore, taxable gift	$6,000
$14,000 to Skip is reduced by $12,000, therefore, taxable gift	$2,000
Loan is less than $100,000 and donee's net investment income is less than $1,000, therefore, imputed interest is not a gift	$0
Total Taxable Gifts	**$8,000**

Examples

- Grace made an interest-free loan of $9,000 to her daughter for the purchase of a car. The daughter had $4,000 of net investment income. There is no imputed interest because the loan is less than $10,000.

- Grace made an interest-free loan to her daughter of $50,000. On the basis of applicable federal rates, the interest would be $4,000. The daughter had net investment income of $500. There is no imputed interest because the loan was not more than $100,000 and the borrower's net investment income is less than $1,000.

- Grace made an interest-free loan to her daughter of $90,000. On the basis of applicable federal rates, the interest would be $7,200. The daughter's net investment income is $3,000. The imputed interest is $3,000. Because the borrower's net investment income is more than $1,000, interest is imputed as the difference between the federal rate ($7,200) and the actual rate ($0), capped by the net investment income ($3,000). Thus, Grace has made a gift of $3,000 to her daughter.

- Grace made an interest-free loan to her daughter of $150,000. The applicable federal interest is $13,000. The borrower's net investment income is $0. Because the loan is more than $100,000, it does not meet any exception. Grace will have interest income of $13,000. Her daughter will have interest expense of $13,000 (deductibility determined by use of loan proceeds). Grace has given a gift of $13,000. Her daughter has received a gift of $13,000. The annual exclusion will apply to the first $12,000.

---

4. Payments made under an obligation of support (usually determined by state law)

5. Donations to political organizations

6. Disclaimer

   a. A disclaimer is a refusal by a person to accept property that is designated to be transferred or passed to her. The effect of the disclaimer is to pass the property to someone else, thereby possibly avoiding the payment of transfer tax.

   b. An effective disclaimer for federal transfer tax purposes:

      1.) Must be in writing and must be irrevocable

      2.) Must be issued within nine months of the later of the date the interest came into being or the date the person named to receive the property reached age 21

      3.) The disclaiming party cannot have previously benefited from the interest disclaimed

      4.) Must pass the interest without the direction of disclaimant

   c. When to use disclaimers

      1.) Property is left to a spouse who does not need it. Spouse can disclaim and let it pass to the contingent beneficiary (usually children).

      2.) Individual wants to make a tax-free gift to the contingent beneficiary

      3.) Parent receives a large bequest from a relative and would like the assets to pass to the next beneficiary in line

---

Example

- John dies on July 1. He leaves his entire estate to his wife Jessie (or to his children if she predeceases him), thus overqualifying the estate. If Jessie does not need the assets and wants to maximize the potential estate tax savings, she can disclaim an amount equal to the exemption equivalent and let it pass to the children. By disclaiming in a timely manner, Jessie has not made a gift to the children.

- Theodore leaves his son, Teddy, $500,000 with the stipulation that if Teddy disclaims, the amount goes to a charity. Teddy has three options: (1) take the $500,000 and keep it; (2) take the $500,000, donate it, and receive the related income tax deduction; or (3) disclaim it and let the estate take the charitable deduction.

J. TRANSFERS THAT ARE DEDUCTIBLE FOR DETERMINING TAXABLE GIFTS

1. Gifts to qualified charities are deductible from gross gifts for donors who are US citizens or residents

2. Gifts and transfers between spouses, provided the transfer is not a terminable interest unless the transfer meets the exception to terminable interest rules (e.g., QTIP)

3. For a noncitizen spouse, only the first $125,000 (for 2007) per year of gifts of a present interest are not subject to gift tax (in effect, a special annual exclusion)

4. For a noncitizen spouse, all gifts of a future interest are subject to gift tax

Example

When Stacey and James became engaged in February 2007, James gave Stacey a ring that had a fair market value of $14,000. After their wedding in October 2007, James gave Stacey $45,000 in cash so Stacey could have her own bank account. James and Stacey are US citizens. James' marital deduction is $45,000. The engagement ring does not qualify because they were not married at the time of the gift. The $14,000 gift is first reduced by the $12,000 annual exclusion, and when the gift tax return is filed, James has utilized $2,000 of his lifetime exemption equivalency.

K. VALUATION OF A GIFT

1. The value of a gift for gift tax purposes is the fair market value on the date of the gift

2. Any consideration received by the donor reduces the value of the gift

3. For securities, the value is the average of the high and low prices on the date of the gift

    a. Value of stocks for Form 706 will be the average of the high and low trading values for the stock on the date of death or alternate valuation date

    b. If the stock is not traded on the date of death or gift, the value of the stock, according to the IRS regulations, should be the stock price following the death multiplied by the number of days from the date of death to the previous stock trade before the date of death. Added to this is the stock price directly preceding the death, multiplied by the number of days (trading days) between the death and the next trading day. This sum should be divided by the sum of the days before and after the death.

Example

On July 11, Lisa gave her sister, Michelle, one share of XYZ stock that was traded on an exchange. July 11 was a Thursday. Below are the quoted prices on Monday the 8th and Friday the 12th. No sales occurred any other day that week.

SALES PRICE

Date	High	Low	Closing
7/08	$60	$56	$58.50
7/12	$62	$58	$59.00

The fair market value of Lisa's gift is $59.50. It is calculated as follows:

$$\frac{\left[\left(\frac{60 + 56}{2}\right) \times 1\right] + \left[\left(\frac{62 + 58}{2}\right) \times 3\right]}{4} = \$59.50$$

Note: The value is not determined by the closing price.

4. Life estate and remainder interests

    a. A life estate is the right to possession, enjoyment, and profit from property during the individual's lifetime

b. A remainder interest is an interest in property that begins in the future

    1.) Gift tax value of a remainder interest is the present value of the remainder interest on the date of the gift

    2.) Use IRS Table S to determine present value factor

Example

John places $500,000 in an irrevocable trust at First National Bank. The trust instrument specifies that John's brother, Ned, (age 65) will receive income for life, and that Sally, John's niece, will receive the assets upon Ned's death. Using Table S, Single Life Remainder Factors, and assuming an interest rate of 8%, the value of Sally's remainder interest is $500,000 × 0.33208 = $166,040. The life interest transferred to Ned will be $500,000 − $166,040 = $333,960.

L. LIABILITY FOR GIFT TAX

1. The donor is liable for any gift tax due

2. The donee is not subject to gift tax or income tax on the gift. However, if the donor fails to pay, the donee may become liable.

3. Net gifts occur where the donor and donee agree, prior to the gift, that the donee will pay any gift tax due

    a. This transaction is considered to be part sale and part gift, causing the donor to realize taxable income to the extent that the gift tax paid exceeds the donor's adjusted basis

    b. Net gifts are an appropriate technique when the donor does not have sufficient liquid investments (cash) to pay the gift tax liability

---

Example

In 2007, Bill gives his friend, Susan, a parcel of land, FMV $3,000,000, basis $50,000. Susan agrees to pay gift tax of $1,275,800. Bill has taxable income of $1,225,800 ($1,275,800 − $50,000).

M. DEEMED PAID ADJUSTMENT

1. All post-1976 taxable gifts are added back in the gift tax calculation formula, and credit is given for the gift tax on the prior taxable gifts

2. Because taxable gifts in the past may have been subject to a lower rate, it would be unfair to give credit for actual taxes paid

3. A donor will be allowed a deemed paid credit on prior gifts, which means the credit is calculated using current tax rates

N. FILING REQUIREMENTS

1. Form 709 (US Gift Tax Return) must be filed for each calendar year in which any of the following occur:

a. The gifts to one donee for one calendar year exceed the annual exclusion of $12,000 (for 2007)

b. Gift of a future interest has been given

c. Gift splitting between spouses has been elected

　　1.) Form 709 must be filed and signed by the consenting spouse

　　2.) This does not apply to gifts of community property

2. The due date of Form 709 is April 15 of the year following the gift but may be extended to the income tax return extended due date

O. DETERMINATION OF BASIS AND HOLDING PERIOD WHEN PROPERTY IS RECEIVED BY GIFT

1. A gift indicates that there is no cost to the recipient. However, a basis to the gifted property is still assigned and depends on the following:

a. The date of the gift

b. The donor's adjusted tax basis of the property gifted

c. The amount of the gift tax paid (if any) by the donor

d. The fair market value of the property on the date of the gift

2. Gift of appreciated property

a. When the donor gives appreciated property to the donee, generally the basis to the donee is the carryover basis of the donor

b. The donor's holding period also carries over to the donee

c. A realized gain occurs if the donee subsequently sells the gifted property at a higher price than the property's adjusted basis

d. If the donor paid gift tax at the time the appreciated property is gifted, the donee can increase his basis by a portion of the gift taxes paid. The following formula is used to determine a donee's basis when the donor has paid gift taxes:

$$\text{donee's basis} = \text{donor's adjusted basis} + \left(\frac{\text{unrealized appreciation}}{\text{FMV}} \times \text{gift tax paid} \right).$$

　　1.) To calculate the FMV of the donated gift used in the above calculation, the donee must first determine whether the donor used all or part of the annual exclusion for the gift. The FMV is reduced by the annual exclusion amount, if used, only for the purposes of the calculation.

Example

Chelsea gave Virginia stock with a FMV of $60,000 and paid gift tax of $15,000. Chelsea originally acquired the stock two years ago for $20,000. This is the only gift Chelsea has made to Virginia this year. Virginia's basis in the gift is $32,500 calculated as follows:

$$\$20,000 + \left(\frac{\$40,000}{\$60,000 - \$12,000} \times \$15,000 \right) = \$32,500 \text{ basis.}$$

Basis includes $20,000 of carryover basis, plus $12,500 of the gift tax paid. Virginia immediately has a holding period of two years, which is the carryover holding period from Chelsea.

---

3. Gift of loss property

    a. When the donor gives loss property to the donee, the double basis rule applies

    b. Basis cannot be determined until the donee subsequently disposes of the gifted property

        1.) Gain basis

            a.) If the donee subsequently disposes of the property at a higher price than the donor's adjusted tax basis, the donee determines the gain on the basis of the donor's basis (carryover basis)

            b.) The donor's holding period also carries over to the donee in determining whether the gain is short term or long term

            c.) If the donor paid gift tax at the time of the gift, the gift tax is not allocated to the donee's basis when the property is subsequently disposed of

        2.) Loss basis

            a.) If the donee subsequently disposes of the property at a lower price than the fair market value of the property at the time of the gift, the donee determines the loss on the basis of the fair market value at the time of the gift

            b.) The donor's holding period does not carryover to the donee in determining whether the loss is short term or long term. The donee's holding period begins on the date of the gift.

            c.) If the donor paid gift tax at the time of the gift, the gift tax is not allocated to the donee's basis when the property is subsequently disposed of

        3.) If the donee sells the gifted property at a price between the donor's adjusted tax basis and the fair market value at the date of the gift, no gain or loss is recognized at the time of the sale

Examples

- Bill received an acre of land as a gift from his father. At the time of gift, the land had a fair market value of $700,000. His father purchased the land four years ago for $800,000 and paid gift tax of $100,000 as a result of the gift. Assume Bill sold the land one week after receiving the gift.

  — If Bill sold the land for $850,000, he would have a long-term capital gain of $50,000 ($850,000 – $800,000) on the sale. Bill will use his father's carryover basis of $800,000 (gain basis) and will use his father's carryover holding period of four years. Gift tax paid by the father will not be allocated to Bill's basis, because this was a gift of loss property.

  — If Bill sold the land for $550,000, he would have a short-term capital loss of $150,000 ($550,000 – $700,000) on the sale. Bill's basis will be the $700,000 fair market value on the date of the gift (loss basis), and Bill's holding period will begin on the date of the gift. Gift tax paid by the father will not be allocated to Bill's basis, because this was a gift of loss property.

  — If Bill sold the land for $730,000, there will be no gain or loss, because he sold the land at a price between the father's adjusted tax basis and the fair market value at the date of the gift. Holding period is irrelevant, because there is no gain or loss.

- Last year, Melissa gave her daughter, Melanie, stock with a fair market value of $20,000. Melissa paid gift tax of $5,000. Melissa purchased the stock several years ago, and her adjusted taxable basis on the date of the gift was $12,000. In the current year, Melanie sold the stock for $24,000. Melanie's basis on the date of sale is $14,000. Melissa gave Melanie a gift of $15,000 earlier this year.

Melissa's basis	$12,000
FMV at date of gift	$20,000
Donee's basis before gift tax	$12,000 (Donor's basis)
Gift tax paid	$5,000
(8,000 ÷ 20,000) × 5,000	$2,000 Gift tax paid adjustment

  Donor's basis of $12,000 + $2,000 gift tax paid adjustment = donee's basis of $14,000.

- Jack gave Emily stock in four different companies. Below are the fair market value and adjusted tax basis for Jack for each of the stocks. (Assume the annual exclusion was unavailable.)

	(No gift tax paid on 1 & 2)		(Gift tax paid on 3 & 4—$34)	
	Stock 1	Stock 2	Stock 3	Stock 4
Fair market value	$68	$3	$68	$68
Adjusted taxable basis	$40	$50	$40	$78
Realized gain/(loss)	$28	($47)	$28	($10)

Here is Emily's adjusted tax basis for each stock.

Stock 1: $40—the carryover basis

Stock 2: $50 for gains and $3 for losses (double basis)

Stock 3: $54—carryover $40 plus $14 gift tax on appreciation

Stock 4: $78 for gains and $68 for losses (double basis). Gift tax is not added to basis because this is a gift of loss property.

Gift Basis Example

The following three examples illustrate the general rule, the gift tax paid rule, the double basis rule, and the double basis with gift tax rule at three different sales prices. (Assume no annual exclusion is available.)

EXAMPLE 1

	General Rule	Gift Tax Paid	Double Basis	DB with Gift Tax
Sales Price $150				
Donor's basis	20	20	100	100
Current FMV	100	100	20	20
Gift tax paid	–	30	–	30
Donee Sells:				
Proceeds	150	150	150	150
Less: Basis	(20)	(44)*	(100)	(100)
Gain/(Loss)	130	106	50	50

EXAMPLE 2

	General Rule	Gift Tax Paid	Double Basis	DB with Gift Tax
Sales Price $80				
Donor's basis	20	20	100	100
Current FMV	100	100	20	20
Gift tax paid	–	30	–	30
Donee Sells:				
Proceeds	80	80	80	80
Less: Basis	(20)	(44)*	(80)	(80)
Gain/(Loss)	60	36	–	–

EXAMPLE 3

	General Rule	Gift Tax Paid	Double Basis	DB with Gift Tax
Sales Price $10				
Donor's basis	20	20	100	100
Current FMV	100	100	20	20
Gift tax paid	–	30	–	30
Donee Sells:				
Proceeds	10	10	10	10
Less: Basis	(20)	(44)*	(20)	(20)
Gain/(Loss)	(10)	(34)	(10)	(10)

$$ *\left(\frac{\$100 - \$20}{\$100}\right) \times \$30 = \$24 \text{ (allocated gift tax)} + \$20 \text{ (carryover basis)} = \$44. $$

1. Holding period

   a. For gain basis—starts on the date the donor acquired the property

   b. For loss basis—starts on the date of the gift

2. Basis for depreciation

   a. The basis for depreciation is the donee's carryover basis

   b. The life for depreciation is the same as if the donee purchased it

P. INCOMPLETE TRANSFERS (A REMINDER)

1. A transfer is not considered a gift if it is incomplete. An incomplete transfer, however, may become a gift upon the later occurrence of some event that makes the transfer complete.

2. A revocable trust becomes a gift when the grantor releases the power of revocation, and the trust becomes irrevocable

---

Example

Lauren sets up a revocable trust and names the bank as trustee. The trust instrument directs the trustee to pay the income to Lauren's friend, Emily, as long as Emily lives, and then the remainder goes to Emily's daughter. Until the first income payment has been made to Emily, Lauren has not made a gift because she could revoke the trust. If five years later Lauren decides to make the trust irrevocable, then she has made a gift of the remaining income interest to Emily, and a gift of the remainder to Emily's daughter.

Q. CRUMMEY POWERS

1. Issue #1—getting the annual exclusion. Gifts of a future interest do not qualify for the $12,000 (2007) annual exclusion. For example, if you put $12,000 into an irrevocable trust for your child where the child gets the income and principal at some later date, then there is not a present interest, and the gift does not qualify for the annual exclusion.

   a. By placing a lapsing power to withdraw (referred to as a Crummey power) in an irrevocable trust, a future interest can be converted to a present interest, which qualifies for the annual exclusion

   b. The present interest gift is usually the lesser of the annual exclusion or the amount contributed to the trust

2. The beneficiary must be given notice that she has the power to withdraw the funds for a limited period of time (generally noncumulative). This power gives her the ability to currently enjoy the interest, thus qualifying the gift as a present interest.

3. Issue #2—does lapsing the power create a gift tax problem? A potential problem in a trust with multiple beneficiaries with Crummey powers is that if a holder of a general power of appointment releases or lets the power lapse, then the holder may be deemed to have made a gift. In other words, if the beneficiary lets his power to withdraw lapse, he may be deemed to have made a gift to the other beneficiaries of the trust.

4. To avoid gift tax consequences of a lapsed power, the annual right to withdraw must be limited to the greater of 5% of the value of the property out of which the withdrawal can be made or $5,000.

Another alternative is to set up multiple trusts where each trust has only one beneficiary. The separate trusts can often be treated as one trust for administrative purposes.

Example—Trust with Crummey provision, one beneficiary

John set up a trust for his only child, Jaimie. The trust is funded with $20,000. Jaimie is given the power to withdraw the lesser of $12,000 or the annual contribution. Jaimie lets his power to withdraw the $12,000 lapse.

Tax consequences: John (father) gets a $12,000 annual exclusion. Because there are no other trust beneficiaries, Jaimie has not made any gifts as a result of letting his power lapse.

Example—Trust with Crummey provision, two beneficiaries, lapse <5/5 lapse rule

Charles sets up an irrevocable trust for his two children, Katty and Passie. The trust is initially funded with $10,000. Each year for a period of 30 days, Katty and Passie have the right to withdraw the lesser of 50% of the amount of property contributed that year or the annual exclusion. Katty and Passie do not exercise their right to withdraw during the current year.

Tax consequences: Charles has included a power to withdraw and, therefore, he gets a $10,000 annual exclusion ($5,000 per child). There are multiple beneficiaries, so Charles needs to address the 5/5 lapse rule to see if there are any gift tax consequences from the lapse. Because the withdrawal was limited to $5,000, and this does not exceed the greater of 5% or $5,000, no gift between Katty and Passie has been triggered by the lapse of power.

Example—Trust with Crummey provision, two beneficiaries, lapse >5/5 lapse rule

In the current year, George and his wife, Helen, contribute $120,000 to a trust established for the benefit of his two children, both equal income and remainder beneficiaries. Each child has the right to withdraw the lesser of the annual exclusion ($24,000) or 25% of the annual contribution (25% × $120,000 = $30,000). The children do not exercise their right of withdrawal during the year, thus causing a lapse and a gift of one-half of the lapse to the other child.

Tax consequences: George and Helen included a Crummey provision, so they get an annual exclusion of $48,000 ($24,000 per child). There are two beneficiaries, so they need to check the 5/5 lapse rule and see whether there are any gift tax consequences resulting from the lapse. Withdrawal was limited to $24,000, which exceeds the 5/5 benchmark of $6,000 (the greater of $6,000 (5% × $120,000) or $5,000). Each of the children made a gift to the other child to the extent that one-half of their lapsed amount exceeded the 5/5 amount ($12,000 − $6,000 = $6,000). The $6,000 gift is a gift of a contingent future interest and is not eligible for the annual exclusion. The gift is between the two children and will require the filing of a gift tax return for each of the two children to the extent of $6,000 taxable gift each.

---

5. Contingent beneficiaries

   a. Estate of Maria Cristofani

     1.) In Cristofani, the taxpayer established a trust where her grandchildren were contingent beneficiaries of the trust in the event that their parents (the primary beneficiaries) died before the trust terminated

     2.) The IRS's position was that there was no reason that the contingent beneficiaries would not be highly motivated to exercise their right to withdraw as the probability of their ever receiving benefit from the trust was quite small

     3.) If the contingent beneficiaries let the power lapse, it must have been because of an understanding that they would do so; therefore, no present interest existed

     4.) The court ruled that the controlling factor was the legal right of a contingent beneficiary to withdraw, not the probability that they would do so

     5.) Therefore, the annual exclusion is available for primary and contingent beneficiaries. However, the IRS acquiesced in result only, meaning that they may continue to challenge contingent beneficiaries.

   b. *Kohlsaat v. Commissioner*

     1.) The use of Cristofani trusts was reinforced in the Kohlsaat case

     2.) Taxpayer set up an irrevocable trust during 1990. Taxpayer's two children were primary beneficiaries.

     3.) Crummey powers were given to the children and to grandchildren and great-grandchildren (total of 18 Crummey powers)

     4.) The IRS claimed that the contingent beneficiaries did not qualify for the annual exclusion

     5.) The Tax Court cited Cristofani and granted the annual gift tax exclusion for all 18 beneficiaries

R. ESTATE FREEZING

1. Revenue Ruling 93-12 (1993-7 IRB 13)—a minority share interest discount will not be disallowed solely because a transferred interest, if combined with interests held by family members, would constitute a controlling interest

---

Example

Father owns 100% of the stock of a closely held corporation, FMV $300,000. He gives one-third to each of three daughters. Because each daughter was given a minority interest, a 25% discount is taken on each transfer. On Form 709, Father reports three gross gifts of $75,000 (total gifts of $225,000). If the stock had been passed at death, 100% of the stock value would have been subject to the estate tax.

---

2. Rev. Rul. 93-12 launched the popularity of family limited partnerships (FLPs) as a planning tool. Taxpayer forms an FLP to hold a closely held business. Taxpayer becomes the general partner and gives limited partnership interests to children/grandchildren. When the limited partnerships are valued for gift tax purposes, they are given discounts for minority interest and lack of

marketability. This is an effective way of saving estate and gift taxes and maintaining family control over assets.

3. IRS has begun to aggressively challenge FLPs as shams created to avoid taxes

4. Recapitalization is an estate-freezing technique for corporations

    a. Common stock is traded for both common and preferred stock

    b. The owner retains the preferred stock and gives the common stock to the children

    c. The idea is to limit the amount included in the owner's estate to the value of the preferred stock

    d. Any appreciation that occurs after the recapitalization and gifting of common stock is attributed to the common stock, thereby keeping the appreciation out of the owner's estate

    e. Section 2701 allows some estate freezing, but generally the preferred stock retained by the senior family member is valued at zero, and so the gift common stock becomes the full value of the business

    f. Under certain conditions (e.g., preferred stock is cumulative), some value may be assigned to the preferred stock

S. GIFT TAX FORMULA

EXHIBIT 4: GIFT TAX FORMULA

(1) Total gifts in current year (fair market value of all gifts)		$ _____
(2) Less:		
(a) One-half of value of gifts split with spouse	$ _____	
(b) Annual exclusions ($12,000 per donee for present interests)	_____	
(c) Marital deduction (can be unlimited if spouse is a US citizen)	_____	
(d) Charitable deduction (can be unlimited)	_____	
(e) Total subtractions	_____	
(3) Equals: Taxable gifts in current year		$ _____
(4) Add: Post-1976 taxable gifts made in prior years		======
(5) Equals: Total taxable gifts to date (tax base)		_____
(6) Tentative tax on total taxable gifts to date		_____
(7) Less: Tax paid or deemed paid on prior taxable gifts		(_____)
(8) Equals: Gift tax on current year taxable gifts before applicable credit amount		_____
(9) Less: Applicable credit amount ($345,800)		(_____)
(10) Equals: Gift tax due on current year taxable gifts		$ ======

Example

Susan and Mike Brown, a happily married couple, made the following gifts during 2007.

Susan's gifts:

- $100,000 to each of their three children
- Leroy Neiman painting FMV $120,000 to her niece
- Paid $14,000 private school tuition for her college roommate's daughter
- Paid $2,000 hospital bill related to co-worker's hospitalization because of food poisoning
- Placed $650,000 in an irrevocable trust with Mike as the income and remainder beneficiary. The trust is funded with 6% coupon bonds. Susan wants to elect to take the marital deduction.

Mike's gifts:

- Federal Express stock, held long term, FMV $40,000, basis $10,000 to the University of Georgia
- $50,000 cash to his high school's homecoming queen

Susan made $750,000 of taxable gifts in 1988 and paid $55,500 in gift tax. Calculate Susan's gift tax liability, assuming the gift-splitting election is made.

Description	Value of Gift	Gift Split	Annual Exclusion	Marital/ Charitable	Taxable Gift
Child One	$100,000	($50,000)	($12,000)		$38,000
Child Two	100,000	(50,000)	(12,000)		38,000
Child Three	100,000	(50,000)	(12,000)		38,000
Painting	120,000	(60,000)	(12,000)		48,000
Irrevocable Trust	650,000	(325,000)	(12,000)	($313,000)	0
Stock (Mike's gift)	40,000	(20,000)	(12,000)	(8,000)	0
Cash (Mike's gift)	50,000	(25,000)	(12,000)		13,000
Total	$1,160,000	($580,000)	($84,000)	($321,000)	$175,000

(1) Total gifts in current year (fair market value of all gifts) $1,160,000

(2) Less:

    (a) One-half of value of gifts split with spouse $580,000

    (b) Annual exclusions ($12,000 per donee for present interests)   84,000

    (c) Marital deduction (can be unlimited if spouse is a US citizen)   313,000

    (d) Charitable deduction (can be unlimited)   8,000

    (e) Total subtractions   (985,000)

(3) Equals: Taxable gifts in current year $175,000

(4) Add: All taxable gifts made in prior years   750,000

(5) Equals: Total taxable gifts to date $925,000

(6) Tentative tax on total taxable gifts to date   316,550

(7) Less: Tax paid or deemed paid on prior taxable gifts   (55,500)

(8) Equals: Gift tax on current year taxable gifts before applicable credit amt $261,050

(9) Less: Applicable credit amount   (261,050)

(10) Equals: Gift tax due on current year taxable gifts $0

Note: The hospital bill and the school tuition were paid directly to providers and, therefore, are excluded because they are qualified transfers. Mike's gift of Federal Express stock is a charitable contribution and is eligible for the charitable deduction.

T. BASIC STRATEGIES FOR TRANSFERRING WEALTH THROUGH GIFTING

1. Generally, if the objective of the transferor is to reduce the size of the transferor's gross estate, the transferor can use the following lifetime gifting techniques to achieve a lower gross estate at death:

   a. Make optimal use of qualified educational transfers (pay tuition for children and grandchildren from private school through professional education directly to provider institutions)

   b. Pay medical costs for children, grandchildren, and heirs directly to provider institutions (not limited to heirs)

   c. Make optimal use of the $12,000 annual gift exclusion ($24,000 if the gift is made jointly with the spouse)

Example

John is married to Joan and has three adult children who all have stable marriages, and there are seven grandchildren. John and Joan can gift $312,000 per year without being subject to gift tax. ($24,000 × 13 transferees—3 children, 3 spouses, 7 grandchildren.)

---

   d. A spouse may make unlimited lifetime gifts to his spouse, if the recipient spouse is a US citizen. Gifts to noncitizen spouses are limited to $125,000 for 2007 annually. Gifts from noncitizen spouses to citizen spouses are still eligible for the unlimited marital deduction.

2. If the above four (*a–d*) are completely exhausted, the transferor can begin using the applicable gift tax exclusion amount ($1 million in 2007) to avoid gift tax until the summation of lifetime taxable gifts exceeds the applicable exclusion amount.

VII. THE FEDERAL ESTATE TAX

A. WHAT IS INCLUDED IN THE GROSS ESTATE?

EXHIBIT 5: WHAT IS INCLUDED IN THE GROSS ESTATE?

Code Section	Property Description
2033	Property owned by decedent or in which decedent had an interest
2034	Dower and curtesy interests
2035	Gift tax on gifts made within three years of death Gifts made within three years of death that would have been included under 2036, 2037, 2038, 2042
2036	Transfers with a retained life interest
2037	Transfers taking effect at death
2038	Revocable transfers
2039	Annuities
2040	Jointly owned property
2041	Powers of appointment
2042	Proceeds of life insurance

1. Section 2033—property owned by the decedent

    a. The gross estate is composed of the value of all property in which the decedent has an interest at his death. It includes the value of properties he transferred during his life if he retained some rights, powers, use, or possession after the transfers (strings).

    b. Property in which the decedent had an interest (e.g., automobile, house, clothes, and savings) will account for most of the property included in the gross estate. Other items also included in the gross estate are:

        1.) Medical insurance reimbursements owed to a decedent on account of hospital and doctor bills paid

        2.) State income tax refunds received after death but relating to tax decedent paid prior to death

        3.) Court award for pain and suffering the decedent experienced as a result of a negligent act caused by another, even if the award was paid to decedent's surviving spouse. Because the cause of action was personal to the decedent, it is includible in the gross estate

        4.) Rental income on rental property paid to the estate

        5.) Property excluded—court award for wrongful death paid to decedent's family. Because a wrongful death suit is based on the wrongdoer's depriving the family of future earnings as a result of the death of the breadwinner, it is an interest that arises after death. Therefore, it is not included in the decedent's gross estate.

2. Section 2034—dower and curtesy interest. Generally, the common law concepts of dower and curtesy have been codified by state statutes that give the surviving spouse a statutory share of the

deceased spouse's estate. The value of this property will be included in the gross estate. Dower and curtesy interests are fully deductible under the marital deduction.

3. Section 2035—certain gifts made within three years of death

   a. Any gift tax paid on gifts made within three years of death must be added to the gross estate. Called the gross-up approach, the procedure prevents the amount of the gift tax from escaping the estate tax.

   b. Gifts made within three years of death are typically not included in the gross estate of the donor. They are, instead, treated the same way as any other post-1976 taxable gift (i.e., added to taxable estate. (See Exhibit 6: Estate Tax Formula on page 58.) Exceptions to this general rule include:

      1.) Property that was given away within three years but otherwise would have been included under Section 2036 (transfers with retained life estate)

      2.) Property that was given away within three years but otherwise would have been included under Section 2037 (transfers taking effect at death)

      3.) Property that was given away within three years but otherwise would have been included under Section 2038 (revocable transfers)

      4.) Property that was given away within three years but otherwise would have been included under Section 2042 (proceeds of life insurance)

   c. These sections deal with gifting of life insurance or severance of a retained interest. Premiums paid within three years by the insured on a policy the insured doesn't own won't be pulled back into the estate under Section 2035. These premiums may constitute a taxable gift if they exceed the annual exclusion.

4. Section 2036—transfers with a retained life estate. Sections 2036, 2037, and 2038 are premised on the notion that the decedent has made a gift of property, but, because she has retained a certain degree of control and enjoyment over such property, the property will be included in the gross estate.

5. Section 2037—transfers taking effect at death

   a. Possession or enjoyment of the property can, through ownership of such interest, be obtained only by surviving the decedent

   b. The decedent must have retained a reversionary interest in the property, and the value of such reversionary interest immediately before the death of the decedent must exceed 5% of the value of such property

6. Section 2038—revocable transfers. Transfers where decedent, at time of death, had power to alter, amend, or revoke the transfer.

7. Section 2042—proceeds of life insurance

   a. Proceeds of a life insurance policy on the life of the decedent will be includible in the decedent's gross estate if, at the insured's death, either the proceeds were receivable by the decedent's executor, or the decedent possessed an incidence of ownership in the policy

---

Note: The entire proceeds under split-dollar arrangements will still be includible, even though a part of the proceeds is payable to a third party, usually the employer.

---

    b.   Under Section 2033 (property owned at death), the terminal value (cash surrender value) of a life insurance policy on the life of someone other than the decedent will be includible in the decedent's gross estate to the extent, at the decedent's date of death, that the decedent had an ownership interest in the policy

> **Note:** These policies are not included under Section 2042.

    c.   Under Section 2035, the proceeds of a life insurance policy on the life of the decedent will be includible in the decedent's gross estate if, within three years of death, the nonowning decedent made a completed transfer of all incidence of ownership in the policy

    d.   Finally, the decedent's adjusted taxable gifts (not gross estate) will include the taxable terminal value of the gift of any life insurance policy (as of the date of the gift) for which the decedent made a completed transfer more than three years before death

8.   Section 2039—annuities

    a.   Straight life annuities—this type of annuity pays the annuitant until his death. In this case, nothing is included in the gross estate because the annuitant's interest in the contract terminates at death.

    b.   Survivorship annuities—this type of annuity provides payments to one person and then provides payments to a second person upon the death of the first

        1.)   When the first annuitant dies, the value of a comparable policy on the second annuitant is included in the first-to-die's estate

        2.)   If the second-to-die has contributed to the purchase of the policy, then only a proportional amount will go into the first-to-die's estate

---

Example

Consider these three different scenarios:

1.   Jeff purchases a straight life annuity. When he dies, the annuity is not included in the gross estate because the annuity extinguishes at Jeff's death.

2.   Jeff purchases a survivorship annuity. Jeff dies and his companion, Nancy, becomes the annuitant. The cost of a comparable policy, based on Nancy's age, will be included in Jeff's estate.

3.   Jeff and Nancy purchase a survivorship annuity together. They each pay half of the premium. When Jeff dies, only half of the value of Nancy's survivor annuity will be included in his estate because he contributed only half of the premiums.

---

9.   Sections 2040—joint interests (JTWROS)

    a.   As a general rule, the gross estate will include the entire value of property held jointly with others.

    b.   Exception—if the only surviving joint owner is the decedent's spouse, the property is a qualified joint interest. In this case, one-half of the total value will always be includible, regardless of that spouse's original contribution and regardless of whether or not that contribution can be proven.

 c. Exception—for jointly owned property held by the decedent and at least one person who is not the decedent's surviving spouse, the decedent's gross estate will include the entire value of the property, reduced only by an amount attributable to that portion of the consideration in money or money's worth that can clearly be shown to have been furnished by the survivors. This is called the consideration furnished test (Contribution Rule).

> **Note:** It is the responsibility of the executor to prove if other contributions were made to the property.

 d. Funds received as a gift from the deceased co-owner and applied to the cost of the property cannot be counted as funds provided by the co-owner

 e. If the owners received the property as a gift from a third party, each owner is considered to have contributed the value of his interest

---

Example

Martha and Raymond are married and hold title as joint tenants to a beachfront lot in Gulf Shores, Alabama. Raymond dies. One-half of the property will be included in his estate.

Suppose now that Martha and Raymond are lifelong companions but not legally married. When Raymond dies, all of the beach property will go into his estate unless Martha can prove that she furnished part of the funds to purchase the property. If Martha can prove she furnished 30% of the funds, then only 70% goes into Raymond's estate. However, if Raymond had gifted her the 30%, her contribution would not count, and Raymond must include 100% of the value of the lot.

---

 10. Sections 2041 and 2514—powers of appointment

  a. A power of appointment is the power to name who will enjoy or own property. The parties are:

   1.) The donor—grants power

   2.) The holder—receives power

   3.) The appointee—person whom the holder appoints to enjoy the property

  b. Powers can be general or limited

   1.) A general power is a power in which the holder can appoint to the holder, to the holder's estate, to the holder's creditors, or to the creditors of the holder's estate to enjoy the property subject to the power. A general power should be given only to a spouse.

   2.) A limited power is any power that is not a general power. A limited power is also called a special power.

  c. Estate tax ramifications

   1.) General power of appointment—the gross estate of a decedent will include any assets under a general power of appointment held by a decedent at the time of death (whether exercised or not). However, there are several exceptions:

    a.) If the right to exercise is limited to an ascertainable standard (health, education, maintenance, or support), then the power is not included in the decedent's gross estate

b.) If the right to exercise requires approval of both the holder and someone else (who is deemed to be an adverse party—someone who has an interest in the property), then the power of appointment is not included in the decedent's gross estate

c.) If the right to exercise is limited to the greater of $5,000 or 5% of the aggregate value of the property each year, then the power of appointment is generally not included in the decedent's gross estate

- This right to withdraw is referred to as a 5-and-5 power

- The 5-and-5 power must be noncumulative. If the withdrawal is not made during the year, that year's right to withdraw is lost.

Example

Mary Sue is the beneficiary of a trust established by her deceased husband, Dennis. The trust includes a 5-and-5 power, allowing Mary Sue to withdraw the greater of $5,000 or 5% of the trust principal each year. If Mary Sue doesn't exercise her right to withdraw this year, she cannot take an extra $5,000 or 5% out of the trust principal next year.

- The value of the 5-and-5 power is includible in the decedent's gross estate in the year of death. Generally, the value of the 5-and-5 power will be 5% of the trust value at death.

Example

Mary Sue is the beneficiary of a trust established by her deceased husband, Dennis. The trust includes a 5-and-5 power, allowing Mary Sue to withdraw the greater of $5,000 or 5% of the trust principal each year. Before exercising the 5-and-5 power for the current year, Mary Sue died. The trust balance at the time of her death was $500,000. Mary Sue must include $25,000 (5% × $500,000) in her gross estate.

- The lapse of a power that exceeds the 5-and-5 power will be included in the decedent's gross estate

---

Example

Mary Sue is the beneficiary of a trust established in the year 2006 by her deceased husband, Dennis. The trust allows Mary Sue to withdraw 8% of the trust principal each year. Mary Sue made no withdrawals from the trust. In 2007, Mary Sue died. The trust balance in years 2006 and 2007 was $1 million. The executor must include 11% of the trust balance ($110,000) in Mary Sue's gross estate.

How is this calculated? The estate must include 3% (8% withdrawal right exceeds the 5-and-5 power by 3%) of the trust balance in Mary Sue's gross estate because of the lapse of the general power in 2006, and must include another 8% because of the 2007 (year of death) unexercised general power.

      2.) Limited power of appointment—assets under a limited power of appointment are not included in the holder's gross estate at death

B. DEDUCTIONS FROM THE GROSS ESTATE

The taxable estate is the gross estate reduced by various deductions. The deductions include:

1. Funeral expenses

2. Administrative expenses

    a. Commissions paid to executors

    b. Attorney fees

    c. Accountant fees

    d. Court costs

    e. Selling expenses for asset dispositions

    f. Appraisal fees

3. Unpaid mortgages

4. Claims against the estate (debts and unpaid taxes)

5. Losses incurred in administering the estate (such as casualty losses)

6. Charitable contributions (unlimited)

7. Transfers to the surviving spouse (unlimited)

8. State death taxes paid (for years 2005–2009)

C. TAXABLE ESTATE AND ESTATE TAX LIABILITY

The tentative estate tax is determined by applying the rate from the estate tax table to the combined value of the taxable estate and post-1976 taxable gifts (tax base)

1. Tax paid or deemed paid on prior taxable gifts—the tentative tax is then reduced by any gift tax paid or payable on gifts included in the tax base

> **Note:** Gift tax paid or payable is a reduction of estate tax and not a credit.

2. Estate tax credits—having determined the tentative estate tax, the next step is to deduct the allowable credits for:

    a. The applicable credit amount (see Federal Gift and Estate Taxation on page 25)

    b. Federal estate taxes on prior transfers—credit is given for estate taxes paid 2 years before and 10 years after death for property included in the gross estate of the decedent. The credit is subject to a percentage limitation that depends on how long the decedent survived the transferor.

Years Between Deaths	Credit Percentage
More than 2, not more than 4	80%
More than 4, not more than 6	60%
More than 6, not more than 8	40%
More than 8, not more than 10	20%
More than 10	0%

    c.   Foreign death taxes—estate taxes paid to other countries

3.   Estate tax liability—the result of these deductions from the tentative estate tax is the net estate tax due

D. DUE DATE OF THE FEDERAL ESTATE TAX RETURN

1.   The federal estate tax return, Form 706, when required, is due nine months after the date of the decedent's death

2.   An extension of time to file can be requested

E. INCLUSION OF AN ITEM IN THE GROSS ESTATE VERSUS ADDING ITEM TO TAXABLE ESTATE

1.   It is difficult to appreciate the difference between the inclusion of an item in the gross estate or adding it to the taxable estate as a prior taxable gift.

    a.   If the gift has to be added to the gross estate, the value of the property must be redetermined. The value of the property included in the gross estate is the fair market value of the property as of the date of death (or alternate valuation date, if elected). The result of this treatment is that all appreciation from the date of the gift will be included and taxed in the estate. If the gift is included in the gross estate, the value of the gift at the time the gift was made must be removed from the category of post-1976 gifts.

    b.   If, on the other hand, the taxable gift is added to the taxable estate, the value at the date of the gift applies. Usually the amount is net of the annual exclusion and net of post-gift appreciation, because only the taxable gift is added.

EXHIBIT 6: ESTATE TAX FORMULA

(1) Gross estate $ _____

(2) Less: Expenses, debts, and losses:

    (a) Funeral and administrative expenses   _____

    (b) Debts of decedent, mortgages, losses   _____

    (c) State death taxes paid   _____

(3) Equals: Adjusted gross estate (AGE)*   _____

(4) Less: Total allowable deductions:

    (c) Charitable deduction   _____

    (d) Marital deduction   _____

    Total allowable deductions   ($ _____)

(5) Equals: Taxable estate $ _____

(6) Add: Adjusted taxable gifts (post-1976)   _____

(7) Compute: Tentative tax base   _____

(8) Compute: Tentative tax   _____

(9) Less: Tax paid or deemed paid on prior taxable gifts   ($ _____)

(10) Equals: Estate tax before reduction for allowable credits   _____

(11) Less:

      Applicable credit amount   _____

      Other credits   _____

(12) Equals: Estate tax liability $ _____

*The term *adjusted gross estate* is not on Form 706; however, this concept applies to Section 6166, Section 303, and Section 2032A and may be tested on the exam.

F. BASIS OF PROPERTY ACQUIRED FROM A DECEDENT

1. When one is receiving property from a decedent, the basis of such property is the FMV at the date of death or, if the alternate valuation date is selected, the FMV six months after the date of death

2. Alternate valuation date requirements

    a. An estate tax return must be filed

    b. Both the value of the gross estate and the estate tax liability must be reduced below what the date of death value would have yielded

    c. The election is made on Form 706 but will not be valid if the return is filed one year after the time prescribed by law (including extension) for filing the Form 706

Example

Ben died recently and left the following assets shown below valued at the date of death (DOD) and at six months after the DOD:

Item	Value at DOD	Value Six Months after DOD
Land	$5,000,000	$4,500,000
Stock	$300,000	$310,000
Annuity	$100,000	$95,000
Condominium	$300,000	Sold 2 months after DOD for $295,000

If Ben's executor elects the alternate valuation date, Ben's total estate will be $4,500,000 + $310,000 + $100,000 + $295,000 = $5,205,000. The land and stock will use the six-month valuation, the annuity (a wasting asset) must be valued at the DOD, and the condominium will be valued as of the sale date.

---

3. Deathbed gifts—if a beneficiary receives property from a decedent that the decedent acquired by gift from the beneficiary within one year of the decedent's death, the donor/beneficiary takes the decedent's basis (which will be the donor's basis). No stepped-up basis is received.

Example

Joey gives property to his son that at the date of gift has a FMV of $7,000. No gift taxes were paid. Joey has an adjusted basis in the property of $2,300. Joey's son dies within one year of the date of the gift. The property was bequeathed to Joey. Hence, Joey's basis in the property is $2,300 (donor's basis).

---

4. Survivor's share of property (JTWROS)—the basis of such property is the FMV at the date of the decedent's death for the portion related to the decedent. This is added to the basis of the survivor.

Example

Michael and Jeff owned, as joint tenants with survivorship, land that they purchased for $60,000. Jeff furnished two-thirds of the purchase price, and Michael furnished one-third. At the date of Jeff's death, the property had a FMV of $100,000. Michael figures his basis in the property as follows:

Interest Michael bought initially	$20,000
Interest Michael received @ Jeff's death ($^2/_3$ of 100,000)(Step to FMV)	$66,000
Michael's basis @ Jeff's death	$86,000

Common law states do not allow an adjustment to the property's basis for excluded property interests (e.g., a spouse's share of jointly held property).

---

5. Community property—receives an adjustment in basis to the FMV on both spouses halves at the death of the first spouse

---

Example

Ted and his wife, Alice, jointly own a mountain retreat. Ted dies and leaves the property, which has a basis of $200,000 and a FMV at DOD of $1 million, to Alice. If Ted and Alice live in a community property state, Alice's new basis is $1 million. If Ted and Alice do not live in a community property state, Alice's new basis is $600,000 (her basis of $100,000 plus his half at FMV $500,000).

---

6. Holding period of property acquired from a decedent is deemed to be long term (i.e., held for the required long-term holding period). This provision applies regardless of whether the property is disposed of at a gain or loss and regardless of decedent's holding period.

VIII. VALUATION OF ASSETS

A. REAL ESTATE

1. Appraisal required

2. Special use valuation (Section 2032A) may be available. (See section titled Special Use Valuation (Section 2032A) on page 103.)

3. If land is sold within a short period after decedent's death to an unrelated party, the sales price will usually be accepted as its value

B. STOCKS

1. Treatment of dividends on Form 706:

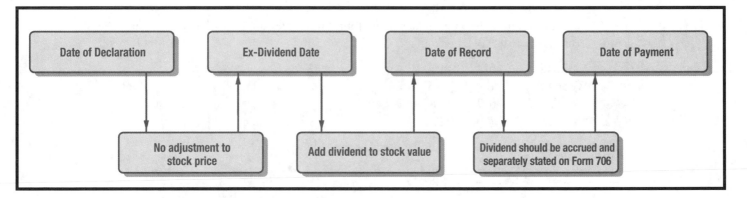

a. Date of declaration—the date the board of directors approves and declares that a dividend will be paid to the shareholders

b. Ex-dividend date—the date that the market price of the stock adjusts for the dividend (i.e., the market price is reduced approximately by the amount of the dividend)

c. Date of record—the date that the company determines who owns stock in the company and is entitled to a dividend, whether or not they own the stock as of the payment date. Shareholders who purchase stock between the date of record and the date of payment are not entitled to the dividend.

d. Date of payment—the date the company pays the dividend to its shareholders

2. Value of stocks for Form 706—the value of the stocks will be the average of the high and low trading values for the stock on the date of death or alternative valuation date. If the stock is not traded on the date of death, the value of the stock according to the IRS regulations should be the stock price following the death multiplied by the number of days from the stock trade before the date of death. Added to this is the stock price directly preceding the death multiplied by the number of days (trading days) between the death and the next trading day. This sum should be divided by the sum of the days before and after the death. (This is the same calculation discussed for gift tax in the section titled Valuation of a Gift.)

Examples

- Bill Cole died on August 29. At that time, he owned stock in XYZ Corporation. The stock traded on both August 28 and August 29. Given the following excerpt from the *Wall Street Journal* for both days, the reported value of XYZ stock on Form 706 will be $59.

August 28	August 29
High - 63	High - 60
Low - 52	Low - 58
Close - 57	Close - 59.5

  The value of the stock reported on Form 706 will be the mean of the high and the low stock price for the date of death. It is not the closing price for stock on the trading day.

- ABC stock does not trade on a regular basis. John Smith dies on Thursday, June 5, and the most recent trades for ABC stock are:

Monday	6/2	27
Wednesday	6/4	25
Monday	6/9	28
Tuesday	6/10	29

  The date of death value that should be used for the federal estate return is $26.

  $$\frac{(1 \times 28) + (2 \times 25)}{3} = \frac{78}{3} = \$26.$$

  According to the IRS regulations, the stock price following the death should be multiplied by the number of days from the stock trade to the date of death (in this case, one day). Added to this is the stock price directly preceding the death, multiplied by the number of days (trading days) between the death and the next trading day (in this case, two days, Friday and Monday). This sum should be divided by the sum of the days before and after the death (2 + 1 = 3 days).

C. LIFE INSURANCE

1. The value of life insurance for gift tax purposes will be the terminal value (cash surrender value) of the policy

2. The value of life insurance included in the gross estate will be the proceeds received. If settlement option is chosen by the beneficiary, the amount includible in the gross estate will be the amount that would have been payable as a lump sum.

D. GOVERNMENT BONDS

1. Series E—valued at redemption price at date of death

E. THE CLOSELY HELD BUSINESS

1. Factors to be considered in closely held company valuation

   a. Nature of the business

   b. Economic outlook

---

    c.   Book value of stock

    d.   Financial condition of business

    e.   Goodwill

    f.   Earning capacity and ability to pay dividends

    g.   Shares that have been sold previously

2.   Estate-freezing techniques—see Estate Freezing on page 47

F. BUY-SELL AGREEMENTS

1.   Benefits of a buy-sell agreement

    a.   Can establish estate value of the business

    b.   Provides cash to the decedent's estate

    c.   Provides for business continuation

    d.   Guarantees that there will be a buyer for the business at the decedent's death

    e.   Reduces a business' credit risk because of continuation plan

2.   Provisions in a buy-sell agreement

    a.   Parties to and purpose of the agreement

    b.   Description of the business interest

    c.   Restrictions on transfers before death

    d.   Method used to determine purchase price

    e.   Funding of the purchase price

    f.   Whether agreement can be modified or terminated

3.   Two types of buy-sell agreements

    a.   Cross-purchase agreement

       1.)   Death or disability of a proprietor, partner, or shareholder of a closely held business may cause serious business problems including liquidation and continuity of management problems. It may even cause dissolution of a partnership. It is appropriate to plan for the sale of the interests of any key person in advance of events such as death or disability.

       2.)   It is possible to have a business buy-sell agreement without funding if the potential buyers have sufficient liquid assets. However, that is not usually the case.

       3.)   A solid buy-sell agreement will have triggering events identified (e.g., death and disability), valuation methodology identified either by formula or process, and a funding mechanism in place. One such funding mechanism is life insurance.

       4.)   Under a cross-purchase agreement funded with life insurance, a partner or shareholder purchases a sufficient amount of life insurance on the lives of each other partner or shareholder to ensure sufficient liquidity to buy out the deceased or disabled partner or shareholder.

Example

A and B are partners. They conclude that the partnership is worth $500,000. Each partner buys a $250,000 policy on the other and enters into an agreement binding on the respective heirs to sell the partnership interest to the surviving partner for $250,000 in the event of one of their deaths.

5.) One problem with cross-purchase agreement funded with life insurance is that when the number of partners or shareholders increases arithmetically, the number of policies increases geometrically. (Four partners equal twelve policies.) The number of policies equals the number of partners times the number of partners minus one, or $n \times (n - 1)$. (Example: 4 partners; $4 \times 3 = 12$ policies)

6.) Another potential problem is the cost difference in funding a policy for older partners or shareholders (more expensive) versus that of funding a policy for younger partners or shareholders (less expensive)

7.) Tax ramifications

    a.) Premiums are not tax deductible, and the proceeds are not includible in taxable income

    b.) Under the cross-purchase method, the estate will have a capital gain on the sale of the decedent's interest

    c.) Because the interest has a step to fair market value at the businessowner's death, there will be very little capital gain

    d.) The purchaser(s) in a cross-purchase agreement will have a basis in the purchased interest equal to the price paid for the interest. Allows increased tax basis for surviving owners.

b. Entity agreement

1.) An entity agreement is also referred to as stock redemption if the entity is a corporation. The shares are typically held by the corporation as treasury stock.

2.) An entity agreement is an alternative to the cross-purchase arrangement. The entity itself buys the insurance policies on each partner or shareholder. The advantage of an entity agreement is that the number of policies is reduced to one per partner or shareholder.

3.) Tax ramifications

    a.) Premiums are not tax deductible, and the proceeds are not includible in taxable income

    b.) Under the entity method, the entity will not receive a deduction for the amounts paid to the deceased owner's estate

    c.) Because the owners are not purchasing the business interest, they do not receive any increase in their basis

EXHIBIT 7: CROSS PURCHASE VERSUS ENTITY AGREEMENT

CROSS PURCHASE		ENTITY	
Advantages	Disadvantages	Advantages	Disadvantages
• Basis adjustment	• Number of policies = n $(n-1)$ • Inequality in policy cost because of differing ages	• Fewer policies if 3 or more owners	• No basis adjustment • Potential corporate AMT • Possible dividend treatment by IRS

4. Choosing the type of buy-sell agreement

    a. The following factors must be considered when choosing a type of agreement:

        1.) Number of partners/shareholders

        2.) Flexibility

        3.) Funding

        4.) Valuation

    b. Number of partners/shareholders

        1.) The entity approach is typically favored if there are many of partners/shareholders

        2.) Entity approach is easier, and the funding is easier to obtain

        3.) Cross purchase will most likely require more policies: $n \times (n-1)$

    c. Flexibility

        1.) A cross purchase agreement can be more flexible, because survivors can change their ownership percentage disproportionately when a partner/shareholder dies

        2.) Under the entity agreement, there is no change in the ratio of ownership after a partner's death

    d. Funding

        1.) A cross-purchase agreement can cause problems when the owners' ages differ

            a.) Younger owners will pay high premiums on the lives of older owners

        2.) The business entity pays the premiums under the entity approach

            a.) With a partnership, older partners may get a lower distributive share from the partnership

            b.) More equitable than cross purchase

    e. Valuation

        1.) Cross purchase—each surviving owner receives insurance proceeds when a partner/shareholder dies

            a.) Surviving owners buy decedent's interest from the estate

        2.) Entity—entity owns policies and receives distribution when a partner dies

5. Disability buy-sell agreements

    a. Overview

1.) A disability buy-sell agreement is similar to a death buy-sell agreement, except the purchase of the business interest occurs when the businessowner becomes disabled

2.) A single buy-sell agreement can be created that addresses both the death and the disability of the businessowner

b. Provisions in a disability buy-sell agreement

1.) Elimination period—time between the onset of disability and the purchase of the stock

2.) Buy-out reversal provision

3.) Definition of disability—the definition of disability for the buy-sell agreement should match the insurance definition of disability to avoid disputes

a.) Own occupation—best definition of disability for buy-sell agreements; the inability to engage in one's regular occupation

b.) Any occupation for which the insured is suited

c.) Any occupation at all

4.) Salary continuation plans—a plan that provides continued income if disability occurs

a.) Disability income protection insurance can be used to provide future income to a disabled businessowner

b.) Disability income protection insurance is different from disability buy-out insurance, which is used to fund the purchase of the business from the disabled businessowner

5.) Disposition of policies provision

6.) Premature death clause

c. Types of disability buy-sell agreements

1.) Cross-purchase agreement

a.) A partner or shareholder purchases a sufficient amount of disability buy-out insurance on the lives of the other partners or shareholders

b.) When a partner or shareholder becomes disabled, the other partners or shareholders purchase the business interest from the disabled partner

c.) Income tax ramifications

- The disability buy-out insurance premiums paid by the partners or shareholders are not deductible

- Disability buy-out proceeds received by a partner or shareholder are not taxable to the recipient partner or shareholder

- The disabled businessowner will recognize capital gain when her business interest is purchased by the other owners

— Capital gain may be significant, because there is no step-up in basis of the business interest

— Step-up occurs only if the businessowner dies

- The purchasing owners will have a basis in the purchased business interest equal to the purchase price of the business

    2.) Entity agreement

        a.) The entity purchases a sufficient amount of disability buy-out insurance on the lives of the partners or shareholders

        b.) When a partner or shareholder becomes disabled, the entity purchases the business interest from the disabled partner

        c.) Income tax ramifications

- The disability buy-out insurance premiums paid by the entity are not deductible

- Disability buy-out proceeds received by the entity are not taxable to the entity

- The disabled businessowner will recognize capital gain when his business interest is purchased by the entity

    — Capital gain may be significant, because there is no step-up in basis of the business interest

    — Step-up only occurs if the business owner dies

  d. Choosing the appropriate type of disability buy-sell agreement

    1.) The same factors used to determine the appropriate type of death buy-sell agreement should be used to determine the appropriate type of disability buy-sell agreement

    2.) Factors include:

        a.) Number of businessowners

        b.) Flexibility

        c.) Funding

        d.) Valuation

Example

Kathy is one of several very active owners of Rebuild, Inc., a successful construction company. It has been proposed to the owners that to insure the future of the company against the loss of one of the owners to death or disability and to provide for the liquidity of each owner's interest in the business in such an event, that they enter into an entity buy-sell agreement for both death and disability. Kathy's basis in her stock in Rebuild is $500,000 and the buy-out value is $2 million. Rebuild, Inc., pays all of the premiums for the insurance, but the premiums are NOT deductible as a business expense. Kathy has asked you to explain what would happen in either event.

A. Kathy dies. Rebuild, Inc., receives the $2 million from the life insurance policy. Her stock receives a step-up in basis to $2 million. Meanwhile the other owners will have increased their ownership in Rebuild, Inc., but will not have increased their basis.

B. Kathy is disabled. Again, Rebuild, Inc., buys the stock from Kathy for $2 million. In this case, upon the sale, Kathy has a capital gain of $1.5 million ($2 million sale price—$500,000 basis), which she must report on her income tax return. As in the case of a death, the owners will have increased their ownership in Rebuild, Inc., but will not have increased their basis.

G. VALUATION DISCOUNTS

1. In general

   a. The transfer tax value of closely held businesses, real estate, and other assets may be significantly reduced by the utilization of various valuation discounts

   b. These discounts are often used in conjunction with a family limited partnership (see Family Limited Partnership on page 92) or a family limited liability company

2. Minority discount

   a. A reduction in value of an asset transferred is often allowed if the asset transferred represents a minority interest in a business

   b. A minority interest is any interest that, in terms of voting, is not a controlling interest

   c. Minority owners cannot manage the business or compel its sale or liquidation. Therefore, outside buyers would not be willing to pay the same amount for a minority interest as they would for a majority or controlling interest.

   d. For transfer tax purposes, minority discounts (when available) often range from 15% to 50%

3. Lack of marketability discount

   a. A reduction in value of an asset transferred is often allowed if the asset transferred has an inherent lack of marketability

   b. Interests in a closely held business and partnership interests are more difficult to sell than interests in other assets such as publicly traded stock. Therefore, a discount is often allowed for the lack of marketability

   c. Lack of marketability discounts typically range from 15% to 50%, and can be utilized for both minority and majority interests

   d. A lack of marketability discount can be used in conjunction with a minority discount to produce a larger overall discount

---

Example

Tom gave his son a 3% interest in his closely held business. The business is valued at $500,000, and Tom applied a lack of marketability discount and a minority discount that totaled 40%. For gift tax purposes, the value of the gift is only $9,000, calculated as follows: ($500,000 × 3%) × (1 – 40%). The $9,000 gift is eligible for the annual exclusion, resulting in a taxable gift of zero.

---

4. Blockage discount

   a. A blockage discount is a discount attributable to the value of large blocks of corporate stock that are listed on a public exchange

   b. A discount may be available because a large block of stock is often less marketable than smaller amounts of stock

   c. The theory behind a blockage discount is that a large amount of stock included in the decedent's gross estate cannot be liquidated at one time without a decrease in the stock's market price

    d.   The discount would be based on the decrease in the realizable price below the current market price of the stock

5.   Key person discount

    a.   A discount may be allowed for a business in which a key person has died or becomes disabled

    b.   The discount is based on the premise that the stock of a closely held business will decline if a key person, such as the founder, dies or becomes disabled

    c.   The discount may be reduced by the value of key person life insurance proceeds payable to the corporation on the death of the key person

IX. THE MARITAL DEDUCTION

A. DEFINITION

The decedent's estate can claim as a deduction an unlimited amount for qualifying bequests or transfers of property to a surviving spouse

1. This treatment parallels the marital deduction for gift tax.

2. The deduction does not apply to surviving spouses who are not US citizens. They have their own separate rules described in the section titled Alien Surviving Spouses on page 72.

B. QUALIFICATIONS FOR DEDUCTION

1. The property must be included in the decedent's gross estate

2. The property must be passed to the decedent's spouse

3. The interest in the property must not be a terminable interest

    a. A terminable interest is defined as an interest that ends upon an event or contingency. In other words, the spouse initially gets the interest in the property, this interest will terminate upon some event (usually death), and then the interest will pass to someone else.

    b. Exceptions to the terminable interest rule

        1.) When the only condition of the bequest is that the survivor live for a period not exceeding six months, the marital deduction is allowed if the surviving spouse actually lives for the period specified

        2.) When there is a life estate coupled with a general power of appointment, the marital deduction is allowed

        3.) When there is a be quest to the spouse of income from a charitable remainder annuity trust or a charitable remainder unitrust and the spouse is the only noncharitable beneficiary, the marital deduction is allowed

        4.) Certain marital trusts

C. STRAIGHT BEQUESTS

1. The first spouse dies and leaves everything to the surviving spouse

2. Estate of the decedent spouse gets 100% marital deduction. The property will be taxed in the estate of the second spouse.

3. Advantages

    a. Simple and inexpensive

    b. Surviving spouse gets unfettered control over the assets

4. Disadvantages

    a. May overqualify estate if the first spouse to die does not take advantage of the applicable credit amount

    b. Total estate tax between the two spouses may be higher if all property is bequeathed to the surviving spouse

D. QUALIFIED TERMINABLE INTEREST PROPERTY (QTIP) TRUST

1. Allows a terminable interest to be passed to a surviving spouse and the property to still qualify for the marital deduction

2. Election is made on Form 706

3. Income from the trust must be payable to the surviving spouse at least annually for life

4. The value of the trust assets must be included in the estate of the surviving spouse when she dies

5. Surviving spouse is not usually given a general power of appointment

6. Usually the first spouse to die has specified in the trust provisions the ultimate disposition of the property

7. Sometimes called a C trust or a Q trust

E. POWER OF APPOINTMENT TRUST

1. Allows a terminable interest to be passed to the surviving spouse and the property to still qualify for the marital deduction

2. No election required as with QTIP

3. Income from the trust must be payable to the surviving spouse at least annually for life

4. The trust will be included in the estate of the surviving spouse when he dies

5. Surviving spouse is given a general power of appointment over the property during life or at death

6. The first spouse to die does not control the ultimate disposition of the property because the surviving spouse has a general power of appointment

7. Sometimes called an A trust

F. BYPASS TRUST

1. The purpose of a bypass trust is to take advantage of the applicable credit amount when the first spouse dies ($780,800 for transfers at death in 2007)

2. The property does not qualify for the marital deduction and is taxed in the estate of the first spouse to die

3. A common scenario is for the first spouse to leave at death everything to the surviving spouse except for the applicable exclusion amount of $2 million for transfers at death in 2007, which is transferred into a bypass trust

   a. The trust can be designed to allow the surviving spouse to invade the trust for health, education, maintenance, and support

   b. When the surviving spouse dies, it does not go into her estate, and the property passes to the children

4. A bypass trust can be used instead of an outright bequest to nonspouse heirs who are not sophisticated or mature enough to handle the property. The choice of the trust over the outright bequest does not save any tax dollars; it simply provides the transferor with some peace of mind.

5. Often, highly appreciating assets are placed in a bypass trust to freeze the value for estate tax purposes at the death of the first spouse

6. Also called a credit equivalency trust, a credit shelter trust, a family trust, or a B trust

G. USE OF DISCLAIMERS

1. Allows spouse to disclaim part of estate, which would then go to the bypass share

2. A specific direction to disclaim is not necessary in the will

3. Allows more flexibility in the estate

4. If spouse disclaims the property, his control over the property is minimized

5. Because disclaimer has to be made within nine months of the spouse's death, the surviving spouse may find it difficult to give up property at a time when the surviving spouse may not be feeling very secure

H. ALIEN SURVIVING SPOUSES

1. The unlimited marital deduction is disallowed if the surviving spouse is not a US citizen. (The unlimited marital deduction is available, however, for a decedent alien spouse leaving assets to a citizen spouse.)

2. If the spouse becomes a citizen before the federal estate tax return is filed (Form 706 within nine months) or has been a resident alien at all times since the decedent's death, the unlimited marital deduction is allowed. The spouse must have been a US resident at the time of the decedent's death.

3. Marital deduction is allowed for property placed in a qualified domestic trust (QDOT) that passes to a non-US surviving spouse

   a. Trust document requires at least one trustee to be US citizen or US corporation

   b. Trustee has a right to withhold estate tax on distribution

   c. Must meet requirements of the Treasury

   d. Executor must make irrevocable election

I. CALCULATION OF MARITAL DEDUCTION

1. An unlimited marital deduction is allowed for testamentary transfers to a surviving spouse

   a. Has the effect of treating a husband and wife as one economic unit for gift and estate tax purposes

   b. Applies in both separate and community property states

2. Generally, the marital deduction is determined on the basis of the gross estate value of the asset transferred to the decedent's surviving spouse

---

Example

At the time of his death, Tom owned a parcel of real estate worth $800,000 and a checking account worth $25,000. His will bequeathed the parcel of land to his surviving spouse, Sandi, and the checking account to his son, Tommie.

Tom will have a gross estate of $825,000 ($800,000 real estate plus $25,000 checking account), and his estate will claim a marital deduction of $800,000, equal to the gross estate value of the real estate transferred to Sandi. Tom's taxable estate will be $25,000 ($825,000 gross estate less $800,000 marital deduction).

---

3. The marital deduction is reduced by any liabilities transferred to the spouse at death

---

Example

Assume the same facts as the previous example, except the parcel of real estate was subject to a $350,000 mortgage at the time of Tom's death. His will bequeathed both the real estate and the associated mortgage to Sandi.

Tom will have a gross estate of $825,000 ($800,000 + $25,000) and will have an adjusted gross estate of $475,000 ($825,000 gross estate less $350,000 debt). However, his marital deduction will be only $450,000 ($800,000 real estate less $350,000 associated debt) because of the liability that was transferred to Sandi. Tom's taxable estate will be $25,000 ($475,000 adjusted gross estate less $450,000 marital deduction).

The marital deduction must be reduced by any associated liabilities transferred to the surviving spouse.

---

4. An interrelated marital deduction is required in the case of some estates

   a. Some states do not allow a marital deduction for certain property transfers, such as qualified terminable interest property

   b. If state death taxes are charged against marital property, the net amount passing to the surviving spouse is reduced, thus reducing the marital deduction

   c. As the marital deduction is reduced, the likelihood of paying federal estate taxes increases, especially if the decedent's applicable credit amount has been exhausted because of prior gifts or bequests to nonspouse heirs

   d. If the additional federal estate tax is paid out of assets transferred to the surviving spouse, the marital deduction is further reduced. In essence, an interrelated marital deduction is required.

X. TRUSTS

A. GENERAL

1. A trust is a legal arrangement that involves three parties

   a. Grantor (settlor)—transfers the property (called the principal or corpus) into the trust

   b. Trustee—holds the legal title to the assets and has a fiduciary responsibility to safeguard the property and distribute corpus and trust income as directed by the trust instrument

   c. Beneficiary—the person or persons the trust benefits. The beneficiary is said to have a beneficial interest.

   d. It is not always the case that three different individuals are involved. In some cases, an individual may serve two or more functions.

      1.) Grantor names herself trustee

      2.) Grantor names himself beneficiary

      3.) Grantor is both trustee and beneficiary. This is called a grantor trust and is not recognized for tax purposes.

2. Types of trust interests

   a. Income interest—beneficiary receives the accounting income (income earned from trust assets) of the trust

   b. Remainder interest—beneficiary receives the trust principal upon termination of the trust. A vested remainder is one that is nonforfeitable. A contingent remainder is where the interest depends on whether a certain future event happens.

   c. Reversionary interest—a grantor who retains the remainder interest is said to have a reversionary interest

3. Duration

   a. The terms of the trust will dictate the length of the trust life

   b. Rule against perpetuities (certain states do not have a rule against perpetuities)

      1.) The rule against perpetuities prevents trusts from having an infinite life

      2.) The rule aims to prevent the transferor of property from controlling the disposition of the property for an unreasonably long period after making the transfer

      3.) This rule states that an interest cannot last longer than 21 years after the death of someone who was alive on the date the interest was created

      4.) The date on which the interest is created is different for revocable and irrevocable trusts. If the trust is an irrevocable trust, the interest is created on the date the trust is created. If the trust is a revocable trust, the interest is created on the date in which the trust becomes irrevocable (usually at the date of death of the settlor).

      5.) To avoid application of the rule against perpetuities, most trusts and wills contain a perpetuities savings clause requiring that the trust terminate no later than the outer limits of the rule (21 years)

      6.) Charitable trusts are exempt from the rule against perpetuities

B. REASONS FOR CREATING A TRUST

1. To avoid probate

2. To avoid or reduce estate and/or income taxes

3. Asset management for an individual who is the grantor and the beneficiary in the case he becomes incapacitated

4. Asset management for beneficiaries who are not grantors. (The grantor may not have confidence in the beneficiaries abilities to invest assets.)

5. To make a charitable contribution while retaining some interest

C. TRUST CHARACTERISTICS

1. When created

   a. Inter vivos—created during life

   b. Testamentary—created by will and included in estate. Gift tax does not apply because transfer occurs at death.

2. Permanency

   a. Revocable—a trust that is able to be rescinded or amended by the grantor (grantor trusts)

   b. Irrevocable—a trust where the grantor has given up all control over the property. The trust cannot be changed by the grantor. All simple and complex trusts are irrevocable trusts.

3. Funding

   a. Funded—trust has property placed in it. There is a principal or corpus amount.

   b. Unfunded—a trust that is legally ready to receive property but has not done so yet

4. Income payout requirements

   a. Simple trust—required to pay out all income to beneficiaries annually

      1.) No amounts may be paid to a charitable beneficiary or charitable purpose

      2.) May not distribute corpus

   b. Complex trust—any trust that isn't a simple trust. A simple trust will be complex in its final year because any corpus remaining is distributed in the final year.

D. TYPES OF TRUSTS

1. Living trust

   a. Grantor creates an inter vivos trust that is funded with part or all of the grantor's property

   b. This property does not pass through probate at death thus the transfer is accomplished with a minimum of publicity, expense, and delays

   c. Revocable living trust—revocable during the grantor's life and becomes irrevocable at grantor's death

      1.) Includible in gross estate

      2.) No gift tax at time of creation because there is not a completed gift

   d. Irrevocable living trust—grantor places property into a trust that he cannot rescind or amend

1.) Transfers constitute completed gifts thus gift tax may apply at the time the trust is created

2.) Has income and estate tax benefits (freeze value of estate assets)

2. Grantor trusts

a. Grantor trust rules rest on the idea that if a grantor has control over the trust, then a completed gift has not been made, the grantor still has ownership of the assets, and the trust is not a separate taxable entity. Therefore, any income is taxed to the grantor.

b. Sections 671–677 state that if a trust is a grantor trust, then the grantor is treated as the owner of the assets. Consequently, all the income, deductions, and credits of the trust are attributable to the grantor.

c. The grantor is deemed owner of the trust if the grantor retains:

1.) A reversionary interest in the corpus or income of the trust

2.) The power to control the beneficial enjoyment of the property or income (withdraw funds or change beneficiaries)

3.) Certain administrative powers, such as borrowing

4.) The power to revoke a portion of the trust

5.) Income for the benefit of the grantor, such as purchasing life insurance on the grantor or paying for support obligations of the grantor

3. Standby trust—a trust (usually revocable) that has been legally created but will not actually function until some event occurs. For example, a trust that will spring upon incapacity to manage the assets when the grantor becomes unable.

4. Pourover trust—assets are poured from another source (e.g., from a will, IRA, or insurance contract) into the trust. May be revocable or irrevocable.

5. Charitable transfers

a. General—in general, a charitable income tax deduction is available for transfers to charities during life. Such transfers may take a variety of forms.

1.) To receive a current income tax deduction, charitable transfers must be in the precise form of one of the following:

a.) Direct outright gift

- A charitable income tax deduction is permitted for direct outright donations to a qualifying charitable organization

— The charitable income tax deduction is generally equal to the value of the cash or property donated

— See income tax section for detailed description of income tax deduction allowed if cash or other property is donated outright to charity

- An unlimited charitable deduction is allowed for estate tax purposes

— Property must be included in the decedent's gross estate

— Estate tax charitable deduction reduces the decedent's adjusted gross estate in arriving at the taxable estate

- An unlimited charitable deduction is allowed for gift tax purposes

— Charitable deduction eliminates any gift taxes

— In most cases, gift tax returns are not required for charitable contributions

b.) Charitable gift annuity—an irrevocable transfer of assets for a charitable annuity. Transfer is for less than a commercial annuity; therefore, a charitable income tax deduction is available for the difference using the IRS method.

c.) Pooled income fund—an irrevocable transfer of assets to a charity for an income stream from the charity's commingled asset management. A charitable deduction is available.

- Pooled income fund—public charity

  — Created and maintained by the charity

  — Donor transfers property including irrevocable remainder interest to charity (must be a 50% type charity and managed by the charitable remainderman)

  — Property commingled with property of other donors

  — Grantor retains income interest for one or more beneficiaries for life (no term trusts)

  — Investments cannot include tax-free municipal bonds

  — Payment to donor is determined by earnings of trust annually

  — Sprinkling is not allowed

d.) Charitable remainder trust (CRT)

- Overview

  — A CRT is an irrevocable trust in which the remainder beneficiary is a qualified charity

  — A CRT can take the form of a charitable remainder annuity trust (CRAT) or a charitable remainder unitrust (CRUT)

- Common features of both a CRAT and a CRUT

  — Trust is irrevocable

  — Remainder interest is paid to charity

  — Trust can last for life of grantor, or for a term of up to 20 years

  — The present value of the remainder interest at the inception of the trust must be at least 10% of the initial fair market value of the property transferred to the trust

  — The charity does not have to know it was named as the remainder beneficiary

  — Annuity/unitrust payout rate must be at least 5%, and less than or equal to 50%

- Unique features of a charitable remainder annuity trust (CRAT)

  — Grantor receives either a fixed percentage of the initial fair market value of the property transferred to the trust or a fixed dollar amount annually

  — Annuity must be paid in spite of necessity to invade principal because of income deficiency

— No additional contributions are permitted after inception

— Very inflexible

- Unique features of a charitable remainder unitrust (CRUT)

    — Grantor receives a fixed percentage of the trust assets, valued annually

    - Unitrust amount may be limited to income earned

    - Trust may provide for catch-up provisions when income does not meet the percentage requirement and then later exceeds the current percentage payout

    - Annual valuation may be expensive if property in trust is not easily valued (e.g., closely held businesses, real estate)

    — Additional contributions to the trust are permitted after inception

    — Very flexible

Example

Virginia, a 70-year-old widow, has charitable inclinations but needs the income from all her assets during her retirement years. She decides to establish a charitable remainder annuity trust with $500,000 cash. Virginia will get a payment of 5% of the principal each year for the rest of her life. Assuming a rate of 10%, Virginia would go to Table S (Single Life PV of Annuity, Life Estate and Remainder Interests) to determine the value of her retained interest: 6.4093 × $25,000 or ($500,000 × 5%) = $160,233. Virginia then receives a charitable contribution deduction for the remainder interest of $339,767 ($500,000 – $160,233).

---

    e.) Charitable lead trust (CLT)

- Income from property transferred to trust is distributed to charity. Remainder reverts to noncharitable beneficiary (often a family member).

- If set up as a grantor trust, a charitable income tax deduction for the present value of the income interest is available at the inception. However, the annual trust income is taxable to the grantor.

- If set up as a nongrantor trust, no charitable income tax deduction is available; however, the gift is valued at FMV less the present value of the charitable income interest. The trust receives an unlimited annual charitable deduction for the gift made to the recipient charity each year.

- Used by high-wealth individuals who have no need for the current income from the assets. Advantageous to fund with high appreciation assets because it will remove appreciation from the estate (if nongrantor type trust is used).

    f.) Private foundations

- Overview of private foundations

    — Private foundations are tax-exempt charitable organizations created to effectively direct charitable contributions

    — Typically created by a family or corporation

— Unlike public charities, private foundations generally do not receive contributions from a wide range of supporters

— Can be operating or nonoperating

- Operating—use their funds in their own charitable activity, including purchasing assets

- Nonoperating—do not engage in charitable activity directly but disburse funds for charitable purposes

- Tax ramifications of private foundations

— Income tax deduction for contributions of cash to private nonoperating foundations is limited to 30% of the donor's contribution base for the tax year

— Tax deduction for contributions of long-term capital gain property to private nonoperating foundations is limited to basis and is limited to 20% of the taxpayer's contribution base

— Net investment income of the private foundation is subject to special income tax

- Advantages of private foundations

— Donor receives a charitable deduction in the year the contribution is made

— Donor can control the investment and distribution of assets

— Allows the donor to address specific charitable objectives that may not be addressed by other organizations

— Provides ability to train heirs to manage wealth

— Accumulation of assets allows for larger charitable gifts

- Disadvantages of private foundations

— Subject to strict reporting requirements

— Can be administratively expensive

— Donations to private foundations are subject to deductibility limitations

— The foundation must generally distribute at least 5% of its net investment assets each year

g.) Donor advised funds

- Overview of donor advised funds

— A donor advised fund is an arrangement in which a donor makes a gift to a charity

- The charity establishes a fund in the donor's name

- The donor or its representative makes future recommendations of grants to charitable beneficiaries

— Usually established by a public charity or community foundation

- Tax ramifications of donor advised funds

  — Donor receives an immediate income tax deduction when initial donation is made

  — Income tax deduction for contributions of cash is limited to 50% of the donor's contribution base for the tax year

  — Income tax deduction for contributions of appreciated property is limited to 30% of the donor's contribution base for the tax year

  — Donor advised funds fall under the tax-exempt classification of the charity offering the fund

- Advantages of donor advised funds

  — Donor receives immediate income tax deduction, even though grants to charities may be spread out over several years

  — Costs to establish the fund are low

  — Donor has ability to name several charitable recipients

  — Fund is generally very simple to understand and use

  — Minimum required contribution is usually relatively low

  — Can be established relatively quickly

  — Charity performs any necessary annual filings

- Disadvantages of donor advised funds

  — Once the donor makes a donation to the fund, it is irrevocable

  — Charity may place restrictions on the grant

  — Occasionally, the annual fees charged by the fund are substantial

  — Donor only has a limited right to control management of fund assets

---

Example

John sets up a CLT with $500,000 that pays a charity a 10% fixed annuity with the remainder going to his children at the end of the trust term. If John uses a grantor trust, John will calculate the present value of the annuity, and he will be able to take a current income tax deduction for the present value of the annuity stream as a charitable contribution. However, John will have to treat the entire annual income of the trust as income during the trust term. John will also have made a taxable gift equal to the present value of the remainder interest. This is a gift of a future interest not subject to the annual exclusion. If John uses a nongrantor trust, he will not get a current charitable deduction, but he will remove the entire asset ($500,000) from his estate at the discounted amount of the taxable gift.

EXHIBIT 8: CHARITABLE REMAINDER TRUSTS

	CRAT	CRUT	Pooled Income Fund
Income Tax Deduction	Total value of property—PV of retained income interest	Total value of property—PV of retained income interest	Total value of property—PV of retained income interest
Income Recipient	Noncharitable beneficiary (usually donor)	Noncharitable beneficiary (usually donor)	Noncharitable beneficiary (usually donor)
Payment	At least 5% of initial FMV of assets paid at least annually for life or term ≤20 years (similar to fixed annuity). Cannot exceed 50% of value of trust.	At least 5% of current FMV of assets (revalued annually) paid at least annually for life or term ≤20 years (similar to variable annuity). Cannot exceed 50% of value of trust.	Trust rate of return for year
Remainder Beneficiary	Charity	Charity	Charity
Additional Contributions	No	Yes	Yes
Sprinkling	Yes	Yes	No
When Income Is Insufficient for Payout	Must invade corpus	Can pay up to income and make up deficiency in subsequent year	N/A
Can Hold Tax-Exempt Securities	Yes	Yes	No

6. Gifts to minors

   a. Uniform Gift to Minors Act (UGMA)

      1.) Adopted in all states

      2.) Gifts can include cash, securities, life insurance, but usually not real property

      3.) No bonding or accounting usually required

      4.) Donees usually must receive property by age of majority

      5.) If donor is custodian and predeceases the beneficiary, then custodial property would be included in donor's estate

   b. Uniform Transfers to Minors Act (UTMA)

      1.) More flexible than Uniform Gift to Minors Act (UGMA)

      2.) Most states have adopted it

      3.) Allows any property interests to be a fiduciary gift

   c. Guardianship

      1.) Very restrictive—requires bonding and accounting

      2.) Court must supervise

      3.) Donee must receive property at age 18

  d. Irrevocable minor's trusts

      1.) Section 2503(b) trust (mandatory income trust)

        a.) All income is required to be distributed annually either to the child/beneficiary directly or to a custodial account where it could be accumulated or used for the child's/beneficiary's benefit

        b.) Not required to end at age 21

        c.) The right to the income qualifies as present interest and the annual exclusion. The income interest is calculated on the basis of the age of the beneficiary and current interest rates at the time of the gift. The remainder interest (corpus) would be subject to gift tax.

        d.) May be excluded from donor's estate

Example

A gift of $12,000 to a 2503(b) trust for a child of 5 and with a trust term of 35 years (until the child is age 40) has both a present interest component and a future interest component. If the prevailing interest rate at the time of the gift is 7%, then the future interest (and taxable gift) would be $1,123.95 and the gift of a present interest would be $10,876.05 which would be eligible for the annual exclusion.

      2.) Section 2503(c) trust

        a.) Income distribution is discretionary

        b.) Principal distribution is discretionary until minor reaches age 21

        c.) While not meeting the requirements of a present interest, the Internal Revenue Code provides an exception in Section 2503(c) whereby gifts to such trusts are deemed to be gifts of a present interest

        d.) If the donee dies before age 21, property must go to the donee's estate, or the donee must hold a general power of appointment

        e.) Trust pays income tax on the undistributed income

      3.) Crummey minor's trust

        a.) Advantageous over Section 2503(b) and Section 2503(c) trusts because income distribution and corpus distribution at age 21 are not mandatory

        b.) See section, Crummey Powers on page 45

7. Grantor retained trust

  a. In a grantor retained trust, a grantor transfers property into a trust but retains some right of enjoyment of the property, usually income. If transferor survives the income period, all beneficial interest in the trust ceases, and the asset is out of the transferor's estate.

  b. The value of the taxable gift is calculated by taking the FMV of the property and reducing it by the retained interest. This equals the remainder interest that is considered a gift.

c. Section 2702 severely limits the advantage of a grantor retained trust by valuing the income interest at zero when the transfer is made for the benefit of a member of the transferor's family and an interest is retained by the transferor or an applicable family member

    1.) Member of transferor's family—ancestors, descendants, spouse, and siblings; ancestors and descendants of spouse; and spouses of transferor's ancestors, descendants, and siblings

    2.) Applicable family member—transferor's spouse, ancestors of the transferor or the transferor's spouse, and any spouse of such ancestor

d. When the retained interest is valued at zero, the remainder interest will be valued at FMV as if an outright gift had occurred

e. Section 2702 carves out exceptions from the zero value rule for qualified personal residence trusts (QPRT), grantor retained annuity trusts (GRAT), grantor retained unitrusts (GRUT), and tangible personal property trusts. Remainder interests can be given to family members for these types of trusts and will escape the zero valuation rules in Section 2702.

f. Grantor retained interest trust (GRIT)—is effective only when used for a personal residence and is sometimes known as a residence GRIT or qualified personal residence trust (QPRT). The grantor transfers a personal residence to a trust and retains the right to live in the residence during the trust term.

    1.) The trust may have an interest in only one residence

    2.) The benefit is that the value of the gift will be equal to the fair market value of the house discounted for the number of years of the term of its trust at the applicable Section 7520 rate. Used most effectively when the residence is expected to rapidly appreciate.

    3.) The residence cannot be occupied by someone other than termholder and family

    4.) The residence may be subject to mortgage

    5.) Prohibits distribution of trust income to anyone but termholder

    6.) At the option of the termholder, may convert to qualified annuity interest (GRAT)

    7.) The house can be rented or repurchased by grantor after trust term

    8.) A QPRT may be an appropriate estate planning technique for a vacation home

    9.) Grantor may be trustee

QUALIFIED PERSONAL RESIDENCE TRUST (QPRT)

Key Features

- Taxable gift occurs when the trust is created

- No limit on trust term

- If transferor lives beyond term of trust, there is no inclusion of the asset in the gross estate

- If the transferor dies before the expiration of the trust term, the property is included in the gross estate at the fair value at the date of death

- This transaction may commonly result in the asset being leased back to the transferor at the end of the term if the transferor is still living. The lease payments will further reduce the transferor's estate, but the beneficiaries will have taxable lease income

- The gift is a future interest (no annual exclusion)

- The trust assets can only consist of a personal residence (maybe a small amount of cash)

- This transaction does not make use of minority discounts

- This is an irrevocable trust

- Purchasing power risk to transferor

- Interest rate risk to transferor

- Reinvestment risk to transferor

- This transaction makes use of the applicable credit amount

- This transaction may require sophisticated valuation at the time of the initial transaction

Example

Virginia, a 70-year-old widow, is in the maximum estate tax bracket. She places her $100,000 personal residence into a QPRT that provides for her to live there 10 years, and then the property passes to her children. Virginia will calculate the present value of her right to live in the house and subtract it from the FMV of her house to calculate the remainder gift to her children. If Virginia dies before 10 years, the FMV of the property at her death will be included in her estate. After 10 years, Virginia could be permitted to remain in the residence provided the agreement is arm's length and rent is charged at market value.

    g. Grantor retained annuity trust (GRAT)

        1.) Income taxed to grantor during lifetime for income tax purposes

        2.) Not taxable in grantor's estate unless grantor dies within income period (term of trust)

        3.) Gift to the extent that the value of the property exceeds income interest calculated at time of creation (this is the remainder interest)

        4.) Remainder passes to family members at end of income term

        5.) Designed to produce estate tax savings for grantor. (Freezes value at trust creation if grantor outlives trust term.)

        6.) Makes fixed payments to grantor at least annually

        7.) Fixed annuity does not have to be the same for each year; however, annuity payment in any year cannot exceed 120% of previous year

        8.) Qualified retained interest is not valued at zero for purposes of Section 2702

        9.) A GRAT is usually used with a family member and where the transferor has a better than average probability to outlive the term of the trust

---

GRANTOR RETAINED ANNUITY TRUST (GRAT)

Key Features

- For any specific term (usually 2–5 years)

- Grantor receives an annual payment from the trust of either a fixed amount or a fixed percentage of the initial FMV of the trust assets

- If transferor lives beyond term of trust, there is no inclusion of the asset in the gross estate

- If the transferor dies before the expiration of the trust term, the property is included in the grantor's gross estate at the FMV at the date of death

- The gift is a future interest (no annual exclusion)

- The trust cannot be used as a personal residence trust

- This transaction does not make use of minority discounts

- This trust is an irrevocable trust

- Purchasing power risk to transferor

- Interest rate risk to transferor

- Reinvestment risk to transferor

- This transaction makes use of the applicable exclusion amount

- This transaction may require sophisticated valuation at the time of the initial transaction

---

h. Grantor retained unitrust (GRUT)

    1.) Makes payments at least annually of a fixed percentage of the net fair market value of the trust assets as determined annually

    2.) All other characteristics are like a GRAT

i. Tangible personal property trusts

    1.) Tangible personal property is transferred to the trust, with the grantor retaining a term certain interest in the trust (retained interest). At the end of the trust term, the beneficiaries receive the remainder interest in the trust.

    2.) Depreciable property cannot be used. Artwork can be used because it is not depreciable.

    3.) The zero valuation rule of Section 2702 does not apply to tangible personal property trusts. The value of the retained interest in the trust will be equal to the amount the interest could be sold for to an unrelated third party.

    4.) The grantor has the burden of establishing the value of the retained interest. Because of the difficulty in valuing the retained interest, tangible personal property trusts are not common.

Example

Kevin established a tangible personal property trust by transferring a $500,000 painting to the trust. Kevin gave his son a remainder interest in the trust, and Kevin retained a 15-year term certain interest. The value of the gift would be $500,000 less the value of the retained interest. Kevin has the burden of establishing the value of the retained interest.

---

8. Credit equivalency trust (bypass trust)

  a. Usually testamentary

  b. Does not ordinarily qualify for the unlimited marital deduction

  c. Ensures that the estate makes use of the applicable exclusion amount ($1 million for inter-vivos gifts and $2 million for transfers at death for 2007). Otherwise, property would automatically be taxed in second spouse's estate if marital deduction was used.

  d. Spouse may be income beneficiary

9. Dynasty trust

  a. Passes a life insurance policy to grandchildren

  b. Avoids GSTT

  c. Transfers substantial wealth

10. Totten trust (similar to POD/TOD)

  a. A trust created by New York statute

  b. When an individual who opens an account in trust for another, it is not a completed transfer. The income is taxed to the grantor until the trust is made irrevocable.

11. Blind trust

   a.   A blind trust can be used to hold assets where ownership of the assets may give rise to conflict of interest issues

   b.   These trusts are commonly used by government officials

   c.   The official, spouse, or dependent child has a beneficial interest, which is certified by the Director of the Office of Government Ethics

   d.   The official has no knowledge or control of the management of the trust assets and only receives the income from the assets

EXHIBIT 9: TRUSTS—SUMMARY OF TRUST CLASSIFICATION AND USE

TRUST	PURPOSE	CHARACTERISTICS	PLANNING OPPORTUNITIES	INCOME / ESTATE / GIFT TAX CONSEQUENCES
QTIP Trust (known as C Trust)	Marital trust that creates a terminable interest for spouse but that DOES qualify for the unlimited marital deduction and gives power to settlor to name remainderman.	All income must be payable to surviving spouse at least annually for life. Surviving spouse is usually not given power of appointment. QTIP election made on Form 706 by executor.	Place assets in QTIP, income to spouse for life, remainder to children.	Assets of the trust are not included in the first decedent's estate but rather in the surviving spouse's estate. Trust pays its pro rata share of estate tax for surviving spouse.
Power of Appointment Trust (known as A Trust or Marital Trust)	Marital trust that creates a terminable interest for spouse but that does qualify for the unlimited marital deduction and gives general power to appoint to surviving spouse to name remainderman.	All income must be payable to surviving spouse at least annually for life. Surviving spouse has general POA. No election required.	Place assets in POA Trust, income to spouse. Spouse is given general POA over property exercisable during life or at death.	Not included in taxable estate of decedent spouse but included in the taxable estate of the surviving spouse (as long as surviving spouse has not gifted or consumed trust corpus during life). If surviving spouse gives the property away (exercises her unlimited POA during life), then surviving spouse has made a taxable gift.
Bypass Trust (known as B Trust or Credit Shelter Trust)	Purpose is to take advantage of the applicable credit amount afforded first decedent spouse. A trust that is sometimes used to pass property to surviving spouse but can be used to give any beneficiary an income interest, with a different remainderman. Does not qualify for the marital deduction.	An alternative to an outright transfer. Takes advantage of the applicable credit of decedent. Useful when a split investment exists between income and remainder.	Instead of leaving an outright bequest to children, decedent spouse puts property into a bypass trust, income to surviving spouse for life, and remainder to children upon surviving spouse's death.	Assets included in first decedent spouse's gross estate.
Charitable Remainder Annuity Trust (CRAT)	Split interest gift where part of an interest is given to charity. Donor receives a fixed annuity and remainder goes to charity. Usually created during life.	Contributions at setup only. Must receive an annuity income of at least 5% of the original value of assets transferred into trust. Can be for life or term ≤20 years. PV of RI ≥10 at inception.	Good for clients who desire certainty of fixed income. As IRS interest rates go up, the deductible charitable remainder interest goes up.	Donor receives an immediate charitable contribution deduction for income tax purposes if created during life. The value of the property is included in the gross estate, but an equivalent charitable deduction reduces the taxable estate amount to zero.
Charitable Remainder Unitrust (CRUT)	Split interest gift where part of an interest is given to charity. Donor receives a variable annuity and remainder goes to charity.	Contributions after initial setup are permitted. Must receive an annuity income of at least 5% of the current fair market value of assets. Can be for life or term ≤20 years. PV of RI ≥10 at inception.	Appeals to clients who want hedge against inflation. Can provide for income on lesser of unitrust amount or amount actually earned on property, with makeup, but net income with makeup CRUTS (NIMCRUTS) are risky.	Donor receives an immediate charitable contribution deduction for income tax purposes if created during life. The value of the property is included in the gross estate, but an equivalent charitable deduction reduces the taxable estate amount to zero.

TRUSTS—SUMMARY OF TRUST CLASSIFICATION AND USE (CONTINUED)

TRUST	PURPOSE	CHARACTERISTICS	PLANNING OPPORTUNITIES	INCOME / ESTATE / GIFT TAX CONSEQUENCES
Pooled Income Fund (PIF)	Investment fund created and maintained by target charity. Pools property from all contributors and pays a return on the basis of earnings of fund.	No tax-free securities may be held by PIF. Sometimes limit donations to cash and cash equivalents.	Preferred by those who want to avoid having to establish and maintain a trust. Frequently maintained by colleges and universities.	Donor receives an immediate charitable contribution deduction for income tax purposes if created during life. The value of the property is included in the gross estate, but an equivalent charitable deduction reduces the taxable estate amount to zero.
Charitable Lead Trust (CLAT or CLUT)	Property is transferred to a trust that distributes income to a charitable beneficiary for a specific term with the remainder reverting to a noncharitable beneficiary (may be grantor or other remainderman).	Noncharitable beneficiary can be grantor, spouse, child, or other.	Good for clients who have a large amount of highly appreciating assets and can forego the income from these assets. When interest rates are low, this increases the valuation of the deductible interest donation because of the lower valuation of the remainder.	If it is a grantor trust, then the grantor claims the income and receives the charitable deduction equal to the amount the trust pays to the charity. However, if the trust is a nongrantor trust where the remainderman is someone other than the grantor, then the grantor does not claim the income and cannot receive an income tax charitable deduction, but the value of the asset is out of the estate.
2503(b) Trust or Mandatory Income Trust	Trust set up for a beneficiary composed of an income interest and a remainder interest. Mandatory distribution of income entitles donor to annual exclusion.	Annual exclusion is available for the income interest. Income must be distributed.	Less attractive since Crummey decision. Often used for gifts to minors.	Income is taxable to beneficiary.
2503(c) Trust	Trust set up for minor that is a gift of a future interest but qualifies for the annual exclusion.	Property and income for benefit of minor. Income distribution is discretionary. Property must be available to beneficiary at age 21. If minor dies before age 21, property goes to minor's estate.	Less attractive since Crummey decision. Created to discourage income payout to immature minors solely to take advantage of annual exclusion.	If minor dies before age 21, property goes to minor's estate.
Crummey Trust	Trust that allows a right to withdraw for a brief period thus creating a present interest that qualifies for the annual exclusion.	Beneficiary usually allowed to withdraw the lesser of the amount of the available annual exclusion or the value of the gift property transferred. Beneficiary must be given notice of right to withdraw.	If the trust has more than one beneficiary, demand right should not exceed greater of $5,000 or 5% of value of property to avoid taxable gift to remainderman. Cristofani decision extended annual exclusion treatment to contingent beneficiaries.	Present interest is created by the right to withdraw.
Irrevocable Life Insurance Trust	Enables donor to control the disposition of life insurance proceeds. The trust may be created to purchase insurance or to receive insurance assigned to it by the grantor.	Excludes insurance proceeds from taxable estate of both spouses. Excludes proceeds from probate.	Transferor must surrender all interest in policy. Can be used as source of funds to pay estate taxes by beneficiaries. Grantor can make annual gifts to trust (qualify for annual exclusion) that will cover policy premiums if Crummey provision is used.	Excluded from transferor's estate if no incidence of ownership. May have gift tax on cash value of policy assigned transferred into trust. Will be included in transferor's estate if he does not live three years after transfer if policy assigned.

E. SPECIAL TRUST PROVISIONS

1. Sprinkling—the power to direct income at the discretion of the trustee for the benefit of the beneficiary. (The trustee can choose when/how much to distribute to the beneficiary.)

2. Beneficiary power to withdraw to limited extent

3. Crummey power—limited power to withdraw (usually 30 to 60 days)

4. Special or limited power of appointment (e.g., the power to invade the principal for the health, education, maintenance, or support of the income beneficiary)

5. General powers of appointment (e.g., the power to appoint income or corpus to the trustee by the trustee)

F. OVERVIEW OF TRUST AND ESTATE TAXATION

1. Trusts are generally treated as separate taxable entities. Remember that grantor trusts are not recognized for tax purposes.

2. A simple trust is one that:

    a. Is required to distribute all of its income currently (each year)

    b. Has no charitable beneficiaries

    c. Does not distribute any corpus

3. A complex trust is any trust that cannot be classified as a simple trust

4. An estate is created when a decedent dies

    a. The estate consists of the probate estate

    b. The estate holds and protects the assets, collects income from those assets, and satisfies obligations of the estate until all the assets are distributed

5. Estates and trusts are subject to the same rate schedule, a very highly progressive structure where the top rate of 35% begins at $10,450 (for 2007)

6. Fiduciaries file Form 1041 on or before the 15th day of the fourth month after the close of the tax year. Grantor trusts may also file a Form 1041.

G. CALCULATING THE TAX

1. Similar to calculating tax for individuals

    a. Gross Income – Deductions = Taxable Income

    b. Deductions include a distribution deduction

    c. Deductions include an exemption

        1.) Exemption for most simple trusts is $300

        2.) Exemption for most complex trusts is $100

2. Fiduciary long-term capital gains rate is no more than 20%

3. Fiduciaries may be subject to AMT

H. HOW INCOME IS TAXABLE

1. Beneficiary is taxed on an amount equal to the distribution deduction

2. Trust is not taxed on this amount because the trust gets a deduction for it

3. The distribution deduction is the lesser of DNI or the amount actually distributed to the beneficiaries

4. Income distributed maintains its character (ordinary, tax exempt, capital)

I. DISTRIBUTABLE NET INCOME (DNI)

1. Equals maximum distribution deduction

2. Equals maximum amount beneficiaries can be taxed on

3. DNI is similar to fiduciary accounting income

    a. Includes most normal income/expense items

    b. Excludes items relating to corpus such as capital gains, stock splits, and depreciation of business assets

XI. OTHER LIFETIME TRANSFERS (OTHER THAN STRAIGHT SALES AND GIFTS)

A. FAMILY LIMITED PARTNERSHIP

1. In general

   a. A family limited partnership is a partnership that is created to transfer assets to younger generations at a reduced gift tax valuation and cost

   b. A major objective is to generate valuation discounts (for estate and gift tax purposes) on the transfer of a limited interest in the partnership. The discounts are available because a limited partner cannot easily sell her partnership interest (lack of marketability discount) and cannot manage the partnership's operations (minority discount). (See Section Valuation Discounts on page 68 for a discussion of minority and lack of marketability discounts.)

   c. Typically, a senior family member transfers an asset (such as a closely held business) to a partnership in exchange for a 1% general partnership interest and a 99% limited partnership interest

   d. The senior family member then makes gifts (over time) of the limited partnership interests to junior family members

   e. The transfer of the limited partnership interests constitute a gift, eligible for the annual exclusion

2. Advantages

   a. The senior family member can retain control of the business, because the senior family member is the only family member with a general partnership interest (limited partners are not allowed to participate in management of the business)

   b. Restrictions can be placed on transfers of limited partnership interests by junior family members

   c. Some creditor protection may be afforded

   d. Transfers can be made at substantial discounts as compared to the value of underlying assets

   e. Gifts of limited partnership interests are eligible for the annual exclusion

3. Disadvantages

   a. Attorney fees will be incurred when the partnership is established

   b. Appraisal fees may be required to support underlying asset valuation and discounts taken

---

FAMILY LIMITED PARTNERSHIP

Key Features

- Used only between loved ones

- Makes use of minority discounts

- Makes use of lack of control discounts

- Minority interest usually has transfer restrictions

- Can allow the transferor to maintain control of the asset with little ownership interest

- Makes use of the annual exclusion

- Makes use of the applicable credit amount

- Gift is of a present interest

- Transaction requires sophisticated and perhaps repeated valuation

---

B. BARGAIN SALES

1. In general

   a. Sale of an asset for less than full consideration, usually made to related parties

   b. Considered part sale and part gift

2. Income and estate tax ramifications

   a. The difference between the sales price of the asset and the seller's basis in the asset will be a taxable gain to the seller for income tax purposes

   b. The difference between the fair market value of the asset and the consideration received is considered a gift

   c. The buyer's tax basis is equal to the greater of the amount paid by the buyer, or the seller/donor's basis in the property at the time of transfer, and the amount of increase, if any, in basis for any gift tax paid

   d. The gift portion will qualify for the annual exclusion if it is a completed gift

   e. The property sold will not be included in the seller's gross estate upon death. However, the portion of the property that is considered a taxable gift will be added back to the seller's taxable estate (as a prior taxable gift) in arriving at the estate tax base.

Example

Steve owns property with a basis of $50,000 and a current value of $140,000, which he sells to his son, Murray, for $90,000. Steve will have a taxable gain of $40,000 ($90,000 sales price less $50,000 basis). Steve has also made a gift of $50,000 ($140,000 value less $90,000 sales price). The gift will be eligible for the annual exclusion.

C. INSTALLMENT SALES AND SCINs

1. Sale for a single or series of installment notes. An installment sale can defer income tax, but because the present value of the notes will be included in seller's estate, no estate tax relief is obtained.

2. A SCIN is an installment note that cancels at the seller's death

   a. The present value of the notes canceled at the death of the seller is not included in the seller's estate, but any payments due, but not yet paid, at the death of the seller are included as an asset in the gross estate

   b. The gain inherent in these notes payable is income in respect of decedent, and the estate's income tax return will be allowed the appropriate deduction for income in respect of decedent (Sec. 691)

   c. SCINs are usually made to family members

SELF-CANCELING INSTALLMENT NOTE (SCIN)

Key Features

- Used between loved ones

- Transaction is a sale—seller will have capital gain, ordinary income (if depreciable property), and return of capital

- The sale is for the full fair market value of the property (buyer pays a risk premium)

- Removes asset from gross estate

- Used when seller is in ill health relative to table life expectancy

- For a specific term

- No step to fair market value at death of seller (buyer's basis is sum of payments to seller)

- Risk to transferee of paying more than fair value (if seller lives the full term)

- Purchasing power risk to seller

- Interest rate risk to seller

- Reinvestment risk to seller

- Indebtedness may be collateralized (secured)

- Does not use minority discounts

- Does not use the annual exclusion (not a gift)

- Does not use the applicable credit amount

- Requires sophisticated valuation only at the time of sale

Example

A.C., age 65, has some land (FMV $200,000, basis $80,000) he wants to sell to his son. A.C. and son enter into a 15-year, self-canceling installment agreement. To avoid gift treatment, A.C. will charge his son either a higher interest rate, a higher payment, or more than $200,000. If A.C. were 75 instead of 65, the SCIN premium would be more than at 65. If A.C. dies before the son pays off the note, the value of the note is not included in A.C.'s gross estate.

D. PRIVATE ANNUITIES

1. The sale of an asset (usually to a related party) in exchange for an unsecured promise to pay a lifetime annuity to the transferor

2. Consequences

    a. There will be no gift and, therefore, no gift tax as long as value of property transferred equals the value of property received (PV of annuity)

    b. No immediate income tax implications, but gain is reported similar to payments received from an installment sale. The gain is recognized using an exclusion/inclusion ratio (similar to an annuity) after recognizing interest income to the extent of market rate

        1.) Ordinary income is the interest component

        2.) Return of basis—based on exclusion ratio

        $$\frac{\text{Investment in contract}}{\text{Total expected return}} = \text{Exclusion ratio}$$

        3.) Capital gain—based on inclusion ratio

    c. Because a private annuity ceases at the seller's death, it is not included in the transferor's (decedent) gross estate

    d. May not have security or be collateralized

    e. If annuitant outlives life expectancy, the buyer will have made a bad bargain and the annuitant will include all the annuity payments not consumed in his estate. However, the transferor could use his annual exclusion and forgive up to $12,000 ($24,000 for split gift) of the payment without incurring any gift tax consequences.

    f. Ordinarily used when transferor is not expected to live the full table life expectancy

---

Example

Assume the same facts as in the previous example. Suppose that A.C. decides to transfer the land under a private annuity arrangement. Using the applicable federal rate (say 8%), A.C. would go to Table S to calculate his annuity payment ($200,000/8.1360) of $24,582. There is no gift and the asset is removed from A.C.'s estate. Each payment made to A.C. will be taxed as part return of basis, part gain, and part ordinary income. If A.C. lives less than his life expectancy, the son has paid less than FMV for the asset. Any unrecovered basis will be a loss deduction on A.C.'s final tax return. If A.C. lives longer than his life expectancy, the son has paid more than the FMV and would probably think he had not made a good deal!

PRIVATE ANNUITY

Key Features

- Used only between loved ones

- Transaction is a sale

- Sale is for full fair market value of the property

- Removes asset from gross estate

- Used when seller is in ill health relative to table life expectancy

- For a full life term

- No basis step to fair market value at death of seller

- Risk to buyer of paying more than fair value (buyer's basis is sum of payment made until death of seller and payments forgiven [gifted] by seller)

- Purchasing power risk to seller

- Interest rate risk to seller

- Reinvestment risk to seller

- Indebtedness may not be collateralized

- Does not use minority discounts

- Does not use control discounts

- Does not use the annual exclusion

- Does not use the credit equivalency

- Transaction requires sophisticated valuation only at the time of sale

XII. THE GENERATION-SKIPPING TRANSFER TAX (GSTT)

A. OVERVIEW

1. The GSTT is designed to tax transfers from an individual to a skip person

   a. The GSTT is applied using a flat rate equal to the highest estate and gift tax rate for the year of the transfer (45% for 2007)

   b. For years beginning after 2009, the GSTT is repealed

2. The GSTT is a tax levied in addition to the gift and estate tax

   a. Lifetime transfers to skip persons may be subject to both gift tax and GSTT

   b. Testamentary transfers to skip persons may be subject to both estate tax and GSTT

   c. There is no additional penalty for skipping more than one generation

3. Exemptions from GSTT:

   a. Trusts that were irrevocable before September 25, 1985

   b. Wills that could not be changed after 1987 (capacity)

B. SKIP PERSON

1. A skip person is any of the following:

   a. A related individual two or more generations below the donor (i.e., grandchild)

   b. A trust, when all beneficiaries are two or more generations below the donor

   c. An unrelated individual younger than the donor by 37½ years or more

2. A skip person does not include:

   a. The donor's spouse or former spouse, regardless of age

   b. A grandchild of the donor, if the donor's child is deceased (predeceased parent rule)

      1.) The grandchild effectively moves up one generation

      2.) Parent may be transferor's child or spouse's child

      3.) Grandchild may be any grandchild

      4.) Exception extends to collateral heirs if a decedent has no living lineal descendents. In other words, grandparent who has no grandchildren can make a gift to a grand nephew or grand niece without incurring GSTT.

C. TYPES OF TRANSFERS SUBJECT TO TAX

1. Direct skip

   a. A direct skip is a direct gift or bequest to a skip person

   b. The transferor, or their estate, is liable for any GSTT due on the transfer

   c. For lifetime transfers, any GSTT paid will be added to the value of the gift to determine the value of which to apply the federal gift tax

---

Example

Grandfather dies and leaves $100,000 to his grandson in his will. A direct skip has occurred. Any GSTT due is the responsibility of the grandfather's estate.

---

2. Taxable distribution

   a. A taxable distribution is a distribution from a trust made to a beneficiary two or more generations below the donor's generation

   b. Taxable amount is the net value of the property received by the beneficiary

   c. Any resulting GSTT is paid by the recipient

Example

Amy Miller created an irrevocable trust in 1995 for the benefit of her son, Rosco, and her grandson, Justin. At the time the trust was created, a direct skip did not occur, because there was a nonskip beneficiary (Rosco) of the trust.

In the current year, the trustee made a distribution of $20,000 of trust income to Rosco and $16,000 to Justin. The distribution to Justin, a skip person, is considered a taxable distribution that triggers GSTT.

---

3. Taxable termination

   a. A taxable termination occurs when an interest in a trust terminates because of death or lapse of time or release of a power that results in a skip beneficiary holding interests in the trust

   b. A taxable termination cannot take place as long as at least one nonskip person has an interest in the property

   c. Taxable amount is value of property transferred, less debts and taxes

   d. Any resulting GSTT is paid by the trust

Example

Amy Miller created an irrevocable trust in 1995 for the benefit of her son, Rosco, and her grandson, Justin. According to the terms of the trust, Rosco will receive all the income from the trust for the remainder of his life. Upon Rosco's death, any remaining trust corpus will pass to Justin. At the time the trust was created, a direct skip did NOT occur, because there was a nonskip beneficiary (Rosco) of the trust.

In the current year, Rosco died and the trust corpus was distributed to Justin. The distribution of the trust corpus to Justin (a skip person) is considered a taxable distribution that triggers GSTT.

D. GSTT CALCULATION

1. GSTT reductions

   a. An annual exclusion of $12,000 (for 2007) per donee per donor is allowed for direct skip transfers

   b. Gift splitting is available if both spouses elect

   c. A lifetime GSTT exemption of $2 million (for 2007) is allowed for every taxpayer. This exemption is equal to the applicable exclusion amount for estate tax purposes.

   d. Qualified transfers (e.g., medical, tuition) are excluded from GSTT

2. Reporting

   a. A lifetime gift that is subject to GSTT is reported on Form 709, Gift Tax Return

   b. A testamentary transfer that is subject to GSTT is reported on Form 706, Estate Tax Return

3. Determination of the GSTT

   a. The GSTT is determined by multiplying the taxable amount by the applicable GSTT rate

      1.) Taxable amount—the value of any direct skip, taxable distribution, or taxable termination

      2.) Applicable GSTT rate—the highest federal estate and gift tax rate (45% for 2007) multiplied by and inclusion ratio

      Inclusion ratio = 1 − (transferor's annual exclusion and exemption allocated to transfer ÷ value of property transferred)

Example

Grandfather makes a gift to grandson of $5 million in year 2007. Grandfather has made no other generation-skipping transfers. After the annual exclusion of $12,000 and the lifetime exemption of $2 million (for 2007), Grandfather has GSTT liability of $1,344,600.

The inclusion ratio is .5976, calculated as follows: 1 − [$2,000,000 + $12,000) ÷ $5,000,000]. The applicable GSTT rate is .26892 (45% × .5976). The tax due is $1,344,600 (.26892 × $5,000,000).

The GSTT will be added back to the $5 million to determine the gift tax liability.

XIII. LIFE INSURANCE AND ESTATE AND GIFT PLANNING (INCLUDING GSTT)

A. THE INCLUSION OF LIFE INSURANCE IN THE GROSS ESTATE

1. Causes for inclusion of the entire proceeds of the policy

2. Incidents of ownership within three years of death (IRC Section 2035)

3. Retained rights or reversionary rights

4. General powers of appointment over the policy (IRC Section 2043)

5. Qualified terminal interest property trusts (QTIPs)(IRC Section 2044)

6. The inclusion of the lifetime value of a policy owned on the life of another person (IRC Section 2033). The value will generally be the replacement cost (permanent product less interpolated terminal reserve plus any unearned premium; if term less the unearned premium [note the following exceptions]).

   a. The election of the alternate valuation date when the insured has died within six months of the owner of a life insurance policy or a person with a general power of appointment over the policy could cause inclusion of the entire proceeds rather than the value of the interpolated terminal reserve (caution)

   b. Second-to-die policies are especially subject to the risk of using the alternate valuation date causing inclusion in the first estate

B. OWNERSHIP OF LIFE INSURANCE POLICIES ON THE INSURED AND INCLUSION IN GROSS ESTATE OF DECEASED

1. Ownership by the insured—result is inclusion in the gross estate of the insured

2. Joint ownership by insureds—inclusion to the extent of the contribution rule (spouse deemed 50%) to the estate of the insured

3. Ownership by someone other than the insured

   a. If the policy was acquired outright by someone other than the insured and with an insurable interest, there is no inclusion in the estate of the decedent insured

   b. If a policy is acquired by transfer or by assignment from the insured, the throwback rule will cause inclusion in the insured's gross estate if such transfer was made within three years of the insured's death. If transfer occurred more than three years before death, the policy will not be included in the gross estate.

   c. If a second-to-die policy is transferred, the death benefit will be included in the gross estate of the second person to die, if the second person to die is deceased within three years of the transfer. If joint life (first-to-die) was transferred, then there is no inclusion (depends on ownership of policy).

Note: If decedent made a completed transfer of ownership of a life insurance policy more than three years before death, then the taxable terminal value, as of the date of the gift, will be included in the decedent's adjusted taxable gifts (if greater than the annual exclusion).

C. LIFE INSURANCE AND GIFT TAXATION

1. Outright transfers

    a. A policy transferred from the original owner to another without adequate consideration is a gift

    b. A policy purchased by one who designates another as owner at the inception has made a gift (if spouse, no consequence)

2. Transfer in trust—when the owner transfers a policy to a trustee, the owner has made a gift to the beneficiaries of the trust, assuming that the gift is a completed gift

3. Indirect gifts

    a. Generally, the direct payments of premiums for a policy owned by another are indirect gifts

    b. Indirect gifts may be avoided by gifting amounts not exceeding the annual exclusion from payor to owner or, if in trust, using a Crummey provision

4. Valuation (actual cost or replacement)

    a. Generally, the valuation of an insurance policy is the fair market value (at the date of the gift). This valuation applies to any paid up or newly issued policy.

    b. However, if the policy has been in force and premiums remain to be paid, the value is the interpolated terminal reserve plus any unearned premium plus dividend accumulations minus loans against the policy. This valuation applies to any policy in force with remaining premiums.

    c. Universal policies and whole life policies with vanishing premiums are valued using the terminal reserve method because there can be no absolute assurance that future premiums will not be necessary to keep the policy in force

D. THE MARITAL DEDUCTION

1. If the entire ownership interest in a life insurance policy is gifted to the donor's spouse, the transaction will qualify for the unlimited marital deduction

2. If a gift is in trust for the spouse, the transfer will qualify for the unlimited marital deduction only if it is made in a trust that qualifies under the terminable interest rules (e.g., POA trust or QTIP)

E. INSURANCE TRUSTS

1. If the trust purchases life insurance directly on the life of the insured, the death benefit is not included in the insured's estate

2. If the life insurance policy is assigned or transferred to the trust, the proceeds will be included in the transferor's estate if the transferor dies within three years of the transfer

3. Advantages

    a. Avoids probate

    b. Can restrict use of funds by beneficiaries

    c. Greater flexibility in distributions

    d. Trustee has more investment policy discretion

4. Revocable—no income tax advantage but still has nontax advantages listed above

5. Irrevocable

    a. Unfunded—grantor contributes the cash to pay premiums at a later time

b. Funded—cash/property contributed to trust to pay premiums

F. LIFE INSURANCE AND THE GSTT

1. Payment of premiums—the use of the annual exclusion may reduce gift tax (in a trust, use a Crummey provision). Lifetime GSTT exemption ($2 million for 2007) may reduce or eliminate GSTT.

2. Transfer of policies—when a life insurance policy is transferred to a skip person, such a transfer triggers GSTT

3. When the grandparent is the owner of the policy, and the payment of insurance proceeds to a skip person (i.e., grandchild), it is a generation-skipping transfer

G. SPECIAL ISSUES

1. Joint life (first-to-die) policies may cost less and provide more for couples with similar income levels or for businesses with several key employees. A joint life policy usually costs less than two policies but has only one death benefit, thus actually costing more per dollar of death benefit. The base policy may include an option of guaranteed insurability for the survivor (insured under a subsequent policy without evidence of insurability, but at current rates).

2. Joint life (second-to-die) policies

   a. Often used for a husband and wife to provide estate liquidity at the death of the second. Expectations are that the marital deduction will be used at the death of the first spouse.

   Inclusion in the gross estate of the decedent should be avoided by eliminating incidents of ownership on the part of the decedent

H. BENEFICIARIES

The selection of owners and beneficiaries of life insurance is of great importance because of the possible inclusion in the decedent's estate

1. Generally, it is wise to make either the beneficiaries or an irrevocable trust the owner of the policy

2. Assignment may be effective, but the three-year lookback rule may defeat the objective of removing the proceeds from the estate

XIV. SPECIAL PROVISIONS FOR SMALL BUSINESSES, FARMS, ILLIQUID ESTATES

A. SPECIAL USE VALUATION (SECTION 2032A)

1. If a decedent owned real property that was used as a farm or in connection with a closely held business, then a reduced gross estate valuation may be available for the property

2. The reduced valuation is made on the basis of the current actual use rather than its highest and best use. The aggregate reduction in value cannot exceed $940,000 (for 2007).

3. Several conditions must be met

    a. Value of the property (real and personal) must be at least 50% of the adjusted gross estate

    b. Value of the real property alone must be at least 25% of the adjusted gross estate

    c. Decedent or family member must have been a material participant in the business for at least five of the last eight years

4. Executor must make the election on Form 706

5. If the special-use property is disposed of to a nonfamily member or if the property discontinues its qualified use within 10 years of the decedent's death, then all or part of the estate tax savings may be recaptured

B. DEFERRED PAYMENT OF ESTATE TAX (SECTION 6166)

1. This is an election available to owners of farms or closely held businesses

    a. Value of the closely held business must exceed 35% of the value of the adjusted gross estate

    b. Applies to proprietorships, partnerships, and corporations

2. Executor may elect to defer for five years any estate tax payment relating to the closely held business. The estate tax can then be paid in 10 annual installments beginning after the five-year deferral period. Interest is paid during the deferral period.

3. A 2% interest rate applies to the taxes attributable to the first $1,250,000 (for 2007) of taxable value. Any value over that has a rate equal to 45% of the regular underpayment interest rate.

4. Unpaid installments will be accelerated if the total dispositions of property from the business is equal to or more than 50% of the estate tax valuation

C. STOCK REDEMPTION (SECTION 303)

1. Permits the estate of a decedent shareholder to redeem the decedent's shares with favorable income tax treatment

2. The transaction will be treated as a disposition of an asset rather than receipt of a dividend

3. Conditions to be met

    a. Stock must be included in the decedent's estate

    b. The value of the stock must be more than 35% of the adjusted gross estate

    c. Redemption proceeds eligible for capital gain treatment cannot exceed death taxes plus deductible funeral and administrative expenses

XV. POSTMORTEM PLANNING

A. JOINT INCOME TAX RETURN

1. Joint income tax return with a surviving spouse is generally advantageous because of the rate schedule and closing period of the surviving spouse

2. A possible disadvantage may be potential tax liability because of joint and several liability

B. WAIVER OF COMMISSIONS

1. Waiver of commissions for executor spouse is generally preferred if the estate is taxable and the unlimited marital deduction is used

2. However, the waiver may not be beneficial if the executor spouse's marginal tax bracket is lower than the applicable estate tax rate

C. MEDICAL EXPENSES

1. Medical expenses paid within one year of death are deductible on the decedent's final income tax return (Form 1040) or as an estate tax deduction (Form 706)

2. If the medical expenses are deducted on the final income tax return, the expenses will be subject to a 7.5% of AGI floor

3. If the expenses are deducted on the estate tax return, there is no limit on the deduction. The estate would not claim this deduction on the estate tax return if no tax is otherwise due.

D. INCOME IN RESPECT OF A DECEDENT

1. In general

    a. Income in respect of a decedent (IRD) is income at death that the decedent had earned and was entitled to but had not been received as of the date of death

    b. IRD will be considered an asset for estate tax purposes (Form 706) and income for federal income tax purposes (Form 1040 or 1041)

    c. Examples of IRD

        1.) Distributions from a qualified plan or IRA made after the date of death. The beneficiary receiving the distribution must report the taxable portion of the distribution in his taxable income

        2.) Forgiveness of debt at death of an installment note. The entire amount of any remaining unrecognized gain will be IRD to the estate.

        3.) Salary earned by the decedent that is paid after the date of death. The party receiving the salary has IRD in the year of receipt.

        4.) Rental income and interest income accrued but unpaid at death

        5.) Annuity payments received after death

2. Estate tax ramifications

    a. IRD items represent assets of the decedent and, therefore, will be included in the decedent's gross estate

b. The decedent's basis of the IRD asset carries over to the new owner of the asset. In other words, no step to fair market value in basis occurs at death.

3. Income tax ramifications

a. IRD will be included in the gross income of the recipient of the IRD. Typically, the recipient would be the decedent's estate or a beneficiary of the estate.

b. The character of the IRD income (e.g., ordinary, tax-exempt, or capital gain) is the same to the recipient as it would have been in the hands of the decedent. For example, a distribution from an IRA received by the decedent's beneficiary will be taxed as ordinary income to the beneficiary.

c. Whoever receives the IRD is entitled to any deductions associated with the IRD

d. An income tax deduction will be allowed for the portion of estate tax attributable to the IRD. The deduction is allowed each year IRD is included in income.

1.) The deduction is calculated in two steps.

a.) Determine the estate tax that is attributable to IRD

Example

When Mike Orentlich died, his gross estate included a qualified plan (IRD asset) worth $700,000. The total estate tax liability for Mike's estate was $2 million. The estate tax liability would have been $1,600,000 if the qualified plan was excluded from his gross estate. Therefore, the estate tax attributable to the IRD (qualified plan) is $400,000 ($2 million − $1,600,000).

---

b.) Calculate the deduction on the basis of the recipient's proportionate amount of IRD

Example

Assume the same facts as the previous example. Mike's son, George, the beneficiary of Mike's qualified plan, received a taxable distribution from the plan in the amount of $350,000. The entire $350,000 will be included in George's taxable income, but George will also be entitled to an income tax deduction of $200,000 ($350,000 ÷ $700,000 × $400,000).

2.) The deduction is available on Form 1041 or may flow to the beneficiary of the property, which generated the IRD, by way of the Form K-1 from Form 1041.

3.) If the deduction is claimed by an individual, it will be an itemized deduction not subject to the 2% of AGI floor.

E. SERIES E AND EE BONDS

It is generally advisable to report accrued interest on Form 1040 by making the election. Failure to make the election results in income in respect of a decedent (IRD). The associated tax liability is deductible on the estate return.

F. QUALIFYING WIDOW(ER)

Does survivor qualify as surviving spouse? If so, then the surviving spouse is eligible for Qualifying Widow(er) filing status on Form 1040 for two years after the close of the year in which the decedent died. There must be a dependent child residing in the household.

G. ADMINISTRATIVE EXPENSES AND CASUALTY LOSSES

There is usually a choice of deducting these on the estate return (Form 706) or fiduciary return (Form 1041). The choice depends on relative tax brackets.

H. INTEREST DEDUCTIONS

1. Personal interest is nondeductible

2. Trade or business interest is deductible

3. Investment interest is deductible to the extent of investment income

4. Qualified residence interest is deductible in a limited manner

I. SELECTING VALUATION DATE FOR ESTATE ACCOUNTS

1. Date of death

2. Alternate valuation date (6 months after date of death) will be permitted when:

    a. There is a decrease in the value of gross estate

    b. There is a decrease in the sum of the estate and GSTT tax

3. Consider partial QTIP election. The executor can make a QTIP election on an asset-by-asset basis.

J. DISCLAIMERS

1. By spouse to children—reduces overqualification

2. By children to spouse—increases use of marital deduction

3. May disclaim general power of appointment

4. Must be irrevocable, in writing, and made within nine months. The disclaiming person must not direct the ultimate beneficiary. The beneficiary disclaiming the property must not have accepted benefits from the property (such as rental income from a rental property) prior to disclaiming the transfer.

K. QUALIFIED TERMINABLE INTEREST PROPERTY

1. In general

    a. A terminable interest to the spouse does not qualify for the marital deduction

    b. Qualified terminable interest property (QTIP) allows a terminable interest transferred to the spouse to qualify for the unlimited marital deduction

    c. QTIP is an alternative to the life income interest plus general power of appointment. However, life income interest plus general power of appointment can result in the risk of loss of control of ultimate disposition.

    d. The primary benefit of a QTIP is that the spouse receives the income from the property for life, and the property is able to pass to the beneficiary designated by the decedent

  e. The QTIP property is usually placed in a QTIP trust

 2. Requirements

  a. The spouse must receive all income from the property at least annually for life

  b. The right to the income cannot be contingent

  c. The executor must make a QTIP election when the estate tax return (Form 706) is filed

  d. The property must be included in the surviving spouse's gross estate at her death

  e. During the surviving spouse's lifetime, the property cannot be appointed to anyone other than the surviving spouse

 3. Reverse QTIP

  a. Under GSTT rules, QTIP property included in the surviving spouse's estate is considered transferred by the surviving spouse, not by the decedent. Therefore, if a decedent transfers property into a QTIP trust, and the trust beneficiaries are grandchildren, the decedent will not be allowed to use his GSTT exemption. The surviving spouse would be required to use her exemption at death.

  b. The reverse QTIP election is a special election available for GSTT purposes. The election treats the QTIP property as if the QTIP election was not made for GSTT purposes.

  c. The marital deduction will be available for estate tax purposes but not for GSTT purposes

  d. The Reverse QTIP election is often made to utilize a decedent's GSTT exemption

---

Example

John died in 2007, owning $2 million of property. Upon his death, $1 million of John's assets were transferred to a credit shelter trust, with his grandchildren as the beneficiaries. The remaining $1 million of John's assets were transferred to a QTIP trust, which qualifies for the marital deduction. The beneficiaries of the QTIP trust are also John's grandchildren. Without a reverse QTIP election, only the assets in the credit shelter trust would be eligible for the GSTT exemption. Therefore, John will have wasted $1 million of his GSTT exemption.

If a reverse QTIP election is made, the $1 million of assets transferred to the QTIP trust will still qualify for the marital deduction for estate tax purposes. These assets will not qualify for the marital deduction for GSTT purposes, but John could use his remaining GSTT exemption to avoid any GSTT. Therefore, with a reverse QTIP election, John could fully utilize the GSTT exemption in the year of death.

L. ALTERNATE VALUATION DATE

 1. Executor can make an election to value the estate six months after the date of death, if such election will decrease both the value of the gross estate and the estate tax liability. Under this election, all assets are valued six months after the date of death or on their date of disposition if earlier. Alternate valuation applies to all assets, not to specific assets. Three key points:

  a. Executor must make the election to use the alternate valuation date

  b. Election must lower both the gross estate and the estate tax

    c.   Election applies to all assets. There are exceptions for:

        1.)   Wasting assets (e.g., annuities, patents, and installment notes) which will be valued at date of death (DOD)

        2.)   Assets disposed of between the date of death and the alternate valuation date that will be valued at the date of disposal

2.   Because a lower valuation will result in a lower income tax basis to the beneficiary, consideration should be given to the marginal estate tax rate versus the beneficiary's marginal income tax rate. Further complicating the picture, an assessment should be made on whether the beneficiary intends to sell the asset.

3.   All assets disposed of between the date of death and the alternate valuation date are valued on the date of disposition if the alternative valuation date is properly elected

4.   All wasting assets (e.g., annuities that have been annuitized, leases, patents, installment sales, and cash accounts) are valued as of the date of death regardless of selecting the alternate valuation date

XVI. COMMON ESTATE PLANNING MISTAKES

A. OVERQUALIFYING THE ESTATE

1. Overqualification occurs when the first decedent spouse in effect uses too much marital deduction at death

    a. Marital deduction reduces the decedent's taxable estate

    b. If too much marital deduction is used, the decedent's taxable estate will be reduced below the applicable exclusion amount, resulting in a waste of the applicable credit amount

2. Overqualification can be avoided by leaving some of the decedent's assets in her taxable estate at death.

    a. A bypass trust can be used to leave assets in the decedent's estate

    b. Alternatively, the decedent can leave assets in his taxable estate by bequeathing the assets directly to an heir other than the surviving spouse

3. See Appendixes 1, 2, and 3 for examples

Example

Sonny dies with an estate worth $4 million. He had a simple will, which left everything he owned to his wife, Bonny. At Sonny's death he will owe no estate tax. However, Bonny must include the entire $4 million (plus appreciation) in her gross estate upon her death. Sonny has failed to take advantage of his applicable credit amount and has therefore overqualified his estate.

Alternatively, assume Sonny's will had left the applicable exclusion amount ($2 million for 2007) to a bypass trust and the remainder to his wife, Bonny. At Sonny's death, he will still owe no estate tax because of the applicable credit amount. However, Bonny must only include $2 million (plus appreciation) in her gross estate upon her death. Sonny has taken advantage of his applicable credit amount and has not overqualified his estate.

B. UNDERQUALIFYING THE ESTATE

1. Underqualification occurs when the first decedent spouse in effect uses too little marital deduction at death

    a. Marital deduction reduces the decedent's taxable estate

    b. If too little marital deduction is used, the decedent's taxable estate will exceed the applicable exclusion amount, resulting in estate tax being due at the first spouse's death

2. Underqualification can be avoided by leaving some of the decedent's assets to her spouse at death

    a. A marital trust can be used to leave assets to the decedent's spouse

    b. Alternatively, the decedent can leave assets to his spouse by bequeathing the assets directly to the surviving spouse

3. See Appendixes 1, 2, and 3 for examples

Example

Sonny dies with an estate worth $4 million. His will left everything he owned to his son, George. At Sonny's death, he will owe estate tax because the entire $4 million will be included in his taxable estate. Sonny has failed to take advantage of the marital deduction and has therefore underqualified his estate.

Alternatively, assume Sonny's will had left the applicable exclusion amount ($2 million for 2007) to a bypass trust, and the remainder to his wife, Bonny. At Sonny's death, he will owe no estate tax because of the applicable credit amount. Sonny has taken advantage of the marital deduction and has not underqualified his estate.

C. INVALID, OUT-OF-DATE, OR POORLY DRAFTED WILL

1. Will does not meet statutory requirements—invalid will makes estate subject to intestacy laws

2. Will does not contemplate changes in tax laws—fails to minimize estate taxes because will is out of date

3. Decedent has moved to another state of residence and domicile. Possibility that the will does not conform to probate laws of new state making estate subject to intestacy laws of new state.

4. Will has no residuary clause or lacks drafting specificities

D. SIMPLE WILLS ("SWEETHEART" OR "I LOVE YOU" WILLS)

Leaving everything to your spouse. (See Appendixes 1, 2, and 3 for examples.)

1. May cause an overqualification of the estate

    a. Fails to take advantage of the applicable exclusion amount for the first spouse who dies

    b. The second spouse to die may pay estate taxes that could have been avoided with a bypass trust or bequest

2. Mismanagement of assets may occur. Assets may be put in the hands of a spouse who does not have the education, experience, training, or desire to manage them efficiently and effectively.

E. IMPROPERLY ARRANGED OR INADEQUATE LIFE INSURANCE

1. Failure to remove proceeds from estate

    a. If the insurance policy is owned by the decedent, the proceeds will be included in the estate

    b. Regardless of ownership, if the decedent has any incidence of ownership in the policy or if the beneficiary is the estate, the proceeds will be included in the estate

    c. Any transfer by the policyowner within three years of death will be included in the policyowner"s estate

2. Leaving proceeds directly to beneficiary

    a. Proceeds left directly to a beneficiary may create a problem if the beneficiary is ill equipped (e.g., emotionally, legal capacity, or a minor) to receive and manage those assets. A trust may provide the needed management of the insurance proceeds.

b. If the insurance policy fails to name a successor contingent beneficiary, the proceeds may end up back in the estate where they may be subject to creditor claims, state inheritance laws, or federal estate taxes (or all three)

3. Inadequate life insurance coverage

a. The proceeds are inadequate to cover the needs of the insured (survivor needs and estate liquidity needs). Generally, the survivor needs are calculated as the present value of the lost income (net of taxes and decedents consumption) over the remaining work life expectancy. An industry standard is to use 10 times salary to offset inflation. However, either or both of these may be inadequate with regards to providing sufficient estate liquidity where the majority of the other assets in the estate are both large in value and illiquid (real estate or a closely held business).

b. Another approach is to calculate the present value of the lost future earnings

F. POSSIBLE ADVERSE CONSEQUENCES OF JOINTLY HELD PROPERTY

1. Joint title may result in state and federal gift and estate tax. If joint title results in a completed gift, consequences may be federal and state gift tax liability.

2. Double estate taxation. For jointly owned property (not by spouses), property value may be included in first decedent's estate, then included in survivor's estate (recall, credit for tax on prior transfer).

3. Property passed by law but not by will, (JTWROS) can thwart the intentions of decedent because property will pass automatically by law.

4. Jointly held property allows survivor to name ultimate remainderman. Decedent may not be able to direct property to person or entity to whom he wishes.

G. ESTATE LIQUIDITY PROBLEMS

1. Insufficient cash assets

a. Estate may be forced to liquidate assets at a time when they are not fully valued or have not reached their potential value

b. Assets may have to be sold at less than full value

c. Closely held businesses may have to be sold to an outsider to generate the cash to pay the estate tax

2. Inadequate planning

Estate may be forced to liquidate assets at a time when they are not fully valued or have not reached their potential value

H. WRONG EXECUTOR/TRUSTEE/MANAGER

Poor estate management always increases costs

1. Potential conflicts of interest

2. Proximity problems/family conflict

3. Named executor/trustee is incapable of administering estate efficiently and effectively

4. Being an executor is work, and the person chosen should be capable and willing

APPENDIX 1: EXAMPLE 1

(ESTATE TAX CALCULATION)

Kurt Smith has the following assets at his death in 2007*:

Boat	$50,000	Owned in his name only
Note receivable (present value)	$650,000	Owned in his name only
Insurance (policy on Kurt at face value)	$125,000	Owned in his name only/spouse beneficiary
Ranch	$400,000	Owned in his name only
House	$120,000	Owned jointly with his spouse (JTWROS) FMV = $120,000 (50% = $60,000)
Annuity	$80,000	Payable to his spouse

*All assets (except the life insurance) are stated at fair market value.

At his death, Kurt also had $45,000 in debt, state death taxes of $15,000, and a $100,000 mortgage on his ranch. His insurance was payable to his spouse. His will gave everything to his daughter and son equally and provided that all debts, expenses, and taxes were to be paid out of his probate residue. The expenses of administering his estate were $40,000. He made no taxable gifts during his life. His estate has no credits against the tax except the applicable credit amount. Calculate the net federal estate tax, if any, due on Kurt's estate. Kurt lives in a separate property state.

EXAMPLE 1—SOLUTION/COMMENT

Estate Tax Formula

(1)	Total gross estate		$1,365,000**
(2)	Less: Expenses, debts, and losses:		
	(a) Funeral and administrative expenses	$40,000	
	(b) Debts of decedent, mortgages, losses	160,000	$(200,000)
(3)	Equals: Adjusted gross estate (AGE)		$1,165,000
(4)	Less: Total allowable deductions:		
	(c) Charitable deduction	0	
	(d) Marital deduction	$265,000***	
	Total allowable deductions		(265,000)
(5)	Equals: Taxable estate		$900,000
(6)	Add: Adjusted taxable gifts (post-1976)		0
(7)	Compute: Tentative tax base		$900,000
(8)	Compute: Tentative tax		$306,800
(9)	Subtract: Gift taxes paid on prior transfers		(0)
(10)	Equals: Estate tax before reduction for allowable credits		$306,800
(11)	Subtract:		
	Allowable applicable credit amount (max $780,800)	$306,800	
	Other credits	0	($306,800)
(12)	Equals: Estate tax liability		$0

> **COMMENT**
> *No estate tax due.*

ASSETS

Probate		Nonprobate			
Boat	$ 50,000	Insurance	$125,000	Total probate	$1,100,000
Note	650,000	House (1/2)	60,000	Total nonprobate	265,000
Ranch	400,000	Annuity	80,000		
	$1,100,000		$265,000	**Total Estate**	$1,365,000**

** Note the $1,365,000 is reconciled to the gross estate.

*** $265,000 qualifies for the marital deduction.

APPENDIX 2: EXAMPLE 2

Kurt Smith has the following assets at his death in 2007*:

Boat	$50,000	Owned in his name only
Note receivable (present value)	$650,000	Owned in his name only
Insurance (policy on Kurt at face value)	$125,000	Owned in his name only/spouse beneficiary
Ranch	$400,000	Owned in his name only
House	$120,000	Owned jointly with his spouse (JTWROS) FMV = $120,000 (50% = $60,000)
Annuity	$80,000	Payable to his spouse

*All assets (except the life insurance) are stated at fair market value.

At his death, he also had $45,000 in debt, state death taxes of $15,000, and a $100,000 mortgage on his ranch. His insurance was payable to his spouse. His will gave everything to his spouse and provided that all debts, expenses, and taxes were to be paid out of his probate residue. The expenses of administering his estate were $40,000. He made no taxable gifts during his life. His estate has no credits against the tax except the applicable credit amount. Calculate the net federal estate tax, if any, due on Kurt's estate. Kurt lives in a separate property state.

EXAMPLE 2—SOLUTION/COMMENT

Estate Tax Formula

(1)	Total gross estate			$1,365,000**
(2)	Less: Expenses, debts, and losses:			
	(a) Funeral and administrative expenses	$40,000		
	(b) Debts of decedent, mortgages, losses	160,000	(200,000)	
(3)	Equals: Adjusted gross estate (AGE)			$1,165,000
(4)	Less: Total allowable deductions:			
	(c) Charitable deduction	0		
	(d) Marital deduction	$1,165,000***		
	Total allowable deductions		$(1,165,000)	
(5)	Equals: Taxable estate			0
(6)	Add: Adjusted taxable gifts (post-1976)			0
(7)	Compute: Tentative tax base			0
(8)	Compute: Tentative tax			0
(9)	Subtract: Gift taxes paid on prior transfers			0
(10)	Equals: Estate tax before reduction for allowable credits			0
(11)	Subtract:			
	Allowable applicable credit amount (max $780,800)	0		
	Other credits	0	0	
(12)	Equals: Estate tax liability			$0

COMMENT

No estate taxes are due. He has overqualified the estate by $1,165,000, the lesser of the adjusted gross estate or the applicable exclusion amount. However, unless the surviving spouse has assets of her own, it is probably unlikely that the assets in the spouse's estate will be large enough to generate an estate tax in excess of the credit afforded to the spouse's estate.

ASSETS

Probate		Nonprobate			
Boat	$50,000	Insurance	$125,000	Total probate	$1,100,000
Note	650,000	House (1/2)	60,000	Total nonprobate	265,000
Ranch	400,000	Annuity	80,000		
	$1,100,000		$265,000	Total Estate	$1,365,000**

**Note the $1,365,000 is reconciled to the gross estate.

***While $1,365,000 qualifies for the marital deduction, only $1,165,000 can be used. The spouse will only receive $1,165,000 in assets because the assets have been reduced by the expenses, debts, and losses.

APPENDIX 3: EXAMPLE 3

Kurt Smith has the following assets at his death in 2007:

Boat	$50,000	Owned in his name only
Note receivable (present value)	$1,150,000	Owned in his name only
Insurance (policy on Kurt at face value)	$125,000	Owned in his name only/son and daughter beneficiary
Ranch	$400,000	Owned in his name only
House	$1,120,000	Owned jointly with his spouse but spouse has no right of survivorship FMV = $1,120,000 (50% = $560,000)
Annuity	$80,000	Payable to his son and daughter

At his death, he also had $45,000 in debt, state death taxes of $15,000, and a $100,000 mortgage on his ranch. His insurance was payable to his children. His will gave everything to his son and daughter and provided that all debts, expenses, and taxes were to be paid out of his probate residue. The expenses of administering his estate were $40,000. He made no taxable gifts during his life. His estate has no credits against the tax except the applicable credit amount. Calculate the federal estate tax, if any, due on Kurt's estate. Kurt lives in a separate property state.

EXAMPLE 3—SOLUTION/COMMENT

Estate Tax Formula

(1)	Total gross estate		$2,365,000**
(2)	Less: Expenses, debts, and losses:		
	(a) Funeral and administrative expenses	$40,000	
	(b) Debts of decedent, mortgages, losses	160,000	(200,000)
(3)	Equals: Adjusted gross estate (AGE)		$2,165,000
(4)	Less: Total allowable deductions:		
	(c) Charitable deduction	0	
	(d) Marital deduction	0	
	Total allowable deductions		0
(5)	Equals: Taxable estate		$2,165,000
(6)	Add: Adjusted taxable gifts (post-1976)		0
(7)	Compute: Tentative tax base		$2,165,000
(8)	Compute: Tentative tax		$855,050
(9)	Subtract: Gift taxes paid on prior transfers		0
(10)	Equals: Estate tax before reduction for allowable credits		$855,050
(11)	Subtract:		
	Allowable applicable credit amount	$780,800	
	Total credits		$(780,800)
(12)	Equals: Federal estate tax liability		$74,250

**See next page.

COMMENT

The federal estate tax liability of $74,250 resulted from the failure to use the marital deduction.

EXAMPLE 3—SOLUTION/COMMENT (CONTINUED)

ASSETS

Probate		Nonprobate			
Boat	$50,000	Insurance	$125,000	Total probate	$2,160,000
Note	1,150,000	Annuity	80,000	Total nonprobate	205,000
Ranch	400,000	Total	$205,000	**Total Estate**	**$2,365,000** **
House (1/2)	560,000				
Total	$2,160,000				

**Note the $2,160,000 is reconciled to the gross estate.

APPENDIX 4: EXAMPLE 4 (2007)

Additional assumption added to Example 1.

Kurt Smith had made $1 million of previously taxable gifts in 1997 and paid gift tax of $153,000. Kurt died in 2007.

	Gross estate	$1,365,000
−	Funeral and admin. exp.	(200,000)
=	AGE	$1,165,000
−	Marital deduction	(265,000)
=	Taxable estate	$900,000
+	Plus post-76 gifts	1,000,000
=	Tentative tax base	$1,900,000
	Tentative tax	$735,800
−	Previous gift tax paid	(153,000)
=	Estate tax before credit	$582,800
−	Applicable credit amount*	(582,800)
=	Estate tax liability	$0

*The applicable credit amount is limited to the lesser of $780,800 or the actual estate tax owed by the estate.

APPENDIX 5: EXAMPLE 5 (2007)

Example 5—same as Example 1 except $2,000,000 gift made in 2005, and gift tax of $435,000 was paid on the gift.

	Gross estate*	$1,800,000	= ($1,365,000 + $435,000)
−	Funeral and admin. exp.	(200,000)	
=	AGE	$1,600,000	
−	Marital deduction	(265,000)	
=	Taxable estate	$1,335,000	
+	Plus post-76 gifts	2,000,000	
=	Tentative tax base	$3,335,000	
	Tentative tax	$1,381,550	
−	Gift tax paid	(435,000)	
=	Estate tax before credits	$946,550	
−	Applicable credit amount	(780,800)	
=	Estate tax liability	$165,750	

*Includes $435,000 of the prior gift tax paid.

This is an application of the gross-up rule for gift tax paid on gifts made within three years of death.

Appendix 6: IRS Form 706

Form **706** (Rev. October 2006) Department of the Treasury Internal Revenue Service	**United States Estate (and Generation-Skipping Transfer) Tax Return** Estate of a citizen or resident of the United States (see separate instructions). **To be filed for decedents dying after December 31, 2005, and before January 1, 2007.**	OMB No. 1545-0015

Part 1—Decedent and Executor

1a Decedent's first name and middle initial (and maiden name, if any)	**1b** Decedent's last name	**2** Decedent's Social Security No.

3a County, state, and ZIP code, or foreign country, of legal residence (domicile) at time of death	**3b** Year domicile established	**4** Date of birth	**5** Date of death

6b Executor's address (number and street including apartment or suite no. or rural route; city, town, or post office; state; and ZIP code) and phone no.

6a Name of executor (see page 4 of the instructions)

6c Executor's social security number (see page 4 of the instructions)

Phone no. (   )

7a Name and location of court where will was probated or estate administered

7b Case number

8 If decedent died testate, check here ▶ ☐ and attach a certified copy of the will. **9** If you extended the time to file this Form 706, check here ▶ ☐

10 If Schedule R-1 is attached, check here ▶ ☐

Part 2—Tax Computation

1	Total gross estate less exclusion (from Part 5—Recapitulation, page 3, item 12)	**1**	
2	Tentative total allowable deductions (from Part 5—Recapitulation, page 3, item 22)	**2**	
3a	Tentative taxable estate (before state death tax deduction) (subtract line 2 from line 1)	**3a**	
b	State death tax deduction	**3b**	
c	Taxable estate (subtract line 3b from line 3a)	**3c**	
4	Adjusted taxable gifts (total taxable gifts (within the meaning of section 2503) made by the decedent after December 31, 1976, other than gifts that are includible in decedent's gross estate (section 2001(b)))	**4**	
5	Add lines 3c and 4	**5**	
6	Tentative tax on the amount on line 5 from Table A on page 4 of the instructions	**6**	
7	Total gift tax paid or payable with respect to gifts made by the decedent after December 31, 1976. Include gift taxes by the decedent's spouse for such spouse's share of split gifts (section 2513) only if the decedent was the donor of these gifts and they are includible in the decedent's gross estate (see instructions)	**7**	
8	Gross estate tax (subtract line 7 from line 6)	**8**	
9	Maximum unified credit (applicable credit amount) against estate tax **9**		
10	Adjustment to unified credit (applicable credit amount). (This adjustment may not exceed $6,000. See page 6 of the instructions.) **10**		
11	Allowable unified credit (applicable credit amount) (subtract line 10 from line 9)	**11**	
12	Subtract line 11 from line 8 (but do not enter less than zero)	**12**	
13	Credit for foreign death taxes (from Schedule(s) P). (Attach Form(s) 706-CE.) **13**		
14	Credit for tax on prior transfers (from Schedule Q) **14**		
15	Total credits (add lines 13 and 14)	**15**	
16	Net estate tax (subtract line 15 from line 12)	**16**	
17	Generation-skipping transfer (GST) taxes payable (from Schedule R, Part 2, line 10)	**17**	
18	Total transfer taxes (add lines 16 and 17)	**18**	
19	Prior payments. Explain in an attached statement	**19**	
20	Balance due (or overpayment) (subtract line 19 from line 18)	**20**	

Under penalties of perjury, I declare that I have examined this return, including accompanying schedules and statements, and to the best of my knowledge and belief, it is true, correct, and complete. Declaration of preparer other than the executor is based on all information of which preparer has any knowledge.

Signature(s) of executor(s)   Date

Signature of preparer other than executor   Address (and ZIP code)   Date

For Privacy Act and Paperwork Reduction Act Notice, see page 28 of the separate instructions for this form. Cat. No. 20548R Form **706** (Rev. 10-2006)

APPENDIX 7: IRS FORM 709

Form **709**

Department of the Treasury
Internal Revenue Service

United States Gift (and Generation-Skipping Transfer) Tax Return

(For gifts made during calendar year 2005)

► See separate instructions.

OMB No. 1545-0020

2005

1 Donor's first name and middle initial	2 Donor's last name	3 Donor's social security number

4 Address (number, street, and apartment number)	5 Legal residence (domicile) (county and state)

6 City, state, and ZIP code	7 Citizenship

Part 1—General Information

		Yes	No
8	If the donor died during the year, check here ► ☐ and enter date of death .... ,.................		
9	If you extended the time to file this Form 709, check here ► ☐		
10	Enter the total number of donees listed on Schedule A. Count each person only once. ►		
11a	Have you (the donor) previously filed a Form 709 (or 709-A) for any other year? If "No," skip line 11b		
11b	If the answer to line 11a is "Yes," has your address changed since you last filed Form 709 (or 709-A)?		
12	**Gifts by husband or wife to third parties.** Do you consent to have the gifts (including generation-skipping transfers) made by you and by your spouse to third parties during the calendar year considered as made one-half by each of you? (See instructions.) (If the answer is "Yes," the following information must be furnished and your spouse must sign the consent shown below. **If the answer is "No," skip lines 13–18 and go to Schedule A.**)		
13	Name of consenting spouse	**14** SSN	
15	Were you married to one another during the entire calendar year? (see instructions)		
16	If 15 is "No," check whether ☐ married ☐ divorced or ☐ widowed/deceased, and give date (see instructions) ►		
17	Will a gift tax return for this year be filed by your spouse? (If "Yes," mail both returns in the same envelope.)		
18	**Consent of Spouse.** I consent to have the gifts (and generation-skipping transfers) made by me and by my spouse to third parties during the calendar year considered as made one-half by each of us. We are both aware of the joint and several liability for tax created by the execution of this consent.		

Consenting spouse's signature ►   Date ►

Part 2—Tax Computation

1	Enter the amount from Schedule A, Part 4, line 11	1	
2	Enter the amount from Schedule B, line 3	2	
3	Total taxable gifts. Add lines 1 and 2	3	
4	Tax computed on amount on line 3 (see *Table for Computing Gift Tax* in separate instructions)	4	
5	Tax computed on amount on line 2 (see *Table for Computing Gift Tax* in separate instructions)	5	
6	Balance. Subtract line 5 from line 4	6	
7	Maximum unified credit (nonresident aliens, see instructions)	7	345,800	00
8	Enter the unified credit against tax allowable for all prior periods (from Sch. B, line 1, col. C)	8	
9	Balance. Subtract line 8 from line 7	9	
10	Enter 20% (.20) of the amount allowed as a specific exemption for gifts made after September 8, 1976, and before January 1, 1977 (see instructions)	10	
11	Balance. Subtract line 10 from line 9	11	
12	Unified credit. Enter the smaller of line 6 or line 11	12	
13	Credit for foreign gift taxes (see instructions)	13	
14	Total credits. Add lines 12 and 13	14	
15	Balance. Subtract line 14 from line 6. Do not enter less than zero	15	
16	Generation-skipping transfer taxes (from Schedule C, Part 3, col. H, Total)	16	
17	Total tax. Add lines 15 and 16	17	
18	Gift and generation-skipping transfer taxes prepaid with extension of time to file	18	
19	If line 18 is less than line 17, enter **balance due** (see instructions)	19	
20	If line 18 is greater than line 17, enter **amount to be refunded**	20	

Attach check or money order here.

Sign Here

Under penalties of perjury, I declare that I have examined this return, including any accompanying schedules and statements, and to the best of my knowledge and belief, it is true, correct, and complete. Declaration of preparer (other than donor) is based on all information of which preparer has any knowledge.

► _____ Signature of donor   Date _____

Paid Preparer's Use Only

Preparer's signature ►	Date	Check if self-employed ► ☐
Firm's name (or yours if self-employed), address, and ZIP code		Phone no. ► ( )

For Disclosure, Privacy Act, and Paperwork Reduction Act Notice, see page 12 of the separate instructions for this form.   Cat. No. 16783M   Form **709** (2005)

Form 709 (2005)   Page **2**

SCHEDULE A	Computation of Taxable Gifts (Including transfers in trust) (see instructions)

A Does the value of any item listed on Schedule A reflect any valuation discount? If "Yes," attach explanation . . . . . . Yes ☐ No ☐

B ☐ ◄ Check here if you elect under section 529(c)(2)(B) to treat any transfers made this year to a qualified tuition program as made ratably over a 5-year period beginning this year. See instructions. Attach explanation.

Part 1—Gifts Subject Only to Gift Tax. Gifts less political organization, medical, and educational exclusions. See instructions.

A Item number	B • Donee's name and address • Relationship to donor (if any) • Description of gift • If the gift was of securities, give CUSIP no. • If closely held entity, give EIN	C	D Donor's adjusted basis of gift	E Date of gift	F Value at date of gift	G For split gifts, enter ½ of column F	H Net transfer (subtract col. G from col. F)
1							
Gifts made by spouse—*complete* **only** *if you are splitting gifts with your spouse and he/she also made gifts.*							

Total of Part 1. Add amounts from Part 1, column H . . . . ►

Part 2—Direct Skips. Gifts that are direct skips and are subject to both gift tax and generation-skipping transfer tax. You must list the gifts in chronological order.

A Item number	B • Donee's name and address • Relationship to donor (if any) • Description of gift • If the gift was of securities, give CUSIP no. • If closely held entity, give EIN	C 2632(b) election out	D Donor's adjusted basis of gift	E Date of gift	F Value at date of gift	G For split gifts, enter ½ of column F	H Net transfer (subtract col. G from col. F)
1							
Gifts made by spouse—*complete* **only** *if you are splitting gifts with your spouse and he/she also made gifts.*							

Total of Part 2. Add amounts from Part 2, column H . . . . ►

Part 3—Indirect Skips. Gifts to trusts that are currently subject to gift tax and may later be subject to generation-skipping transfer tax. You must list these gifts in chronological order.

A Item number	B • Donee's name and address • Relationship to donor (if any) • Description of gift • If the gift was of securities, give CUSIP no. • If closely held entity, give EIN	C 2632(c) election	D Donor's adjusted basis of gift	E Date of gift	F Value at date of gift	G For split gifts, enter ½ of column F	H Net transfer (subtract col. G from col. F)
1							
Gifts made by spouse—*complete* **only** *if you are splitting gifts with your spouse and he/she also made gifts.*							

Total of Part 3. Add amounts from Part 3, column H . . . . ►

(If more space is needed, attach additional sheets of same size.)   Form **709** (2005)

Form 709 (2005)   Page **3**

Part 4—Taxable Gift Reconciliation

1	Total value of gifts of donor. Add totals from column H of Parts 1, 2, and 3	**1**
2	Total annual exclusions for gifts listed on line 1 (see instructions)	**2**
3	Total included amount of gifts. Subtract line 2 from line 1	**3**

Deductions (see instructions)

4	Gifts of interests to spouse for which a marital deduction will be claimed, based on items .... of Schedule A	**4**	
5	Exclusions attributable to gifts on line 4	**5**	
6	Marital deduction. Subtract line 5 from line 4	**6**	
7	Charitable deduction, based on items .... less exclusions . .	**7**	
8	Total deductions. Add lines 6 and 7		**8**
9	Subtract line 8 from line 3		**9**
10	Generation-skipping transfer taxes payable with this Form 709 (from Schedule C, Part 3, col. H, Total) .		**10**
11	Taxable gifts. Add lines 9 and 10. Enter here and on line 1 of the Tax Computation on page 1 . . .		**11**

12 Terminable Interest (QTIP) Marital Deduction. (See instructions for Schedule A, Part 4, line 4.)

If a trust (or other property) meets the requirements of qualified terminable interest property under section 2523(f), and:

a. The trust (or other property) is listed on Schedule A, and

b. The value of the trust (or other property) is entered in whole or in part as a deduction on Schedule A, Part 4, line 4, then the donor shall be deemed to have made an election to have such trust (or other property) treated as qualified terminable interest property under section 2523(f).

If less than the entire value of the trust (or other property) that the donor has included in Parts 1 and 3 of Schedule A is entered as a deduction on line 4, the donor shall be considered to have made an election only as to a fraction of the trust (or other property). The numerator of this fraction is equal to the amount of the trust (or other property) deducted on Schedule A, Part 4, line 6. The denominator is equal to the total value of the trust (or other property) listed in Parts 1 and 3 of Schedule A.

If you make the QTIP election, the terminable interest property involved will be included in your spouse's gross estate upon his or her death (section 2044). See instructions for line 4 of Schedule A. If your spouse disposes (by gift or otherwise) of all or part of the qualifying life income interest, he or she will be considered to have made a transfer of the entire property that is subject to the gift tax. See *Transfer of Certain Life Estates Received From Spouse* on page 4 of the instructions.

13 Election Out of QTIP Treatment of Annuities

☐ ◄ Check here if you elect under section 2523(f)(6) **not** to treat as qualified terminable interest property any joint and survivor annuities that are reported on Schedule A and would otherwise be treated as qualified terminable interest property under section 2523(f). See instructions. Enter the item numbers from Schedule A for the annuities for which you are making this election ▶

SCHEDULE B   **Gifts From Prior Periods**

If you answered "Yes" on line 11a of page 1, Part 1, see the instructions for completing Schedule B. If you answered "No," skip to the Tax Computation on page 1 (or Schedule C, if applicable).

A Calendar year or calendar quarter (see instructions)	**B** Internal Revenue office where prior return was filed	**C** Amount of unified credit against gift tax for periods after December 31, 1976	**D** Amount of specific exemption for prior periods ending before January 1, 1977	**E** Amount of taxable gifts

1	Totals for prior periods	**1**	
2	Amount, if any, by which total specific exemption, line 1, column D, is more than $30,000		**2**
3	Total amount of taxable gifts for prior periods. Add amount on line 1, column E and amount, if any, on line 2. Enter here and on line 2 of the Tax Computation on page 1		**3**

(If more space is needed, attach additional sheets of same size.)   Form **709** (2005)

Form 709 (2005)   Page **4**

| **SCHEDULE C** | **Computation of Generation-Skipping Transfer Tax** |

Note: *Inter vivos direct skips that are completely excluded by the GST exemption must still be fully reported (including value and exemptions claimed) on Schedule C.*

Part 1—Generation-Skipping Transfers

A Item No. (from Schedule A, Part 2, col. A)	B Value (from Schedule A, Part 2, col. H)	C Nontaxable portion of transfer	D Net Transfer (subtract col. C from col. B)
1			
Gifts made by spouse (for gift splitting only)			

Part 2—GST Exemption Reconciliation (Section 2631) and Section 2652(a)(3) Election

Check box ▶ ☐ if you are making a section 2652(a)(3) (special QTIP) election (see instructions)

Enter the item numbers from Schedule A of the gifts for which you are making this election ▶ -

1	Maximum allowable exemption (see instructions)	1	
2	Total exemption used for periods before filing this return	2	
3	Exemption available for this return. Subtract line 2 from line 1	3	
4	Exemption claimed on this return from Part 3, col. C total, below	4	
5	Automatic allocation of exemption to transfers reported on Schedule A, Part 3 (see instructions)	5	
6	Exemption allocated to transfers not shown on line 4 or 5, above. **You must attach a Notice of Allocation.** (see instructions)	6	
7	Add lines 4, 5, and 6	7	
8	Exemption available for future transfers. Subtract line 7 from line 3	8	

Part 3—Tax Computation

A Item No. (from Schedule C, Part 1)	B Net transfer (from Schedule C, Part 1, col. D)	C GST Exemption Allocated	D Divide col. C by col. B	E Inclusion Ratio (subtract col. D from 1.000)	F Maximum Estate Tax Rate	G Applicable Rate (multiply col. E by col. F)	H Generation-Skipping Transfer Tax (multiply col. B by col. G)
1					47% (.47)		
2					47% (.47)		
3					47% (.47)		
4					47% (.47)		
5					47% (.47)		
6					47% (.47)		
					47% (.47)		
					47% (.47)		
					47% (.47)		
					47% (.47)		
					47% (.47)		
Total exemption claimed. Enter here and on line 4, Part 2, above. May not exceed line 3, Part 2, above		**Total generation-skipping transfer tax.** Enter here; on Schedule A, Part 4, line 10; and on line 16 of the Tax Computation on page 1					

(If more space is needed, attach additional sheets of same size.)   Form **709** (2005)

ESTATE PLANNING

Questions

Estate Planning

BASIC CONCEPTS

1. Which of the following would be included in a broad definition of estate planning?

    1. Wealth accumulation.
    2. Management of assets.
    3. Conservation of assets.
    4. Transfer of assets.
        a. 2 only.
        b. 3 only.
        c. 2 and 4.
        d. 2, 3, and 4.
        e. 1, 2, 3, and 4.

2. Which of the following persons need estate planning?

    1. John, who has a wife and one small child, and a net worth of $250,000.
    2. Dean, married with ten children, five grandchildren, and a net worth of $5,000,000.
    3. Marge, divorced, whose only son is severely mentally challenged.
    4. Cynthia, who is single, has a net worth of $100,000, and has two dogs that are like children to her.
        a. 2 only.
        b. 3 only.
        c. 2 and 3.
        d. 1, 2, and 3.
        e. 1, 2, 3, and 4.

3. What is the proper order for the process of estate planning?

    1. Establish priorities for estate objectives.
    2. Prepare a written plan.
    3. Define problem areas including liquidity, taxes, etc.
    4. Gather client information and establish objectives.
        a. 1, 2, 3, 4.
        b. 2, 1, 3, 4.
        c. 4, 3, 1, 2.
        d. 3, 2, 1, 4.
        e. 4, 1, 3, 2.

4. What is the main benefit of estate planning?

    a. Peace of mind.

    b. To avoid probate.

    c. To ensure property passes to intended persons.

    d. To plan health care treatment.

BASIC DOCUMENTS INCLUDED IN AN ESTATE PLAN

5. Making arrangements to deal with possible physical or mental incapacity is a rapidly developing area of estate planning. Which of the following arrangements is/are plausible when dealing with unanticipated incapacity?

    1. Springing durable powers of attorney.
    2. Revocable living trusts.
    3. Joint tenancies.
    4. Living wills.
        a. 1 only.
        b. 2 and 4.
        c. 2, 3, and 4.
        d. 1, 2, 3, and 4.

6. Which of the following is/are considered potential problems of an estate plan?

    1. Ancillary probate.
    2. The rule against perpetuities.
    3. A will that includes funeral instructions.
    4. A will that attempts to disinherit a spouse and/or a minor child.
        a. 1 only.
        b. 3 only.
        c. 1 and 3.
        d. 1, 3, and 4.
        e. 1, 2, 3, and 4.

7. Which of the following is/are common provisions in a well-drafted will?

    1. Establishment of the domicile of testator.
    2. An appointment and powers clause.
    3. A survivorship clause.
    4. A residuary clause.
        a. 1 only.
        b. 3 only.
        c. 1 and 3.
        d. 1, 2, and 3.
        e. 1, 2, 3, and 4.

8. Alan and Nona Ivey are both age 38. Alan is a successful surgeon, and Nona just made partner in a large law firm. Since their wealth has increased substantially over the last three years, they have begun focusing on estate planning. One of the estate planning attorneys at Nona's law firm assisted the Iveys in generating an estate plan, which included appropriate wills and trusts. However, incapacity planning was not addressed in the estate plan, so the Iveys have started researching some of the more widely used tools for incapacity planning. They have come to you with questions regarding these tools. Which of the following statements is/are correct?

   1. A durable power of attorney for health care is always a direct substitute for a living will.

   2. A living will only covers a narrow range of situations.

   3. A living will must generally meet the requirements of state of domicile.

   4. Many well-intentioned living wills have failed due to vagueness and/or ambiguities.

     a. 3 only.

     b. 2 and 3.

     c. 1, 2, and 3.

     d. 2, 3, and 4.

     e. 1, 2, 3, and 4.

9. Which of the following statements is/are correct regarding durable powers of attorney?

   1. The power survives disability.

   2. The power survives the death of the principal.

   3. The power may be springing.

   4. A principal must be 18 and competent at the time the durable power of attorney is created.

     a. 4 only.

     b. 1 only.

     c. 1 and 4.

     d. 1, 3, and 4.

     e. 1, 2, 3, and 4.

10. Patty, who is single, is diagnosed with a serious disease. Patty expects to be completely incapacitated in two years. Patty has one son, one daughter, and two grandchildren. She has $500,000 in net worth including her principal residence. Which of the following should Patty do?

   1. Set up a durable power of attorney.

   2. Set up a gifting program, gifting annual exclusion amounts to her children and grandchildren.

   3. Set up a revocable living trust.

   4. Set up an ABC trust arrangement for her estate.

     a. 1 only.

     b. 1 and 3.

     c. 1, 2, and 3.

     d. 2, 3, and 4.

     e. 1, 2, 3, and 4.

11. Mary has a general power of appointment over her mother's assets. Which of the following is/are true regarding the power?

    1. Mary can use her mother's money to pay for the needs of her mother.

    2. Mary can pay her own creditors with her mother's assets.

    3. Mary must only appoint money using an ascertainable standard relating to her health, education, maintenance, and support.

    4. If Mary were to die before her mother, Mary's gross estate would include her mother's assets although they were not previously appointed to Mary.

        a. 1 only.

        b. 1, 3, and 4.

        c. 2, 3, and 4.

        d. 1, 2, and 4.

        e. 1, 2, 3, and 4.

12. Doris Jenkins is a 71-year-old widow with a son, age 43, a daughter, age 45, and six grandchildren. Doris has an estate currently worth $572,000, which includes her home worth $250,000 and a life insurance policy on her life with a face value of $160,000. Her children are named as primary beneficiaries. Doris recently suffered a severe stroke that left her paralyzed on her right side. She is home from the hospital but her health will continue to decline, and she will need to go into a nursing home within one year. The only estate planning she has done to date is to write a will in 1989 that left all her assets to her children equally.

    Of the following estate planning considerations, which is/are appropriate for Doris at this time? (CFP® Certification Examination, released 12/96)

    1. Transfer ownership of her home to her children so it will <u>not</u> be counted as a resource should she have to go into a nursing home and apply for Medicaid.

    2. Execute a durable general power of attorney and a durable power of attorney for health care.

    3. Place all of her assets in an irrevocable family trust with her children as beneficiaries.

    4. Start a gifting program transferring assets up to the annual exclusion amount to each of her children and grandchildren.

        a. 1, 2, 3, and 4.

        b. 2 and 3.

        c. 1 and 4.

        d. 4 only.

        e. 2 only.

13. A durable power of attorney for health care will achieve which of the following objectives?

    a. Provide for management of assets upon incapacity.

    b. Appoint a surrogate decision-maker for health care.

    c. Help reduce the value of the gross estate.

    d. Make the creation of a living will unnecessary.

    e. All of the above.

OWNERSHIP OF PROPERTY AND HOW IT IS TRANSFERRED

14. Which of the following estate transfer methods is the least appropriate for a relationship of same-sex individuals who each have the intent to bequeath their property exclusively to each other?

    a. Qualified pension plan assets with a named beneficiary.

    b. Intestate probate.

    c. Testate probate.

    d. Named beneficiary of contract for life insurance.

    e. Property held joint tenancy with rights of survivorship (JTWROS).

15. Larry and Eric were each single men who have been together for over 10 years. They are currently living together, and plan on spending the rest of their lives together. Larry is a successful architect, and his assets are valued at over $2,000,000. He wants to ensure that in the event of his untimely death, Eric would be taken care of for the rest of his life. Larry does not have a will. Which of the following options illustrates appropriate methods of property transfer at death between persons of the same sex who are committed to a long-term relationship?

    1. Tenancy in common with each other, no will.

    2. Fee simple ownership with no will.

    3. Tenancy by the entirety.

    4. Community property.

        a. 1 only.

        b. 1 and 3.

        c. 2 and 3.

        d. 1, 2, and 4.

        e. None of the above.

16. Robert and his long-time companion, Ted, are single men who have come to you for estate planning advice. Robert would like to create an estate plan that will ensure that Ted will be taken care of in the event of Robert's untimely death. Which of the following recommendations would you make to Robert?

    1. Transfer the ownership of Robert's real estate investments into Tenancy by the Entirety.

    2. Name Ted as the beneficiary of Robert's retirement plan.

    3. Make sure Robert creates a will, specifically bequeathing his property to Ted.

    4. Name Ted as the beneficiary of Robert's life insurance policy.

        a. 1 and 4.

        b. 2 and 3.

        c. 1, 2, and 4.

        d. 1, 3, and 4.

        e. 2, 3, and 4.

17. Of the following property ownership arrangements, which may be entered into by spouses only?

    1. Tenancy in common.
    2. Joint tenancy with right of survivorship.
    3. Tenancy by the entirety.
    4. Community property.
        a. 3 only.
        b. 2 and 4.
        c. 3 and 4.
        d. 2, 3, and 4.
        e. 1, 2, 3, and 4.

18. Steve and Susan live together but are unmarried. Which of the following is/are true with respect to the estate and gift tax ramifications of this living arrangement?

    1. If Steve gifts some stock to Susan, the gift tax marital deduction will be unavailable.
    2. If Steve gifts some stock to Susan, the gift tax annual exclusion will be unavailable.
    3. If Susan dies first, the executor of her estate can make a QTIP election to take advantage of the estate tax marital deduction.
    4. If Susan dies without a will, Steve may not receive any of Susan's property.
        a. 1 only.
        b. 1 and 4.
        c. 3 and 4.
        d. 1, 3, and 4.
        e. 1, 2, 3, and 4.

19. Which of the following statements regarding joint tenancy is/are correct?

    1. Under a joint tenancy, each tenant has an undivided interest in the property.
    2. Joint tenancies may only be established between spouses.
    3. Community property is the same as joint tenancy and has been adopted in many states.
    4. Assuming a spousal joint tenancy, the full value of the property will be included in the gross estate of the first spouse to die without regard to the contribution of each spouse.
        a. 1 only.
        b. 1 and 2.
        c. 1 and 3.
        d. 2 and 3.
        e. 1, 2, 3, and 4.

20. Which of the following statements regarding joint tenancy is/are correct?

    1. Each tenant owns the same fractional share in the property.

    2. Joint tenants have the right to sever their interests in the property during life without the consent of the other joint tenant(s).

    3. Upon the death of one joint tenant, property passes to the surviving tenants unless the decedent's will directs a different disposition.

    4. JTWROS property avoids probate.

        a. 1 only.

        b. 1 and 4.

        c. 2 and 3.

        d. 1, 2, and 4.

        e. 2, 3, and 4.

21. Which of the following statements regarding community property is/are correct?

    1. Assets inherited by one spouse in the course of a marriage generally are not community property.

    2. Assets purchased with community assets by either spouse in the course of marriage are community property.

    3. Community property avoids probate.

    4. Assets acquired by either spouse before marriage generally become community property upon their marriage.

        a. 1 only.

        b. 1 and 2.

        c. 2 and 4.

        d. 1, 2, and 3.

        e. 2, 3, and 4.

22. Which of the following types of ownership are only held by married couples?

    a. JTWROS.
    b. Tenancy in Common.
    c. Tenants by the Entirety.
    d. Tenants by Marriage.

23. Which of the following is true with respect to community property?

    a. If a couple lives in a common law state, they can elect to treat their property as community property in order to get a full step-up in basis upon the death of the first spouse.

    b. Upon the death of one spouse, community property will automatically pass to the surviving spouse by operation of law, thus avoiding probate.

    c. If a couple moves from a common law state to a community property state, separate property will generally become community property.

    d. If a couple moves from a community property state to a common law state, separate property will generally remain separate property.

24. John started a manufacturing business in a community property state. John owned 100% of the stock of the corporation. John gifted 50% of the business outright to his son, Chris. Chris and his wife Jennifer also live in Texas. Which of the following statements is/are true with respect to the transfer of the business interest?

    1. The business interest transferred to Chris will be owned by Chris outright, and will not be considered community property.

    2. The business interest transferred to Chris is community property, owned equally by Chris and Jennifer.

    3. If Chris dies tomorrow, the entire value of the business interest transferred to Chris would be included in his gross estate.

    4. If Jennifer dies tomorrow, both her share of the business interest and Chris' share of the business interest would receive a step-up in basis.

    a. 2 only.

    b. 1 and 3.

    c. 1 and 4.

    d. 2 and 4.

    e. 1, 3, and 4.

25. Stephen purchased a tract of land for $100,000. Two years after the purchase, when the land was valued at $160,000, Stephen added his daughter's name to the title as a joint tenant with rights of survivorship. Stephen died when the land was worth $200,000. How much is included in Stephen's gross estate?

    a. $80,000.

    b. $100,000.

    c. $160,000.

    d. $200,000.

26. Stephen purchased a tract of land for $100,000. Two years after the purchase, when the land was valued at $160,000, Stephen added his daughter's name to the title as a joint tenant with rights of survivorship. Stephen died when the land was worth $200,000. What is his daughter's basis in the land after Stephen's death?

    a. $50,000.

    b. $80,000.

    c. $100,000.

    d. $200,000.

27. Which of the following is a correct statement regarding property owned as joint tenants with rights of survivorship?

    a. The property will receive a full step-up in basis upon the first spouse's death.

    b. The property will avoid probate upon the first spouse's death.

    c. In order for a tenant to sever the interest in the joint property, he or she must have the consent of the other tenant(s).

    d. If the JTWROS is between spouses, the property will not be eligible for the marital deduction upon the first spouse's death.

THE PROBATE PROCESS

28. Generally, which of the following property is included in the probate estate?

    1. Property owned outright in one's own name at the time of death.

    2. An interest in property held as a tenant in common with others.

    3. Life insurance, proceeds payable to one's estate at death.

    4. The decedent's half of any community property.

        a. 1, 2, and 4.

        b. 1 and 2.

        c. 2, 3, and 4.

        d. 1, 2, and 3.

        e. 1, 2, 3, and 4.

29. It is sometimes argued that having property included in a probate estate is unwise. Which of the following statements regarding disposition of property through a probate estate is/are true?

    1. Creditors can never attach to the probate estate.

    2. Disgruntled heirs have a better chance of attaching to nonprobate property rather than probate property.

    3. Overall, state and federal taxes are less in reference to a probate estate than to nonprobate assets.

    4. The contents of the probate estate can become public knowledge.

        a. 2 only.

        b. 4 only.

        c. 1 and 2.

        d. 2, 3, and 4.

        e. 1, 2, 3, and 4.

30. Although the probate system is a common method for disposing of property after death, it is by no means the only way to transfer property. Which of the following methods illustrate excellent nonprobate transfer devices?

    1. Life insurance with a named beneficiary.

    2. Payable-on-death bank accounts.

    3. A living trust.

    4. Joint tenancy with rights of survivorship.

        a. 1 and 3.

        b. 3 and 4.

        c. 1, 3, and 4.

        d. 1, 2, and 4.

        e. 1, 2, 3, and 4.

31. Which of the following statements is/are correct regarding the probate process?

    1. The probate process may be costly and create delays in the distribution of assets.

    2. The probate process is open to public scrutiny.

    3. The probate process protects creditors.

    4. The probate process provides heirs and/or legatees with clear title to property.

      a. 1 only.

      b. 2 only.

      c. 1 and 2.

      d. 1, 2, and 3.

      e. 1, 2, 3, and 4.

32. Which of the following property interests of a decedent will pass through probate?

    1. Property held in fee simple.

    2. Life insurance proceeds with decedent's spouse as beneficiary.

    3. Property owned with the brother of the decedent as tenants in common.

    4. Pension plan assets with a named beneficiary.

      a. 1 only.

      b. 2 and 4.

      c. 1 and 3.

      d. 1, 2, and 4.

      e. 1, 2, 3, and 4.

33. Which of the following is/are considered a disadvantage of probate?

    1. The process may be costly.

    2. The process can result in delays.

    3. The process is open to public scrutiny.

    4. The process provides clear title to heirs and legatees.

      a. 1 only.

      b. 1 and 2.

      c. 2 and 4.

      d. 1, 2, and 3.

      e. 1, 2, 3, and 4.

34. Which of the following would be an alternative to probate regarding disposition of property?

    1. Property held tenants by the entirety.
    2. Property held within a revocable living trust.
    3. Property held within an irrevocable trust.
    4. Proceeds of a second-to-die life insurance policy with a named beneficiary.
        a. 1 only.
        b. 1 and 2.
        c. 1 and 3.
        d. 1, 2, and 3.
        e. 1, 2, 3, and 4.

35. Of the following items of property, which would be included in a decedent's probate estate?

    1. Solely owned securities held in a brokerage account.
    2. An interest in a business held as tenants in common with a brother of the decedent.
    3. Life insurance policy death proceeds made payable to the decedent's estate.
    4. A stamp collection owned Joint Tenants with Rights of Survivorship (JTWROS) with the decedent's spouse.
        a. 1 only.
        b. 2 only.
        c. 1 and 2.
        d. 1, 2, and 3.
        e. 1, 2, 3, and 4.

36. Which of the following items will pass through probate?

    a. Bank accounts with named beneficiaries (POD).
    b. Investment accounts with named beneficiaries (TOD).
    c. Property held Joint Tenants with Rights of Survivorship (JTWROS).
    d. Insurance policy on life of decedent, owned by decedent, with a named beneficiary.
    e. None of the above will pass through probate.

FEDERAL GIFT AND ESTATE TAXATION

37. The applicable credit amount can offset the tax liability for which of the following transfers?

    1. A gift to a US citizen spouse.
    2. Lifetime gifts to children.
    3. Testamentary transfers to friends.
    4. A gift to a public charity.
        a. 1 and 2.
        b. 1 and 3.
        c. 2 and 3.
        d. 1, 2, and 3.
        e. 1, 2, 3, and 4.

38. Which of the following is an advantage of giving a lifetime gift as opposed to bequeathing assets at death?

    a. A larger applicable credit amount is available.
    b. The annual exclusion is available.
    c. A charitable deduction is available.
    d. A qualified domestic trust (QDOT) can be used for lifetime gifts to a non-US Citizen spouse.

THE FEDERAL GIFT TAX

39. Last year, Al gave his son a Mercedes worth $80,000 and his daughter a Lexus worth $60,000. He also gave his wife a rare painting that he purchased for $35,000. Al paid gift tax of $25,000 on the gifts he gave last year. In the current year, Al transferred $100,000 to his son and $100,000 to his daughter. Al's wife also transferred $5,000 to their son. No other gifts were made during the current year. Al and his wife elected to split the gifts on their prior and current year gift tax returns. What is the amount of taxable gifts made by Al and Al's wife in the current year?

	Al	Al's Wife
a.	$78,500	$78,500
b.	$91,500	$91,500
c.	$156,000	$5,000
d.	$178,000	$0
e.	$200,000	$5,000

40. Which of the following situations would <u>not</u> constitute a completed gift for federal gift tax purposes?

   1. Father creates an irrevocable trust under the terms of which his son is to receive income for life and his grandson the remainder at his son's death.

   2. Father, with personal funds, purchases real property and has title conveyed to himself and his brother as joint tenants with right of survivorship.

   3. Father creates a trust giving income for life to wife and providing that, at her death, the corpus is to be distributed to their daughter. Father reserves the right to revoke the trust at any time.

   4. Father, with personal funds, purchases a US Savings Bond made payable to himself and his wife. His wife surrenders the bond for cash to be used for her personal benefit.

      a. 1 only.

      b. 2 only.

      c. 3 only.

      d. 3 and 4.

      e. 1, 2, 3, and 4.

41. Jeff created a joint bank account for himself and his friend, Kim. There is a gift to Kim when:

   a. The account is created.

   b. Jeff dies.

   c. Kim draws on the account for her own benefit.

   d. Kim is notified by Jeff that the account has been created.

42. Which of the following represents a taxable gift?

    1. Transfer of $9,000 to a dependent family member that represents legal support.

    2. Payment of $30,000 to the law school for a child's tuition.

    3. Payment of $16,000 of medical bills to the hospital for a friend.

        a. None of the above are taxable gifts.

        b. 2 only.

        c. 1 and 2.

        d. 2 and 3.

        e. 1, 2, and 3.

43. Which of the following statements relating to qualified transfers for gift tax purposes is not correct?

    a. The exclusion for a qualified transfer is in addition to the annual exclusion.

    b. A qualified transfer is allowed without regard to the relationship between the donor and the donee.

    c. Only that part of a payment to a qualified educational institution that applies directly to tuition costs is a qualified transfer.

    d. A payment made directly to an individual to reimburse him for his medical expenses is a qualified transfer.

44. During this year, Mr. and Mrs. B made joint gifts of the following items to their son:

    1. A bond with an adjusted basis of $12,000 and a fair market value of $40,000.

    2. Stock with an adjusted basis of $22,000 and a fair market value of $33,000.

    3. An auto with an adjusted basis of $12,000 and a fair market value of $14,000.

    4. An interest-free loan of $6,000 for a computer (for the son's personal use) on January 1st, which was paid by their son on December 31st. Assume the applicable federal rate was 8% per annum.

    What are Mr. and Mrs. B's gross gifts for this year?

        a. $87,480.

        b. $87,000.

        c. $46,480.

        d. $46,000.

        e. $52,000.

45. December 1st, Rosario gave her son, Alex, stock with a fair market value of $20,000. This was Rosario's only gift to Alex during the year. She paid gift tax of $5,000. Rosario had purchased the stock two years ago, and her adjusted basis on the date of the gift was $12,000. On January 10th of the following year, Alex sold the stock for $24,000. What was Alex's basis on January 10th?

    a. $12,000.

    b. $14,000.

    c. $17,000.

    d. $20,000.

    e. $24,000.

46. Janet made the following gifts for 2007:

Gift	Donee	Value
Cash	Jack, nephew	$12,000
6-month CD	Jill, niece	$8,000
Antique rifle	George, friend	$20,000
Bonds gifted to irrevocable trust:		
Present Value of Life estate	Joel, father	$60,000
Present Value of Remainder Interest	Jill, niece	$18,000

For 2007, Janet's taxable gifts total:

    a. $63,000.

    b. $66,000.

    c. $72,000.

    d. $74,000.

    e. $118,000.

47. During the year, Mary Sue, who is single, made the following gifts:

1. Paid $16,000 in medical bills for her friend, Vicki. The payments were paid directly to her friend's hospital.

2. $19,000 to her mother to pay for her apartment rent, utilities, and food.

3. $15,000 to her nephew, Mike, to get him started in business.

4. Mary Sue made a $30,000 interest-free demand loan to her nephew, Mike, the previous year. The loan is still outstanding at the end of this year. The applicable federal interest rate during the year remained constant at 8%, and Mike's net investment income is $500.

What is the amount of Mary Sue's taxable gifts?

    a. $10,000.

    b. $12,400.

    c. $18,000.

    d. $20,400.

    e. $50,400.

48. Mr. Baker, a US citizen, made the following gifts:

1. $20,000 cash to his son
2. $60,000 cash to his wife, who is a US citizen.
3. Auto to his brother (fair market value $15,000, adjusted basis $9,000).
4. $100,000 in land to the city of Springfield for a new library.

Without considering gift splitting, what is the total of Mr. Baker's exclusions and deductions for his gift tax return for 2007?

   a. $48,000.
   b. $82,000.
   c. $133,000.
   d. $160,000.
   e. $184,000.

49. Which of the following transfers made by John would be considered a taxable gift?

   a. John pays University of South Texas $40,000 in college tuition for his 22-year-old daughter.
   b. John donates $10,000 to the United Church.
   c. John pays $25,000 of medical expenses to Specific Hospital for his invalid niece.
   d. John gives a $20,000 necklace to his fiancée nine months before they are married.
   e. John gives a car to his friend. The car was worth $2,500 on the date of the gift.

50. Scott, a single taxpayer, made the following cash gifts in 2007:

To the United Way	$22,000
To his daughter, Susan	$26,000
To the Democratic Party	$18,000
To his friend, Tom	$6,000

What is the total amount of taxable gifts made by Scott?

   a. $0.
   b. $6,000.
   c. $14,000.
   d. $28,000.
   e. $32,000.

51. Which one of the following statements regarding the federal gift tax treatment of life insurance policies is false?

    a. If a policy is transferred immediately after purchase, the gift tax value of the policy is equal to the gross premium paid to the insurer.

    b. The annual exclusion is unavailable when a life insurance policy is transferred.

    c. If a policy is transferred while in a premium-paying state, the gift tax value of the policy is equal to the sum of the interpolated terminal reserve and the unearned premium.

    d. If a policy is paid up when transferred, the gift tax value is equal to the amount of the premium that the company would charge for the same type of single-premium policy.

52. After their wedding in October, Ron gave Bonnie $45,000 in cash so that Bonnie could have her own bank account. Ron and Bonnie are US citizens. What is the amount of Ron's gift tax marital deduction?

    a. $0.

    b. $33,000.

    c. $45,000.

    d. $112,000.

    e. $345,800.

53. Clint Rogers made the following gifts:

    1. $2,000 each month to a university to pay tuition costs for his friend, Ernesto.

    2. Tract of land to his mother that had an adjusted basis to Clint of $7,000 and a fair market value of $32,000.

    3. Stock to his wife (a US citizen) that had an adjusted basis to Clint of $30,000 and a fair market value of $50,000.

Clint's spouse did not consent to gift splitting. What is his total amount of taxable gifts?

    a. $20,000.

    b. $32,000.

    c. $38,000.

    d. $57,000.

    e. $109,000.

54. Which of the following statements regarding gift splitting is/are true?

 1. The annual gift tax exclusion allows spouses who consent to split their gifts to transfer up to $24,000 (for 2007) to any one person during any calendar year without gift tax liability, if the gifts are of a present interest.

 2. To qualify for gift splitting, a couple must be married at the time the gift is made.

 3. For gift tax purposes, a husband and wife must file a joint income tax return to qualify for the gift-splitting benefits.

 4. Both spouses must consent to the use of gift splitting and at least one gift tax return must be filed.

 a. 1 only.

 b. 1 and 2.

 c. 1, 2, and 4.

 d. 2, 3, and 4.

 e. 1, 2, 3, and 4.

55. Ron made the following gifts:

Cash to his son, Ron, Jr.	$60,000
Stock to his wife, Bonnie	$120,000
Cash to his church	$40,000
Auto to his nephew	$30,000
Cash to his mother	$30,000

 Ron and Bonnie elect gift splitting. Bonnie's only gift during the year is a $30,000 cash gift to her mother. What is the amount of the taxable gifts to be reported by Ron in 2007?

 a. $0.

 b. $24,000.

 c. $48,000.

 d. $100,000.

 e. $140,000.

56. For transfers by gift, one must file a gift tax return (Form 709) for which of the following?

 a. A transfer of a present interest in property that is less than the annual exclusion.

 b. A qualified transfer for educational or medical expenses.

 c. A transfer to one's spouse that qualified for the unlimited marital deduction.

 d. A transfer of $18,000 to a son for which one's spouse has agreed to gift splitting.

 e. A transfer of $12,000 by a father to his son.

57. George and his spouse, Mary, made joint gifts to their daughter as follows:

    - Stock with an adjusted basis of $20,000 and a fair market value of $50,000.
    - Bonds with an adjusted basis of $27,000 and a fair market value of $35,000.
    - A truck with an adjusted basis of $16,000 and a fair market value of $8,000.
    - An interest-free loan of $10,000 to purchase a sailboat. The applicable federal rate was 9%. Loan was outstanding for the entire year.

    What is the total amount of gross gifts includible in George's and Mary's gift tax returns?

    a. $63,900.
    b. $73,900.
    c. $93,000.
    d. $103,900.
    e. $113,000.

58. William and his spouse, Betty, made joint gifts to their daughter as follows:

    - Stock with an adjusted basis of $20,000 and a fair market value of $50,000.
    - Bonds with an adjusted basis of $27,000 and a fair market value of $35,000.
    - A truck with an adjusted basis of $16,000 and a fair market value of $8,000.
    - An interest-free loan of $10,000 to purchase a sailboat. The applicable federal rate was 9%. The loan was outstanding for the entire year.

    What is the amount of total taxable gifts made by William and Betty to their daughter?

    a. $59,000.
    b. $69,000.
    c. $89,000.
    d. $101,900.
    e. $111,000.

59. Which, if any, of the following transfers is subject to the federal gift tax?

    a. Donations to political organizations.
    b. Payments of a nephew's tuition directly to the university.
    c. A taxpayer pays the hospital for medical care provided to her aunt.
    d. In advance of their marriage, the husband pays $50,000 to the wife as a prenuptial settlement.

60. Which, if any, of the following transfers would be subject to the federal gift tax?

    1. Tom designates his wife, Shannon, as beneficiary of his life insurance policy.

    2. Tom dies and the insurance company pays the $300,000 life insurance proceeds to Shannon (the designated beneficiary of Tom's policy).

    3. Tom makes a donated capital contribution to Z Corporation. The stock of Z Corporation is held equally by Tom and Sue (Tom's daughter).

    4. Tom creates a revocable trust for the benefit of his son, Mark, and funds it with $25,000.

        a. 2 only.

        b. 3 only.

        c. 1 and 2.

        d. 2 and 3.

        e. 1, 2, 3, and 4.

61. Shannon loans her daughter, Sue, $200,000. Sue signs a note promising to repay the loan in five years. No interest is provided for. Which, if any, of the following is not a tax consequence of this arrangement?

        a. Shannon has made a gift to Sue of the imputed interest.

        b. Shannon has an interest expense deduction as to the imputed interest.

        c. Shannon has interest income as to the imputed interest.

        d. Sue may be allowed an income tax deduction as to the imputed interest.

62. Which of the following situations constitutes a transfer that comes within the gift tax statutes?

    1. Kurt creates a trust under the terms of which his son is to get income for life and his grandson the remainder at his son's death.

    2. Kurt purchases real property and has the title conveyed to himself and to his brother as joint tenants.

    3. Kurt creates an irrevocable trust giving income for life to his wife and providing that upon her death the corpus is to be distributed to his daughter.

    4. Kurt purchases a US Savings Bond made payable to himself and his wife. The wife surrenders the bond for cash to be used for her benefit.

        a. 1 only.

        b. 1 and 2.

        c. 2, and 3.

        d. 1, 2, and 4.

        e. 1, 2, 3, and 4.

63. Which of the following situations would not constitute a transfer that comes within the gift tax statutes?

    a. A mother creates a trust under the terms of which the daughter is to get income for life and her granddaughter will get the remainder at the daughter's death.

    b. Bill purchases real property and has title conveyed to himself and to his brother, Joe, as joint tenants.

    c. A father creates an irrevocable trust giving income for life to his wife and providing that at her death the corpus is to be distributed to his son.

    d. Joe purchases a US Savings Bond made payable to himself and his wife, Mary. Mary cashes the bond to be used for her own benefit.

    e. Mary Sue creates a joint bank account for herself and her daughter, Rachel. There have been no withdrawals from the account.

64. Which of the following statements regarding qualified transfers for gift tax purposes is/are true?

    1. The exclusion for a qualified transfer is in addition to the annual exclusion.

    2. A qualified transfer is allowed without regard to the relationship between donor and donee.

    3. Only that part of a payment to a qualified educational institution that applies to direct tuition costs is qualified.

    4. A payment made directly to reimburse an individual for medical expenses is a qualified transfer.

    a. 1 only.

    b. 3 only.

    c. 1 and 3.

    d. 1, 2, and 3.

    e. 1, 2, 3, and 4.

65. In 2007, George decided to begin a program of lifetime giving to his 5 grandchildren and 3 great-grandchildren. He wants to control the amount of annual gifts to avoid the imposition of federal gift tax, and he does not desire to use any of his or his wife, Sue's, applicable credit amount. Sue is willing to split each gift over a period of 10 years. George can give a total amount of gifts (ignoring future indexing of the annual exclusion), including the gift splitting, over the 10-year period of:

    a. $1,376,000.

    b. $1,920,000.

    c. $960,000.

    d. $600,000.

    e. $900,000.

66. Which, if any, of the following statements correctly reflects the rules regarding the federal gift tax return (Form 709)?

    1. A donor who uses a fiscal year for income tax purposes uses the same filing date for Form 709.

    2. For a calendar-year taxpayer, an extension of time for filing Form 1040 also extends the time for filing Form 709.

    3. A father gives $24,000 of separate property to his son in 2007. If the father's wife elects to split gifts with the father, they must file a gift tax return.

    4. A father and mother give $24,000 of community property to their son in 2007. No gift tax return need be filed.

        a. 1 only.

        b. 2 only.

        c. 1, 2, and 3.

        d. 2, 3, and 4.

        e. 1, 2, 3, and 4.

67. Which of the following statements correctly reflects the rules regarding the federal gift tax return Form 709?

    1. For a calendar-year taxpayer, an extension of time for filing Form 1040 also extends the time for filing Form 709.

    2. George gives $5,000 of separate property to his son. If Mary, George's wife, elects to split the gift with George, George must file a gift tax return.

    3. George and Mary give $20,000 of community property to their son. No gift tax return need be filed.

    4. An extension of time for filing the gift tax return does not extend the time for payment of the gift tax.

        a. 1 and 2.

        b. 2 and 3.

        c. 1, 2, and 3.

        d. 2, 3, and 4.

        e. 1, 2, 3, and 4.

68. Lifetime gifts can be an attractive estate planning and tax-saving technique. Which of the following statements is/are true regarding lifetime gifts?

    1. Amounts qualifying for the annual exclusion will escape gift taxation and will not be included in the donor's gross estate.

    2. Future appreciation in the value of gifted property will escape gift taxation and estate taxation.

    3. Income from gift property generally will be taxed to the donor for income tax purposes.

    4. Generation-skipping transfer taxes do not apply to "lifetime" gifts.

        a. 1 only.

        b. 1 and 2.

        c. 3 and 4.

        d. 2, 3, and 4.

        e. None of the above.

69. Roy and his wife have 2 children, each over the age of majority, 1 grandchild age 21 and 3 minor grandchildren. Roy and his wife want to make gifts to their children and grandchildren sufficient to make maximum use of the tax provisions providing for annual exclusions from federal gift tax. Considering that desire only, Roy and his wife can make gifts during 2007 totaling:

    a. $36,000.

    b. $72,000.

    c. $144,000.

    d. $345,800.

    e. $1,000,000.

70. Generally, gift property:

    a. Has a zero basis to the donee because the donee did not pay anything for the property.

    b. Has the same basis to the donee as the donor's adjusted basis if the donee disposes of the property at a gain.

    c. Has the same basis to the donee as the donor's adjusted basis if the donee disposes of the property at a loss, and the fair market value on the date of gift was less than the donor's adjusted basis.

    d. Has a zero basis to the donee if the fair market value on the date of gift is less than the donor's adjusted basis.

71. Jan is a 55-year-old nurse with Community Hospital. She was divorced from her husband, Steven, 10 years ago, and she retained custody of their only son, Jonathan, who was 14 years old at the time of the divorce. As part of the divorce decree, Jan received a property settlement from her ex-husband. At the time the property was transferred to Jan (10 years ago), it had a basis of $35,000 and a fair market value of $40,000. In the current year, Jan gifted the property to Jonathan, who is now 24 years old. The fair market value of the property on the date of the gift was $30,000. No gift tax is paid. Jonathan subsequently sells the property for $33,000. What is his recognized gain (or loss)?

    a. No gain or loss.

    b. $2,000 loss.

    c. $3,000 gain.

    d. $33,000 gain.

    e. None of the above.

72. Bill gifts his daughter bonds with a basis to Bill of $1,800 and a fair market value of $1,000. Bill's daughter subsequently sells the bonds for $2,000. What is her recognized gain or loss?

    a. No gain or loss.

    b. $200 gain.

    c. $1,000 gain.

    d. $2,000 gain.

    e. None of the above.

73. Ana received a gift of real estate with an adjusted basis of $80,000 to the donor and fair market value of $55,000 on the date of gift. The donor paid gift tax of $3,000. Ana subsequently sold the property for $65,000. What is her recognized gain or loss?

    a. $10,000 gain.

    b. $7,000 gain.

    c. $15,000 loss.

    d. $12,000 loss.

    e. None of the above.

74. James was given a house during the current year. At the date of the gift, the house had a fair market value of $175,000, and its adjusted basis to the donor (his father, Michael) was $105,000. The donor paid gift tax of $12,000 on the gift. James has made no other gifts to Michael this year. What is James' basis in the house?

    a. $105,000.

    b. $109,800.

    c. $110,153.

    d. $175,000.

    e. $187,000.

75. Tom received a gift of bonds from his cousin. The bonds had a 10-year maturity, and were selling at a premium due to their high 9% coupon rate. The basis of the bonds to the cousin was $42,000, and the fair market value on the date of the gift was $60,000. The cousin paid gift tax of $4,500. What is Tom's basis for the bonds? (Assume the annual exclusion is unavailable.

    a. $0 for gains and $0 for losses.

    b. $43,350 for gains and $43,350 for losses.

    c. $48,000 for gains and $40,000 for losses.

    d. $50,000 for gains and $42,000 for losses.

76. Matt gives Jim securities. Matt's adjusted basis for the securities is $48,000, and the fair market value is $40,000. Matt pays gift tax of $2,000. What is Jim's basis for the stock for gain and for loss?

    a. $0 for gain and $0 for loss.

    b. $40,000 for gain and $40,000 for loss.

    c. $48,000 for gain and $40,000 for loss.

    d. $50,000 for gain and $42,000 for loss.

77. Three months ago, Ryan received a gift of land from his father-in-law. His father-in-law gave him the land because he expects it to appreciate significantly in the future. Ryan doesn't trust his father-in-law's opinions regarding the future of the real estate market and is interested in selling the land in order to purchase some blue-chip stocks. Ryan's father-in-law purchased the land four years ago, and Ryan wants to know whether he can use his father-in-law's holding period in determining whether any gain or loss will be short term or long term for tax purposes. The holding period of property acquired by gift begins on:

   a. The date the property was acquired by the donor only.

   b. The date of gift only.

   c. The date the property was acquired by the donor or the date of gift, depending on whether the property was sold at a gain or a loss.

   d. a, b, or c as elected by donee.

78. Jack gives John a machine to use in his business with a fair market value of $4,500 and a basis to Jack of $4,800. What is John's basis for depreciation?

   a. $0.

   b. $4,500.

   c. $4,650.

   d. $4,800.

79. Which of the following transactions requires the donor to file a gift tax return?

   1. Donor lends $125,000 to son interest free. The federal rate is 10%.

   2. Donor and wife using split-gift technique and give son $12,500 for son's birthday.

   3. Donor transfers $15,000 to revocable inter vivos trust for son who is both income and remainder beneficiary.

   4. Donor gifts jointly with spouse community property worth $14,500 to daughter for daughter's birthday.

   a. 4 only.

   b. 1 and 2.

   c. 1, 2, and 3.

   d. 1, 2, and 4.

   e. 1, 2, 3, and 4.

80. Which of the following is correct regarding a net gift?

   a. In a net gift, the donor pays the gift tax prior to the gift.

   b. A net gift is by definition a gift of a future interest.

   c. A net gift will cause the donor taxable income to the extent the gift tax paid by the donee exceeds the donor's adjusted basis in the gift.

   d. Net gifts do not qualify for the annual exclusion.

81. Which of the following circumstances would definitely cause the date-of-death value of the gifted property to be included in the donor's gross estate?

    1.   Donor transfers property to a revocable trust.

    2.   Donor retains a life estate in the gift property.

    3.   Donor gives $35,000 to his sister.

    4.   Donor dies within three years of the date of the gift.

        a.   1, 2, and 3.

        b.   1 and 2.

        c.   2 and 4.

        d.   3 and 4.

        e.   1, 2, 3, and 4.

82. Mario has accumulated significant wealth over his lifetime, and he is currently implementing techniques to lower his gross estate. He would like to take advantage of the annual exclusion available for certain lifetime gifts. Transfers to which of the following trusts/accounts would allow Mario to utilize the gift tax annual exclusion?

    1.   Uniform Gift to Minors Account (UGMA).

    2.   Grantor Retained Annuity Trust.

    3.   Qualified Tuition Plan.

    4.   2503(c) Trust.

        a.   1 and 4.

        b.   2 and 3.

        c.   1, 2, and 4.

        d.   1, 3, and 4.

        e.   2, 3, and 4.

83. Transfers to which of the following trusts would allow the donor to utilize the gift tax annual exclusion?

    1.   Crummey Trust.

    2.   Revocable Trust.

    3.   Qualified Personal Residence Trust.

    4.   2503(b) Trust.

        a.   1 and 4.

        b.   2 and 3.

        c.   1, 2, and 4.

        d.   1, 3, and 4.

        e.   2, 3, and 4.

84. William Barnhill gave his son, James, a house on August 1st. The fair market value of the house on January 1st, August 1st, and December 31st of the same year were as follows: $130,000, $140,000, and $150,000. Mr. Barnhill had purchased the property in 1992 for $60,000 and had used it as rental property the entire time he held it. He had taken cumulative straight-line depreciation through July 31st of the current year of $10,000. What is James Barnhill's adjusted tax basis?

    a. $0.

    b. $50,000.

    c. $60,000.

    d. $130,000.

    e. $150,000.

85. William Barnhill gave his son, James, a house on August 1st. The fair market value of the house on January 1st, August 1st, and December 1st of the same year were as follows: $130,000, $140,000, and $150,000. Mr. Barnhill had purchased the property in 1992 for $60,000 and had used it as rental property the entire time he held it. He had taken cumulative straight-line depreciation through July 31st of the current year of $10,000. What is James Barnhill's adjusted tax basis if William had paid $30,000 in gift tax? (assume the annual exclusion is not available)

    a. $0.

    b. $50,000.

    c. $69,286.

    d. $65,000.

    e. $130,000.

86. John and Mary are married and have two children, Patrick and Kurt. In 2007, they would like to gift to their children the maximum amount of cash possible without paying any gift tax. They have made no previous gifts during their lifetime and are willing to make maximum usage of whatever techniques are available to make these gifts as long as they don't have to pay any gift tax. How much total can they gift to Patrick and Kurt?

    a. $12,000.

    b. $24,000.

    c. $48,000.

    d. $2,024,000.

    e. $2,048,000.

87. Jeannine transferred, by gift, $100,000 to her son and $100,000 to her daughter. Jeannine's husband, Scott, also transferred, by gift, $50,000 to their son. No other gifts were made. Jeannine and Scott elected to split the gifts on their gift tax returns. What is the total amount of taxable gifts made by Jeannine and Scott?

	Jeannine	Scott
a.	$101,000	$101,000
b.	$114,000	$114,000
c.	$164,000	$36,000
d.	$206,000	$44,000
e.	$198,000	$48,000

88. Robin inherited 10 acres of land at the death of her father during the current year. A federal estate tax return was filed, and the land was valued at $25,000, its fair market value at the date of the father's death. The father had originally acquired the land in 1962 for $5,000. What is Robin's basis in the land she inherited?

    a. $5,000.

    b. $10,000.

    c. $15,000.

    d. $25,000.

89. Gift splitting:

    1. Can utilize another person's applicable credit amount.

    2. Applies to all gifts in a given year.

    3. Doubles the annual exclusion for gifts of a present interest.

    4. Requires the filing of a gift tax return.

    a. 3 only.

    b. 3 and 4.

    c. 2, 3, and 4.

    d. 1, 2, 3, and 4.

90. Husband and wife own property JTWROS, and they are contemplating a transfer from wife to husband. Assuming the transfer occurs, which of the following is/are correct?

    1. A taxable gift occurs.

    2. The transfer avoids capital gain tax.

    3. If the wife dies within 3 years of the transfer, the value of the gift she transferred is included in her gross estate.

    a. 1 only.

    b. 2 only.

    c. 1 and 2.

    d. 2 and 3.

    e. 1, 2, and 3.

91. What is the maximum gift that Bob and Sue Thompson can give to a single third-party recipient in 2007 without paying any gift tax, assuming they have not made any previous taxable gifts?

    a. $12,000.

    b. $24,000.

    c. $1,270,000.

    d. $1,370,000.

    e. $2,024,000.

92. Which of the following statements is/are true regarding lifetime gifts?

    1. Annual exclusion gifts will escape gift taxation and will not be included in the donor's estate.

    2. Future appreciation in the value of gifted property will escape gift taxation and estate taxation.

    3. Income from gift property will generally be taxed to the donee for income tax purposes.

    4. Generation-skipping transfer taxes do not apply to "lifetime" gifts.

    a. 1 only.

    b. 1, 2, and 3.

    c. 2, 3, and 4.

    d. 3 and 4.

    e. None of the above.

93. Donna received a gift of rental real estate with an adjusted basis of $75,000 to the donor and fair market value of $50,000 on the date of gift. Gift tax of $3,000 was paid by the donor. Donna subsequently sold the property for $60,000. What is her recognized gain or loss?

    a. $10,000 gain.

    b. $7,000 gain.

    c. $15,000 loss.

    d. $12,000 loss.

    e. None of the above.

94. Paul gifts a piece of land (basis $100,000, FMV $300,000) on January 1, 2006 to his father. Which of the following statements is true?

    a. If Paul's father dies on February 1, 2007 and leaves the land to Paul, Paul will have to take his father's basis in the property.

    b. Paul's father's basis in the property will be $100,000.

    c. If Paul had sold the land to his father for $50,000 instead of gifting it, he would have had a deductible loss of $50,000.

    d. Paul should not gift appreciating property since it will be added back to the taxable estate at the date-of-death value.

95. Robin Jackson is 75 years old, is in very ill health, and would like to give a gift to her son, Jack. Assuming that the fair market value of each of the properties is $30,000 and that each of the properties produces the same amount of income, which of the following assets should Robin gift to Jack?

    a. Savings account.

    b. Common stock with an adjusted basis of $4,000.

    c. A mutual fund with an adjusted basis of $35,000.

    d. A 401(k) plan from Robin's former employer.

96. Robin Jackson is 75 years old, and would like to give a gift to the United Fund, her favorite charity. Assuming that the fair market value of each of the properties is $30,000 and that each of the properties produces the same amount of income, which of the following assets should Robin gift to charity?

    a. Savings account.

    b. Common stock with an adjusted basis of $4,000.

    c. A mutual fund with an adjusted basis of $35,000.

    d. A 401(k) plan from Robin's former employer.

97. Joe's mother is in need of income, and Joe and his wife are considering gifting some investments to her. He expects that she will live at least several more years and will leave the property to him in her will. Joe has already made lifetime gifts in excess of $800,000. Which of the following assets would be most suitable for such a gift?

    a. Stock A, which is a common stock, paying no dividend for which significant capital appreciation is expected. Basis is $20,000 and FMV is $60,000.

    b. Stock B, which is a highly rated preferred stock, paying an 8% dividend. Basis is $20,000 and FMV is $20,000.

    c. Stock C, which is a common stock, paying a small dividend. Basis is $60,000 and FMV is $20,000.

    d. A zero-coupon corporate bond maturing in 20 years, sold at a discount to yield 9%.

98. Which of the following statements about Crummey trusts is true?

    a. They require notification of withdrawal rights only for beneficiaries who have reached majority.

    b. They provide a catch-up provision if the annual exclusion is not utilized in a prior year.

    c. They usually provide a withdrawal right of the lesser of the amount of available annual exclusion or the value of the gift property transferred.

    d. There are no gift tax consequences to the beneficiaries.

THE FEDERAL ESTATE TAX

99. Which of the following items is/are included in the gross estate?

   1. Medical insurance reimbursements that were due the individual at death.

   2. The value of the part of a deceased husband's real property allowed to his widow for her lifetime (dower interest).

   3. Proceeds of life insurance on the decedent's life if the decedent possessed incidents of ownership in the policy.

   4. Outstanding dividends declared to decedent after the date of death.

      a. 1 only.

      b. 2 only.

      c. 1 and 3.

      d. 1, 2, and 3.

      e. 1, 2, 3, and 4.

100. Which of the following annuities would be included in the annuitant's gross estate at death?

      a. An annuity payable to the annuitant for life, then payable to a beneficiary.

      b. A single life annuity for the decedent's life.

      c. An annuity payable to a decedent for a period that ends before the decedent's death.

      d. An annuity payable for a five-year fixed term. The annuitant lives beyond the five-year term.

101. Several years ago, Tom and his sister, Laura, purchased a tract of real property as joint tenants with right of survivorship (JTWROS). Tom contributed $50,000 toward the $200,000 purchase price and Laura contributed the remaining $150,000. Laura died in the current year, and her will provided that all of her assets would pass to her daughter, Kate. The real property was worth $1,000,000 on the date of Laura's death. The value of Laura's interest in the property includible in her gross estate is:

      a. $250,000.

      b. $500,000.

      c. $600,000.

      d. $750,000.

      e. $1,000,000.

102. Which of the following items of property would be included in the gross estate of a decedent who died during the current year?

    1. Jewelry of the decedent.

    2. Cash of $200,000 given to decedent's friend in two years ago. No gift tax was paid on the transfer.

    3. Stock purchased by decedent and titled as joint tenants with rights of survivorship with decedent's brother.

        a. 1 only.

        b. 1 and 3.

        c. 2 only.

        d. 2 and 3.

        e. 1, 2, and 3.

103. Which of the following is *not* includible in the gross estate of a decedent?

    1. Life insurance proceeds payable to the decedent's children. The policy was transferred to an Irrevocable Life Insurance Trust (ILIT) five years ago.

    2. Real estate located in Mexico owned by the decedent.

    3. Trust assets over which the decedent held a limited power of appointment.

    4. Assets owned by the decedent at death that are distributed to the decedent's surviving spouse.

    5. Gift tax paid on gifts made two years before the decedent's death.

        a. 1 only.

        b. 1 and 3.

        c. 2, 4, and 5.

        d. 1, 3, and 5.

        e. 3, 4, and 5.

104. Bobbie is the holder of a power of appointment over some trust property. Bobbie's gross estate will *not* include the value of the property if the appointment of property she may make to herself is limited by the trust instrument to the sole purpose of her:

        a. Well-being.

        b. Entertainment.

        c. Happiness.

        d. Comfort.

        e. Support.

105. Fifteen months before his death, Eddie Lee Roth gave a painting valued at $600,000 to his son and paid gift tax of $30,000 on the transfer. At the date of Eddie's death, the art was worth $700,000. Based on these facts, what amount is includible in Eddie's gross estate as a result of the gift?

        a. $0.

        b. $30,000.

        c. $600,000.

        d. $700,000.

        e. $730,000.

106. Omar died on September 8th. His will called for the transfer of all of his possessions to his mother. At the date of death, the assets transferred were:

	Adjusted Tax Basis	Fair Market Value
Personal Residence	$140,000	$180,000
Common stock	$20,000	$50,000
Dividends on above stock (declared 9/30)	$2,000	$2,000
Medical insurance reimbursement (check received 8/31 but not cashed)	$2,500	$2,500
Cash	$42,000	$42,000

The executrix did not elect the alternate valuation date. What is Omar's gross estate for purposes of an estate tax return?

    a. $125,000.

    b. $272,000.

    c. $274,500.

    d. $276,500.

107. The fair market values of Art's assets at the date of death were:

Personal effects	$125,000
Real estate bought by Art 5 years prior to death and held with Art's brother as joint tenants with right of survivorship (brother made no contribution)	$700,000

The executor of Art's estate did not elect the alternate valuation date. The amount includible in Art's gross estate on the federal estate tax return is:

    a. $125,000.

    b. $525,000.

    c. $700,000.

    d. $825,000.

108. Dr. Goodbar died on July 31st. His assets and their fair market value at the time of his death were:

Cash	$20,000
Personal residence	$200,000
Life insurance payable to Dr. Goodbar's estate	$100,000
Series EE bonds	$100,000
State of Louisiana bonds	$250,000

Dr. Goodbar had a balance on his residence mortgage of $15,000. What is Dr. Goodbar's gross estate?

a. $305,000.

b. $555,000.

c. $605,000.

d. $620,000.

e. $670,000.

109. Dave died during the current year. Dave has always been a giving person, and as such, gave many gifts during his life and in his will. At the time of his death, Dave had a wife of 30 years and three fully-grown children. His oldest son, Jerome, has asked you to prepare Dave's estate tax return. Which of the following items would be includible in Dave's gross estate at the full date-of-death fair market value?

1. A gift of stock worth $50,000 made to Dave's nephew two years before Dave's death.

2. Assets in a grantor retained annuity trust (GRAT) that was established for a five-year term. Dave, the grantor, died four years after the trust was created.

3. Assets over which Dave held a general power of appointment.

4. Dave's assets donated to charity upon his death.

a. 1 only.

b. 1 and 3.

c. 2 and 3.

d. 1, 2, and 3.

e. 2, 3, and 4.

110. Mrs. Bea Bingham died on August 1 of the current year. What is Mrs. Bingham's gross estate?

- Last year, Bea gave cash of $30,000 to her friend. No gift tax was paid on the gift.

- Bea held property jointly with her brother. Each paid $45,000 of the total purchase price of $90,000. Fair market value of the property at date of death was $200,000.

- Last year, Bea purchased a life insurance policy on her own life and gave it as a gift to her sister. Bea retained the right to change the beneficiary. Upon Bea's death, her sister received $200,000 under the policy.

- In 1983, Bea gave her son a summer home (fair market value in 1982, $100,000). Bea continued to use it until her death pursuant to an understanding with her son. The fair market value at date of death was $190,000.

  a. $200,000.

  b. $250,000.

  c. $375,000.

  d. $425,000.

  e. $490,000.

111. Mary Sue died during the current year. Which of the following would be includible in Mary Sue's gross estate at the full date-of-death value?

1. A gift of property worth $80,000 given by Mary Sue to her cousin four years ago. Mary Sue retained a life estate in the gifted property.

2. A residence that was purchased by Mary Sue and transferred into joint tenancy with rights of survivorship (JTWROS) with her daughter several years ago.

3. A gift of $30,000 cash from Mary Sue to her son, given last year.

4. A life insurance policy that Mary Sue transferred to an Irrevocable Life Insurance Trust two years ago.

   a. 1 only.

   b. 2 and 3.

   c. 1, 2, and 4.

   d. 1, 3, and 4.

   e. 2, 3, and 4.

112. Sonny died three weeks ago. His assets included substantial real estate holdings, and some closely held stock worth approximately $2,000,000. In preparing the estate tax return (Form 706) for Sonny, you have concluded that his total gross estate is $6,500,000. Which of the following items is not an allowable deduction against the gross estate?

   a. Administration and funeral expenses.

   b. Claims against the estate.

   c. Penalty incurred as the result of a late payment of the federal estate tax.

   d. Casualty and theft losses.

113. Which of the following is a deduction from the gross estate in arriving at the adjusted gross estate?

    a. Federal estate tax charitable deduction.

    b. Funeral costs.

    c. Federal estate tax marital deduction.

    d. Gift tax paid on prior taxable gifts.

    e. Income in Respect of a Decedent (IRD).

114. Which of the following is a deduction from the adjusted gross estate in calculating the taxable estate?

    a. Deductible casualty losses.

    b. Deductible funeral costs.

    c. Federal estate tax charitable deduction.

    d. Prior taxable gifts.

    e. Attorney fees associated with maintaining estate assets.

115. Which of the following is *not* deductible in computing the taxable estate of a decedent?

    a. Funeral expenses.

    b. Legal fees to the attorney representing the decedent's estate during probate.

    c. A personal debt owed by the decedent to a friend.

    d. A payment of property to the decedent's children in accordance with the will.

    e. A mortgage on the decedent's principal residence.

116. Kelly died during the current year. The state of residence and domicile was not a community property state. From the items listed below, what are the allowable deductions on the estate tax return?

Funeral expenses	$4,500
Executor and administrative fees	$6,000
Total mortgage on jointly held property, one-half purchase price paid by decedent	$90,000
Bequest of cash to spouse	$75,000
Expense of filing estate's fiduciary income tax return	$1,000

    a. $56,500.

    b. $130,500.

    c. $131,500.

    d. $175,500.

    e. $176,500.

117. A United States citizen died on July 4 during the current year, leaving an adjusted gross estate with a fair market value of $1,400,000 at the date of death. Under the terms of the will, $375,000 was bequeathed outright to his widow, who is also a US citizen. The remainder of the estate was left to his mother. No taxable gifts were made during his lifetime. In computing the taxable estate, the executor should claim a marital deduction of:

    a. $0.

    b. $375,000.

    c. $700,000.

    d. $975,000.

    e. $1,025,000.

118. What amount of a decedent's taxable estate is effectively estate tax free in 2007 if the maximum applicable credit amount is utilized?

    a. $555,800.

    b. $780,800.

    c. $1,000,000.

    d. $1,500,000.

    e. $2,000,000.

119. Form 706, United States Estate Tax Return, was filed for an estate in the current year. The gross estate tax was $350,000. All of the following items are credited against the tentative estate tax to determine the net estate tax payable, except:

    a. Applicable credit amount.

    b. Prior gift taxes paid.

    c. Marital deduction.

    d. Credit for foreign death taxes.

    e. Credit for estate tax on prior transfers.

120. Roger died in 2007 of pancreatic cancer. At the time of his death, his gross estate was $3,800,000, comprised mostly of publicly traded blue chip stocks that had appreciated greatly over the last few years. In preparing his estate tax return, it was determined that he had debts and other administrative expenses of $800,000, resulting in a taxable estate of $3,000,000. He had made no taxable gifts during his lifetime. Roger's federal estate tax due is:

    a. $450,000.

    b. $575,800.

    c. $637,000.

    d. $780,800.

    e. $828,000.

121. Jack died in 2007 with a taxable estate of $1,600,000. During his life, he gave several taxable gifts, causing him to utilize $80,000 of his applicable credit amount. The applicable credit amount that his estate will subtract from tentative estate tax due is:

    a. $15,200.
    b. $265,800.
    c. $345,800.
    d. $555,800.
    e. $780,800.

122. Which of the following rules do not apply to the filing of an estate tax return of a US citizen?

    a. Form 706 is the form that is used to file an estate tax return.
    b. The return is due nine months after the date of death unless an extension of time for filing has been granted.
    c. The return is filed with the Internal Revenue Service Center for the state in which the decedent was domiciled.
    d. For 2007, the value of the gross estate must be over $1,500,000.

123. If a citizen or resident of the United States dies during 2007, an estate tax return must be filed if the gross estate at the date of death was valued at more than:

    a. $650,000.
    b. $1,000,000.
    c. $1,500,000.
    d. $2,000,000.
    e. $3,000,000.

124. Unless an extension of time to file is granted, an estate tax return, Form 706 (United States Estate and Generation-Skipping Transfer Tax Return) is due:

    a. 3 months after the date of the decedent's death.
    b. 6 months after the date of the decedent's death.
    c. 9 months after the date of the decedent's death.
    d. 12 months after the date of the decedent's death.

125. An extension of time to pay estate tax may be granted if the executor can show reasonable cause for requesting the extension. Which of the following would be an illustration of reasonable cause?

    1. Litigation is required to collect assets of the decedent.

    2. Liquid assets of the estate are located in several jurisdictions and are not, nor will be, within the immediate control of the executor due to ancillary probate.

    3. The estate would have to borrow funds at an interest rate higher than generally available to satisfy claims against the estate that are currently due and payable.

    4. Payment of estate taxes would require the liquidation of almost 50% of the assets of the estate.

       a. 1 only.

       b. 1 and 3.

       c. 1 and 2.

       d. 1, 2, and 3.

       e. 1, 2, 3, and 4.

126. The applicable credit amount allowed against federal gift and estate tax for 2007 is:

       a. $12,000 per donee per year.

       b. $345,800 for federal gift and estate tax.

       c. $345,800 for federal gift tax and $780,800 for federal estate tax.

       d. $1,500,000 for federal gift and estate tax.

127. Which of the following alternatives is an effective method of limiting, reducing, or avoiding federal estate taxes:

    1. Use of the annual gift tax exclusion.

    2. Creation of an irrevocable life insurance trust.

    3. Use of gift tax exclusions for tuition and medical expense payments made directly to the provider.

    4. Use of the unlimited marital deduction.

       a. 2 and 4.

       b. 1, 2, and 4.

       c. 1 and 3.

       d. 1, 3, and 4.

       e. 1, 2, 3, and 4.

128. Which of the following statements regarding the federal estate tax marital deduction is false?

       a. If the decedent received a marital deduction, the property must be included in the surviving spouse's gross estate (unless consumed) upon the surviving spouse's death.

       b. A QTIP trust will qualify for the marital deduction, if the executor makes the appropriate election.

       c. The surviving spouse must be a US citizen for the decedent to qualify for the marital deduction.

       d. The marital deduction only applies in separate property states.

129. Which of the following techniques would be used when a surviving spouse is not a US citizen?

    a. Qualified Personal Residence Trust (QPRT).

    b. Qualified Domestic Relations Order (QDRO).

    c. Qualified Domestic Trust (QDOT).

    d. Qualified Terminable Interest Property (QTIP).

    e. Qualified Foreign Citizen Trust (QFCT).

130. Bill, a US citizen, owns a life insurance policy on his life. His latest statement from the life insurance company revealed the following:

Face Amount of Policy	$2,000,000
Interpolated Terminal Reserve	$300,000
Cash Value	$280,000
Gross Premiums Paid	$250,000
Beneficiary	Heidi (his wife)

If Bill died today, and the insurance proceeds were paid to his wife, Heidi (a resident alien), what amount will qualify for the estate tax marital deduction?

    a. $0.

    b. $250,000.

    c. $280,000.

    d. $300,000.

    e. $2,000,000.

131. A husband and wife reside in a community property state. Their community property consists of real property with an adjusted basis of $90,000 and a fair market value of $300,000 and other property with an adjusted basis of $50,000 and a fair market value of $20,000. The husband dies and leaves his estate to his wife. What is the wife's adjusted basis in the real property and other property after the husband's death? (Assume no children).

	Real	Other
a.	$90,000	$50,000
b.	$195,000	$50,000
c.	$195,000	$35,000
d.	$300,000	$20,000

132. Three months ago, Tom gave some land to his son, Junior. At the date of gift, the land had a fair market value of $70,000 and an adjusted taxable basis to Tom of $30,000. No gift taxes were paid. Junior died last week, bequeathing all of his property to Tom. If the land had a fair market value of $80,000 on the date of Junior's death, what is Tom's adjusted tax basis in the land after inheriting the property from Junior?

    a. $0.

    b. $30,000.

    c. $70,000.

    d. $80,000.

    e. $80,000 plus a pro rata portion of estate taxes paid.

133. Val has a basis in an asset of $150,000. He gives the asset to his father who is terminally ill. His father died six months later when the asset was worth $250,000. His father's will leaves the asset to Val. Val sells the asset for $310,000. What is Val's capital gain?

    a. $0.

    b. $60,000.

    c. $100,000.

    d. $160,000.

    e. $310,000.

134. Which of the items below represent deductions from the gross estate to arrive at the taxable estate on Form 706?

    1. Medical (last illness) and funeral expenses.

    2. Debts of the decedent.

    3. Bequests to a spouse.

    4. Charitable bequests.

        a. 1 only.

        b. 2 only.

        c. 1 and 2.

        d. 1, 2, and 3.

        e. 1, 2, 3, and 4.

135. On which IRS form are funeral expenses deducted?

    1. Form 706 estate tax return.

    2. Personal income tax return Form 1040.

    3. Form 1041 fiduciary return.

        a. 1 only.

        b. 2 only.

        c. 3 only.

        d. 1 or 3.

        e. 1, 2, or 3.

136. Which of the following Internal Revenue Code sections might be beneficial to an estate with a closely held corporation as an asset of the estate?

    1. IRC Section 303.
    2. IRC Section 6166.
    3. IRC Section 2032.
    4. IRC Section 2032A.

    a. 1 only.
    b. 2 only.
    c. 1 and 2.
    d. 1, 2, and 3.
    e. 1, 2, 3, and 4.

137. Which of the following will be included in Harry's gross estate if Harry died on 7/1/07?

    a. The proceeds of life insurance transferred to son on 10/1/04.
    b. House transferred to daughter on 12/1/06.
    c. CRAT established in 2001 where Harry was the income beneficiary and the Boy Scouts are the charitable remainder.
    d. a and c.

VALUATION OF ASSETS

138. On July 13, Michael gave his brother, James, one share of XYZ stock, which was traded on an exchange. July 13 was a Thursday, and these were the quoted prices on Wednesday the 12th and Friday the 14th. The market was closed on Thursday:

	Sales Price		
Date	High	Low	Closing
7/12	60	56	58.5
7/14	62	58.5	59

What is the fair market value of Michael's gift?

 a. $58.00.

 b. $58.75.

 c. $59.50.

 d. $59.13.

 e. $60.25.

139. Bill Cole died on August 29th. At that time, he owned stock in XYZ Corporation. The stock traded on both August 28th and August 29th. Given the following excerpt from the *Wall Street Journal* for both days, what is the reported value of XYZ stock on Form 706?

August 28th				August 29th		
High	Low	Close		High	Low	Close
63	52	57		60	58	59.5

 a. 57.00.

 b. 58.00.

 c. 59.00.

 d. 59.50.

 e. 60.00.

140. ABC stock does not trade on a regular basis. If John Smith dies on Thursday, June 5th, and the most recent trades for ABC stock are as follows:

Mon., 6/2   27

Wed., 6/4   25

Mon., 6/9   28

Tues., 6/10   29

What is the date-of-death value that should be used for the Federal Estate Return?

    a. 25.00.

    b. 25.60.

    c. 26.00.

    d. 27.00.

    e. 28.00.

141. Buy-sell agreements:

    a. Can be used to try to establish valuation at date of death.

    b. Are used with both closely held stock and publicly traded stock.

    c. Can be structured only as a cross-purchase plan.

    d. Are useful only for corporations.

142. Susan and John each own a 50% interest in XYZ Inc. The business has just been valued at $4 million, and Susan and John have just entered into a cross-purchase buy-sell agreement. With respect to the policy on Susan's life, who is the owner of the policy, the beneficiary of the policy, and the amount of the insurance?

	Owner	Beneficiary	Amount
a.	Susan	Susan	$4 million
b.	Susan	John	$2 million
c.	John	Susan's spouse	$2 million
d.	John	John	$2 million
e.	John	John	$4 million

143. Three partners have an equal 1/3 interest in a partnership valued at $900,000. If a cross-purchase agreement is selected, how much coverage should each partner have on the life of each of the other partners?

    a. $150,000.

    b. $200,000.

    c. $300,000.

    d. $450,000.

144. How many insurance policies will be required under a partnership entity buy-sell agreement if the partnership has seven partners?

    a. 1.

    b. 7.

    c. 42.

    d. 49.

145. Which one of the following provisions should NOT be included in a buy-sell agreement for an unincorporated business?

    a. Provisions allowing for Section 303 stock redemption.

    b. Parties to the agreement.

    c. Modification or termination agreement.

    d. Funding.

146. Which of the following statements is correct regarding buy-sell agreements?

    a. The agreement must be funded with life insurance.

    b. With a corporate entity-redemption buy-sell agreement, life insurance premiums paid by the corporation on the lives of shareholders are deductible by the corporation.

    c. If the corporation is designated as the owner and irrevocable beneficiary of the life insurance policy used to fund the agreement, the death benefit from the policy should not be includible in the decedent shareholder's gross estate.

    d. In a partnership cross-purchase buy-sell agreement, the partnership purchases life insurance on the lives of each partner.

147. Life insurance purchased to fund a two-person partnership buy/sell agreement utilizing the entity method:

    a. Will be the same total amount as the amount under a cross-purchase plan.

    b. Will be paid for with tax-deductible dollars.

    c. Will be a greater amount than the total amount under a cross-purchase plan.

    d. Will be taxable as income to beneficiaries when received.

    e. Will benefit the partnership with a tax deduction for the premiums that are paid for by the partners.

148. A business that has a value of $1,200,000 has 4 partners. If each of the 4 partners buys a $100,000 life insurance policy on each of the other partners, this is an example of:

    a. A business insurance equity plan.

    b. An insurable interest plan.

    c. A cross-purchase plan.

    d. An entity plan.

    e. A key person plan.

149. The MAD2 partnership has 4 partners. The partners have entered into a binding buy/sell agreement that binds the surviving partners to purchase the partnership interest of the first partner to die. The partnership has chosen to use an entity approach to establish this agreement. How many life insurance policies are necessary to accomplish this agreement?

    a. 1.

    b. 3.

    c. 4.

    d. 8.

    e. 12.

150. MB Partnership is considering creating a buy-sell agreement wherein each partner purchases a life insurance policy on each of the other partners. Which of the following statements is/are correct given this information?

    1. The partners are entering into a cross-purchase buy-sell agreement.

    2. The partners are entering into an entity redemption buy-sell agreement.

    3. Upon the death of an owner, the life insurance proceeds will be used to buy out the decedent's share of the partnership. Those life insurance proceeds are taxable as ordinary income.

        a. 1 only.

        b. 3 only.

        c. 1 and 3 only.

        d. 2 and 3 only.

151. Sally dies during the current year holding a $200,000 note receivable. Which of the following items will not affect its valuation in her estate?

    a. The rate of interest.

    b. The borrower's financial health.

    c. The note is forgiven in the will.

    d. The maturity date.

    e. All of the above.

152. Mary Markert is the founder and 70% owner of the stock of MM Industries, a closely held corporation. She currently works full-time for the corporation and is responsible for all new product development. If Mary were to die, which of the following valuation discounts might her estate be able to claim?

    1. Minority discount.

    2. Blockage discount.

    3. Key personnel discount.

    4. Lack of marketability discount.

        a. 1 and 4.

        b. 3 and 4.

        c. 2 and 3.

        d. 1, 2, and 3.

        e. 2, 3, and 4.

153. In a typical family limited partnership:

    a. The owners of the closely held business transfer general partnership interests to the children or grandchildren.

    b. No discount is allowed on the gifts since the children's interest as a group will be more than 50%.

    c. The children receive limited partnership interests.

    d. The family limited partnership should be funded with assets that are not expected to appreciate.

THE MARITAL DEDUCTION

154. Which of the following qualify for the unlimited marital deduction?

   1. Outright bequest to resident alien spouse.

   2. Property passing to citizen spouse in QTIP.

   3. Income beneficiary of CRUT is a nonresident alien spouse (Trust is not a QDOT).

   4. Outright bequest to resident spouse who, prior to the decedent's death was a noncitizen, but who after the decedent's death and before the estate return was filed, became a US citizen.

      a. 2 only.

      b. 2 and 4.

      c. 2, 3, and 4.

      d. 3 and 4.

      e. 1, 2, 3, and 4.

155. Which of the following illustrate an exception to the terminable interest rule regarding property that qualifies for the marital deduction?

   1. An outright bequest of $100,000 to spouse with a condition that the spouse must survive decedent husband by 6 months and she dies within 3 months of spouse.

   2. An outright bequest of $100,000 to a spouse with a condition that the spouse must survive the decedent husband by 6 months and she lives three years.

   3. Spouse is the sole income beneficiary of a CRAT; charity is the remainderman.

   4. Spouse is the sole income beneficiary of a CRUT; charity is the remainderman.

      a. 2 only.

      b. 1 and 3.

      c. 1, 2, and 4.

      d. 2, 3, and 4.

      e. 1, 2, 3, and 4.

156. Which of the following statements regarding a qualified domestic trust (QDOT) is/are true?

   1. A QDOT would be appropriate when there has been a second marriage.

   2. At least one trustee of the QDOT must be a US Citizen.

   3. All income from the trust must be distributed to the surviving spouse each year.

   4. An election must be made by the decedent prior to death to treat the trust as a QDOT

      a. 1 and 2.

      b. 2 and 3.

      c. 1, 3 and 4.

      d. 2, 3 and 4.

      e. 1, 2, 3 and 4.

157. John, who had a gross estate valued at $3,000,000, died last month. His will created a bypass trust, and transferred assets equal to the applicable exclusion amount into the trust. Assets not transferred to the bypass trust were transferred to John's surviving spouse, Margaret. Which of the following statements is true?

    a.   John has overqualified his estate because of the bypass trust.

    b.   The assets transferred to the bypass trust will be eligible for the estate tax marital deduction.

    c.   Income from the bypass trust must be paid to Margaret each year for the remainder of her life.

    d.   The assets in the bypass trust will not be included in Margaret's gross estate upon her death.

    e.   Margaret will have a general power of appointment over property in the bypass trust.

158. Stan died recently, leaving his investment real estate to his 35-year old son, Oscar. Since Oscar is in the highest estate tax bracket, he executed a valid disclaimer over the real estate. Stan's will leaves all residual property to his spouse, Della. Which of the following statements regarding this arrangement is correct?

    a.   The investment real estate will qualify for the marital deduction.

    b.   Oscar has made a taxable gift to Della.

    c.   Oscar could retain the income from the investment real estate, while disclaiming the actual property.

    d.   The investment real estate will be included in Oscar's gross estate upon his death.

TRUSTS

159. A Marital Power of Appointment Trust:

    a. Cannot qualify for the federal estate tax marital deduction.

    b. Can be elected for the federal estate tax marital deduction.

    c. Qualifies automatically for the federal estate tax marital deduction provided the surviving spouse is a US citizen.

    d. Can qualify for the federal estate tax marital deduction only if the trust produces reasonable income that the trustee, at the trustee's discretion, decides to distribute.

    e. None of the above.

160. A springing power of attorney is:

    a. One which springs from a 1st agent to a 2nd agent after the 1st agent resigns.

    b. Springs back to the principal upon revocation.

    c. Springs into existence upon the incompetency of the principal.

    d. Authorizes only one of two named agents to act, depending upon the power to be exercised.

    e. None of the above.

161. Which type of charitable remainder trusts permit additional contributions to the trust after its inception?

    1. CRATs.

    2. CRUTs.

        a. 1 only.

        b. 2 only.

        c. 1 and 2.

        d. None of the above.

162. Which of the following charitable trusts allow investments in securities that are exempt from taxes?

    1. CRATs.

    2. CRUTs.

    3. Pooled income fund.

        a. 1 only.

        b. 2 only.

        c. 1 and 2.

        d. 1 and 3.

163. Which of the following charitable trusts allow sprinkling provisions?

 1. CRATs.
 2. CRUTs.
 3. Pooled income fund.

    a. 1 only.
    b. 2 only.
    c. 1 and 2.
    d. 2 and 3.
    e. 1, 2, and 3.

164. Which of the following charitable trusts allow both term certain for up to 20 years, and life annuities?

 1. CRATs.
 2. CRUTs.
 3. Pooled income funds.

    a. 1 only.
    b. 2 only.
    c. 1 and 2.
    d. 1, 2, and 3.

165. On January 15th, Glennon transfers property to a trust over which he retains a right to revoke one-fourth of the trust. The trust is to pay Connie 5% of the trust assets valued annually for her life with the remainder to be paid to a qualified charity. On September 1st, Glennon dies and the trust becomes irrevocable. Which of the following trusts does this qualify as?

    a. A CRAT.
    b. A CRUT.
    c. A pooled income fund.
    d. All of the above.
    e. None of the above.

166. On January 15th, Linval transfers property to a trust over which he retains a right to revoke one-fourth of the trust. The trust is to pay Desiree 5% of the trust assets valued annually for her life with the remainder to be paid to a qualified charity. On September 1st, Linval dies and the trust becomes irrevocable. Which of the following statements is/are correct?

    1. The trust is created January 15th.

    2. The trust is created when it becomes irrevocable on September 1st.

    3. Linval receives a charitable deduction equal to the present value of 25% of the remainder interest.

    4. Linval receives a charitable deduction equal to the present value of 75% of the remainder interest.

        a. 1 only.

        b. 1 and 2.

        c. 3 only.

        d. 3 and 4.

        e. None of the above.

167. Of the statements below regarding trusts, which is/are incorrect?

    1. A trust has only two parties: the grantor and the trustee.

    2. A revocable trust's assets pass through probate.

    3. A testamentary trust is created at the grantor's death.

    4. Asset management is a valid reason for creating a trust.

        a. 1 only.

        b. 2 and 4.

        c. 1 and 2.

        d. 3 and 4.

        e. 1, 2, 3, and 4.

168. What are the parties to a guardianship?

    1. The ward.

    2. The guardian.

    3. The state government.

    4. The federal government.

        a. 1 only.

        b. 1 and 2.

        c. 1, 2, and 3.

        d. 2 and 3.

        e. 1, 2, 3, and 4.

169. Which of the following charitable techniques allow the grantor/transferor to manage the transferred assets?

    1. CRATs.
    2. CRUTs.
    3. Pooled income fund.
        a. 1 only.
        b. 2 only.
        c. 3 only.
        d. 1 and 2.
        e. 1, 2, and 3.

170. Troy and Anne have the following in their combined estate. Assume that in 2007, Troy wants to set up the optional standard A B trust arrangement for himself, which of the following would be correct?

Troy separate property	$1,900,000
Anne separate property	$700,000
Community property	$1,600,000

	A Trust	B Trust
a.	$1,200,000	$1,500,000
b.	$2,000,000	$700,000
c.	$700,000	$2,000,000
d.	$2,100,000	$2,100,000

171. Which of the following statements regarding a Grantor Retained Annuity Trust (GRAT) is/are true?

    1. At the end of the GRAT term, a taxable gift will occur when the trust assets are transferred to the beneficiary.
    2. If the grantor dies during the trust term, a pro rata portion of the trust assets will be included in the grantor's estate.
    3. Interest and dividends earned by assets in a GRAT will be taxed to the grantor.
    4. If the grantor survives the trust term, none of the trust assets will be included in the grantor's gross estate.
        a. 1 and 4.
        b. 2 and 3.
        c. 3 and 4.
        d. 1, 2, and 4.
        e. 2, 3, and 4.

172. Which of the following statements regarding a Grantor Retained Annuity Trust (GRAT) is/are true?

1. When the trust is established, a taxable gift will occur based on the present value of the remainder interest of the trust assets.

2. The gift that occurs when the GRAT is created is eligible for the annual exclusion.

3. For estate planning purposes, a GRUT (Grantor Retained Unitrust) would be preferable to a GRAT if the assets in the trust are expected to appreciate in value.

4. The beneficiaries will not receive a step-up in basis of the trust property if the grantor survives the trust term.

    a. 1 and 4.
    b. 2 and 3.
    c. 3 and 4.
    d. 1, 2, and 4.
    e. 2, 3, and 4.

173. Which of the following statements regarding a Qualified Personal Residence Trust (QPRT) is/are true?

1. With a QPRT, the grantor must survive the trust term to realize any estate tax savings.

2. After the trust term, the house will revert back to the grantor.

3. The grantor will have a taxable gift upon the creation of the QPRT.

4. A QPRT is generally inappropriate for vacation homes.

    a. 1 only.
    b. 1 and 2.
    c. 1 and 3.
    d. 2 and 4.
    e. 2, 3, and 4.

174. Which statement below is true regarding charitable remainder trusts?

    a. The annuity payment received from a Charitable Remainder Annuity Trust (CRAT) will increase each year, providing a good hedge against inflation.

    b. The grantor who establishes a Charitable Remainder Unitrust (CRUT) will receive an income tax deduction in the year the trust is created.

    c. Payments received by the grantor from a CRAT or CRUT will be tax free to the grantor.

    d. The rule of perpetuities prevents a CRAT or CRUT from having a term greater than 21 years.

175. Which statement below is true regarding charitable trusts?

    a. A Charitable Lead Unitrust (CLUT) provides a periodic payment to the grantor that increases each year, provided that the assets in the trust appreciate in value.

    b. A grantor who transfers $1,000,000 to a Charitable Remainder Annuity Trust (CRAT), and receives a $40,000 annuity each year is entitled to an immediate income tax deduction.

    c. A Charitable Lead Annuity Trust (CLAT) provides a fixed-income stream to charity.

    d. Property that has appreciated significantly should generally not be transferred to a CRAT or CRUT.

176. Stacy is working with her estate planning attorney to devise methods to transfer assets to her children. She is very concerned about gift taxes, and is looking to find a way to transfer the assets without incurring gift taxes. Last year, she gifted a sufficient amount of property to fully utilize her applicable credit amount. Which of the following techniques, if used in the current year, will not result in a taxable gift to Stacy?

    a. Grantor Retained Annuity Trust (GRAT).

    b. Tangible Personal Property Trust.

    c. Qualified Personal Residence Trust (QPRT).

    d. Self-Canceling Installment Note (SCIN).

    e. Grantor Retained Unitrust (GRUT).

177. Which of the following techniques are generally implemented to lower an individual's gross estate?

    1. Family Limited Partnership.

    2. Totten Trust.

    3. Qualified Personal Residence Trust (QPRT).

    4. Irrevocable Life Insurance Trust.

        a. 1 and 3.

        b. 2 and 4.

        c. 1, 2, and 3.

        d. 1, 3, and 4.

        e. 2, 3, and 4.

178. Which of the following techniques are generally implemented to lower an individual's gross estate?

    1. Grantor Retained Annuity Trust (GRAT).

    2. Revocable Living Trust.

    3. Lifetime Gifting Program.

    4. Pay-on-Death Arrangements (POD).

        a. 1 and 3.

        b. 2 and 4.

        c. 1, 2, and 3.

        d. 1, 3, and 4.

        e. 2, 3, and 4.

OTHER LIFETIME TRANSFERS

179. John is 67 years old, and would like to transfer some of his assets to his adult son, Murray. John does not want to incur a gift tax liability, and also needs some cash flow, so he is considering selling the assets to his son. A friend recently informed John that a self-canceling installment note (SCIN) is a good planning strategy for many reasons. Which of the following statements regarding self-canceling installment notes (SCINs) is/are correct?

   1. To be effective, a SCIN must reflect a risk premium to compensate the seller for the possibility of cancellation.

   2. A seller who accepts a SCIN may accept security without jeopardizing the installment sale treatment.

   3. At the seller's death, the present value of any remaining SCIN balance is excluded from the seller's gross estate.

   4. A SCIN is a debt that ordinarily is extinguished at the seller's death.

   a. 1 only.

   b. 3 only.

   c. 1 and 3.

   d. 1, 2, and 3.

   e. 1, 2, 3, and 4.

180. Which of the following statements are false with respect to a bargain sale?

   1. The difference between the fair market value of the asset and the consideration received is considered a gift.

   2. The gift portion of a bargain sale will not qualify for the annual exclusion even if the gift is considered a completed, present-interest gift.

   3. A bargain sale is generally inappropriate if the buyer of the property is a family member.

   4. If the property is sold for more than the seller's basis in the property, a taxable gain will result.

   a. 1 only.

   b. 2 and 3.

   c. 3 and 4.

   d. 1 and 4.

   e. 1, 2, and 3.

181. Which of the following statements is correct regarding a family limited partnership?

   a. The general partnership interests will qualify for minority discounts.

   b. The transfer of the limited partnership interests to the junior family members is considered a future interest gift and is therefore not eligible for the gift tax annual exclusion.

   c. The transfer of the partnership interests to the junior family members may qualify for both a minority discount and a lack of marketability discount for gift tax purposes.

   d. After the transfer to the junior family members, the senior family member will relinquish control of the business in order to effectively remove the value of the business from his or her gross estate upon death.

---

182. Stan owns property with a basis of $50,000 and a current value of $140,000, which he sells to his son, Marvin, for $90,000. Which of the following statements is correct regarding this bargain sale arrangement?

    a. If Stan dies within three years of the bargain sale, the property will be included in his gross estate.

    b. Stan will have a taxable gain of $40,000 for income tax purposes.

    c. Stan will not be entitled to claim a gift tax annual exclusion on the gift portion of the bargain sale.

    d. Stan has made a gift of $90,000 to Marvin.

183. Rosanne sold some investment land to Harry, and unrelated individual, under the installment method for $500,000. She originally purchased the land for $100,000 six years ago. If Rosanne receives a $100,000 down payment this year from Harry, what will be the amount of the capital gain Rosanne must recognize as a result of the down payment?

    a. $0.

    b. $80,000.

    c. $125,000.

    d. $400,000.

184. Which of the following statements concerning installment sales of property is correct?

    a. An installment note must be unsecured if the seller wishes to avoid gift tax consequences.

    b. The seller will receive installment payments for the remainder of his or her life.

    c. The purchaser may receive an income tax deduction for interest paid to the buyer.

    d. If the seller dies within three years of the establishment of the installment sale, the property sold will be included in the seller's gross estate.

185. Leah had closely-held stock with a basis of $58,000 and a fair market value of $100,000. She sold the stock to her son, Rob, in exchange for a private annuity. Based upon Leah's life expectancy and IRS interest rates, the monthly annuity payment to be made by Rob is $800. Which of the following statements is correct?

    a. The annuity payments will continue to Leah's estate if she dies during her table life expectancy.

    b. Rob can claim an income tax deduction for the interest portion of the annuity payments made to Leah.

    c. The annuity payments received by Leah are taxed entirely as ordinary income.

    d. There will be no gift tax consequences to Leah as a result of this transaction.

186. Wendy Erwin would like to sell $3,000,000 of investment land to her cousin, Lisa. In return, Wendy would like to receive secured periodic payments for a period of 10 years. She does not want to pay gift tax on the transaction, would also like to ensure that nothing will be included in her gross estate if she dies before the 10 year period. Which of the following techniques would be most appropriate for Wendy?

    a.   Bargain sale.

    b.   Installment sale.

    c.   Self-cancelling instalment note.

    d.   Private annuity.

LIFE INSURANCE IN ESTATE PLANNING

187. Proceeds of a life insurance policy on the decedent's life payable to the decedent's estate are:

   a. Includible in the decedent's gross estate only if the premiums had been paid by the insured.

   b. Includible in the decedent's gross estate only if the policy was taken out within 3 years of the insured's death under the "contemplation of death" rule.

   c. Always includible in the decedent's gross estate.

   d. Never includible in the decedent's gross estate.

188. Which of the following would result in the inclusion of life insurance policy proceeds in the insured's gross estate?

   a. The insured is required to pay the monthly premiums.

   b. The insured is permitted to borrow against the policy.

   c. The insured transfers the policy to an Irrevocable Life Insurance Trust (ILIT), and dies five years later.

   d. The insured's spouse owns the policy.

   e. The death benefit is payable to the insured's son.

189. A buy/sell agreement was funded by a cross-purchase insurance arrangement. John bought a policy on Jack's life to finance the purchase of Jack's interest in the event of Jack's death. John, the beneficiary, paid the premiums and retained all incidents of ownership. On the death of Jack, the insurance proceeds will be:

   a. Includible in Jack's gross estate if Jack owns 50% or more of the stock of the corporation.

   b. Includible in Jack's gross estate only if Jack had purchased a similar policy on John's life at the same time and for the same purpose.

   c. Includible in Jack's gross estate if John has the right to veto Jack's power to borrow on the policy that Jack owns on John's life.

   d. Excludable from Jack's gross estate.

190. John, a terminally ill patient, transferred his $600,000 ($200,000 basis) life insurance policy to a viatical settlement provider for $350,000. Which of the following statements is/are true with respect to the life insurance transfer?

1. John will be subject to income tax on this transaction if he lives more than two years.

2. Regardless of how long John lives, he will be subject to income tax on $150,000, the difference between the amount received from the viatical company and John's basis in the policy.

3. If John dies within three years of the transfer, the entire $600,000 of life insurance proceeds on his life will be included in his gross estate.

4. The proceeds of the policy will be excluded from John's gross estate regardless of when he dies (assuming the proceeds were consumed during life).

    a. 1 only.

    b. 4 only.

    c. 1 and 3 only.

    d. 2 and 4 only.

    e. 1, 2, and 3 only.

THE GENERATION-SKIPPING TRANSFER TAX (GSTT)

191. The generation-skipping transfer tax is imposed:

    a. Instead of the gift tax.

    b. Instead of the estate tax.

    c. As a separate tax in addition to the gift and estate taxes.

    d. On transfers of future interest to beneficiaries who are more than one generation above the donor's generation.

192. Which of the following is subject to the generation-skipping transfer tax?

    a. Vicki wrote her will in 1985 establishing a generation-skipping trust. Her will was unchanged when she died on December 31, 1986.

    b. Orion wrote his will in 1970, but amended it in 1984 to add a generation-skipping trust. Orion was permanently mentally incompetent from December 1986 until his death in July 1996.

    c. Bill wrote a will in July 1986 that established a generation-skipping trust. He made no changes in his will before his July 1996 death.

    d. In 1984, Thad established a generation-skipping trust as a gift for the benefit of his grandchildren. The irrevocable trust was unchanged, and no corpus was added prior to his death in 1996.

    e. None of the above are subject to GSTT.

193. Which of the following is a correct statement about what a generation-skipping transfer tax applies to?

    a. A taxable termination only.

    b. A taxable distribution only.

    c. A taxable termination or a taxable distribution, but not a direct skip.

    d. A taxable termination, a taxable distribution, or a direct skip.

    e. None of the above.

194. James (age 63) established a trust and named his wife, Carol, (age 40) as income beneficiary for 20 years. After 20 years, James' son, Bill, (age 30) and nephew, Bob, (age 22) are to receive lifetime income interests. After the death of both Bill and Bob, the remainder passes equally to James' granddaughter, Allison, (age 20) and great-grandson, Michael, (age 1). How many younger generations are there in this trust arrangement?

    a. 4.

    b. 3.

    c. 2.

    d. 1.

    e. 0.

195. James (age 63) established a trust and named his wife, Carol, (age 40) as income beneficiary for 20 years. After 20 years, James' son, Bill, (age 30) and nephew, Bob, (age 22) are to receive lifetime income interests. After the death of both Bill and Bob, the remainder passes equally to James' granddaughter Allison (age 20) and great-grandson Michael (age 1). Assume Bill died 22 years after the trust was established, and Bob died 34 years after the trust was established. Assuming both Allison and Michael were alive when Bob died, how many times is the generation-skipping transfer tax levied?

    a. Never.

    b. Once.

    c. Twice.

    d. Three times.

    e. Four times.

196. Julie, age 53 years exactly, wants to provide for the financial security of her secretary, Carolyn, and other unrelated friends. She establishes a trust. Carolyn, age 66, will receive income from the trust for her life. Upon Carolyn's death, Abe, another friend who is currently 58, will receive income for his lifetime. Upon his death, the remainder interest will be divided equally between Peter (age 36) and Jimmy (age 40). How many times will this trust be subject to a GSTT?

    a. None. No GSTT will be assessed.

    b. One.

    c. Two.

    d. Three.

    e. Four.

197. For the year 2007, $2,000,000 is the:

    a. Aggregate lifetime exemption from gift tax, for annual exclusion of gifts.

    b. Applicable credit amount.

    c. GSTT aggregate, lifetime exemption.

    d. Maximum marital deduction for non-QTIP transfers.

    e. None of the above.

198. Which of the following types of transfers are subject to the GSTT?

    1. Direct skips.

    2. Taxable terminations.

    3. Taxable distributions.

    a. 1 only.

    b. 1 and 2.

    c. 1 and 3.

    d. 2 and 3.

    e. 1, 2, and 3.

199. Who among the following would be skip persons for purposes of the GSTT? Bill is the transferor and is 82 years old.

    1. John, the grandson of Bill whose mother, Donna, is living but whose father, Frank, is deceased. (Frank is Bill's son).

    2. Mary is the great-grandchild of Bill. Both Mary's parents and grandparents are living.

    3. Hazel is the 21-year-old wife of Bill's second son, Mike, age 65.

        a. John only (1 only).

        b. Mary only (2 only).

        c. John and Mary (1 and 2).

        d. Mary and Hazel (2 and 3).

        e. John, Mary, and Hazel (1, 2, and 3).

200. Which of the following statements is/are correct regarding the GSTT for the year 2007?

    1. The annual exclusion is allowed.

    2. Gift splitting is permitted.

    3. Qualified transfers are excluded from GSTT.

    4. Each person is allowed a $2,000,000 lifetime exemption against all skips.

        a. 1 and 4.

        b. 1, 2, and 4.

        c. 1, 2, and 3.

        d. 1, 3, and 4.

        e. 1, 2, 3, and 4.

201. Connie dies insured by a $2,000,000 life insurance policy that her husband, Glennon, owns. Their daughter, Lexie, is the named beneficiary. What are the tax consequences?

        a. Lexie and Glennon would be subject to estate tax liability on the life insurance proceeds.

        b. Connie's estate would be subject to federal income tax liability on the life insurance proceeds.

        c. Glennon would be subject to gift tax liability on the life insurance proceeds.

        d. Lexie would be subject to gift tax liability on the life insurance proceeds.

202. John owns a small business worth $1.2 million. How should life insurance be held if John is trying to benefit his minor grandson with the insurance policy?

        a. John should be the owner.

        b. John's spouse should be the owner.

        c. The grandson should be the owner.

        d. An irrevocable trust should be set up with the grandchild as beneficiary.

        e. A revocable life insurance trust should be established for the grandchild.

203. Which of the following gifts made by Wes, age 60, is subject to the generation-skipping transfer tax?

 a. $10,000 to his grandson.

 b. $100,000 to niece, age 6.

 c. Payment of law school tuition for granddaughter, paid directly to institution.

 d. $100,000 to daughter (age 6) of his college roommate.

SPECIAL PROVISIONS FOR SMALL BUSINESS, FARMS, ILLIQUID ESTATES

204. George's father died recently and left his farm to George. If the father's adjusted gross estate is $2,000,000, what would be the minimum adjusted value of the farm to qualify for special-use valuation?

     a. $500,000.

     b. $700,000.

     c. $1,000,000.

     d. $1,500,000.

     e. $2,000,000

205. Mary Elizabeth, a closely-held business owner, died recently of a long illness. After reviewing her estate tax information, you ascertain the following:

Adjusted gross estate:	$750,000
Value of closely-held stock:	400,000
Admin. and funeral expenses:	50,000
Federal estate taxes due:	70,000
Debts of the decedent:	90,000

What amount of closely held corporate stock can be redeemed under IRC Sec. 303 so that the redemption will be treated as a disposition of an asset rather than receipt of a dividend?

     a. $0; the estate does not qualify under Section 303.

     b. $70,000

     c. $120,000

     d. $210,000

     e. $400,000

206. Which one of the following is true regarding Section 6166 deferral of estate taxes?

     a. To qualify, the value of the closely-held business must comprise at least 50% of the decedent's adjusted gross estate

     b. Under section 6166, estate tax is delayed for 5 years and then paid over 5 equal annual installments.

     c. Interest on the deferred tax is calculated based on the fed funds rate.

     d. The deferred tax will be accelerated if the heirs dispose of the business interest.

POSTMORTEM PLANNING

207. With regard to the federal estate tax, the alternate valuation date:

    a. Is required to be used if the fair market value of the estate's assets has increased since the decedent's date of death.

    b. If elected on the first return filed for the estate, may be revoked in an amended return provided that the first return was filed on time.

    c. Must be used for valuation of the estate's liabilities if such date is used for valuation of the estate's assets.

    d. Can be elected only if it decreases the value of the gross estate as well as the estate tax liability.

208. Mr. Blue died on July 10th. The assets in his estate were valued on his date of death and on an alternate valuation date, respectively, as follows:

Asset	Date-of-Death Valuation	Alternate Valuation
Residence	$300,000	$350,000
Common Stock	$1,800,000	$1,850,000
Municipal Bonds	$180,000	$90,000
Patent	$80,000	$65,000

The patent had 8 years of life remaining at the time of Mr. Blue's death. The executor sold the residence on August 1st for $325,000. If Mr. Blue's executor properly elects the alternate valuation date method, what is the value of Mr. Blue's gross estate?

    a. $2,340,000.

    b. $2,345,000.

    c. $2,355,000.

    d. $2,360,000.

    e. $2,370,000.

209. Ordinary and necessary administration expenses paid by the executor of an estate are deductible:

    a. Only on the fiduciary income tax return (Form 1041) and never on the federal estate tax return (Form 706).

    b. Only on the federal estate tax return and never on the fiduciary income tax return.

    c. On the fiduciary income tax return only if the estate tax deduction is waived for these expenses.

    d. On both the fiduciary income tax return and on the estate tax return by adding a tax computed on the proportionate rates attributable to both returns.

210. Upon the death of the grantor of a revocable or living trust, the trust assets receive:

    a. A carryover basis with capital gains tax consequences but no estate tax consequences.

    b. A carryover basis with no capital gains tax consequences but with estate tax consequences.

    c. A step to FMV basis with no capital gain or loss tax consequences but with estate tax consequences.

    d. A step to FMV basis with capital gain or loss tax consequences but with no estate tax consequences.

    e. A step to FMV basis with capital gain or loss tax consequences and estate tax consequences.

211. If the executor of a decedent's estate elects the alternate valuation date, and none of the property included in the gross estate has been sold or distributed, the estate assets must be valued as of how many months after the decedent's death?

    a. 3.

    b. 6.

    c. 9.

    d. 12.

212. Section 6166 contains provisions for extending the time for paying estate taxes when the estate consists largely of an interest in a closely held business. An interest in a closely held business could include:

    1. An interest as a proprietorship in a business carried on as a proprietorship.

    2. An interest in a partnership carrying on a trade or business if 20% or more of the capital interest in such partnership is included in the gross estate or there are less than or equal to 45 partners.

    3. Stock in a corporation carrying on a trade or business if 20% or more in value of the voting stock of such corporation is included in the gross estate or there are less than or equal to 45 shareholders.

    4. Stock in an S corporation carrying on a trade or business if 15% or more of the value of the voting stock of such corporation is included in the gross estate or there are less than or equal to 100 shareholders.

    a. 1 only.

    b. 1 and 2.

    c. 2, 3, and 4.

    d. 1, 2, and 3.

    e. 1, 2, 3, and 4.

213. Which of the following statements correctly reflects the rules applicable to the alternate valuation date?

1. The general rule is the election covers all assets included in the gross estate and cannot be applied to only a portion of the property.

2. Assets disposed of within six months of decedent's death must be valued on the date of disposition.

3. The election can be made even though an estate tax return does not have to be filed.

4. The election must decrease the value of the gross estate and decrease the estate tax liability.

    a. 1 only.

    b. 2 and 4.

    c. 1 and 2.

    d. 1, 2, and 4.

    e. 1, 2, 3, and 4.

214. Which of the following is/are correct regarding disclaimers?

1. Must be in writing.

2. Disclaiming party could not have previously benefited from interest.

3. Must be disclaimed within 9 months of interest creation.

4. Disclaiming party cannot direct the interest to other parties.

    a. 1 only.

    b. 2 only.

    c. 1 and 2.

    d. 1, 2, and 4.

    e. 1, 2, 3, and 4.

215. A Section 6166 election to pay federal estate taxes on an installment basis includes or permits:

1. An executor to pay the federal estate tax, but not the generation-skipping transfer tax which corresponds to a decedent's interest in a closely held business in installments over a period not extending beyond 12 years.

2. Payments during the first four years may be for interest only on unpaid federal estate tax including GSTT tax.

3. The value of a decedent's closely held business must exceed 35% of the value of a decedent's adjusted gross estate both inclusive and exclusive of transfers made within three years of the decedent's death.

4. Multiple businesses may not be aggregated for determining the minimum percentage that qualifies as a closely held business.

    a. 1 only.

    b. 2 only.

    c. 2 and 3.

    d. 1, 2, and 3.

    e. 1, 2, 3, and 4.

216. Joe dies owning a closely held business (a proprietorship). The total business is valued at $350,000, the real estate in the business is valued at $250,000, and Joe's total adjusted gross estate is $900,000. Which of the following postmortem provisions can Joe's executor elect?

    a. Section 2032A.

    b. Section 6166.

    c. Section 303.

    d. Section 2057.

    e. The executor can elect all of the above.

217. Assuming the following facts about Davidson Corporation's annual dividend:

Date declared	June 5th
Ex-dividend	August 7th
Dates of record	August 15th
Date of payment	September 1st

Which of the following statements is/are true about the treatment of the Davidson dividend with respect to the Federal Form 706?

    1. If the decedent dies on June 15th, the dividend should be ignored for purposes of the 706.

    2. If the decedent dies on August 12th, the dividend should be simply added to the date-of-death stock price.

    3. If the decedent dies on August 28th, the dividend should be accrued and listed separately on the 706.

    4. If the decedent dies after September 1st, the dividend should be ignored for purposes of the stocks and bonds section of the 706.

        a. 1 and 4.

        b. 2 and 3.

        c. 1, 2, and 3.

        d. 1, 3, and 4.

        e. All of the above are true.

218. George dies and leaves his son, Jeb, a farm. At its current use, the farm is worth $1,400,000. The FMV at highest and best use is $2,000,000. If George's executor elects Section 2032A, which of the following statements is <u>not</u> true?

    a. The farm will be valued at $1,400,000 in the estate.

    b. Recapture only occurs if Jeb sells the farm within the next ten years.

    c. If recapture occurs, Jeb, and not the estate, is liable for the tax.

    d. If the election is made, the payment of estate tax can be deferred for five years.

219. Special-use valuation is available for real property if certain requirements are met. Which of the following is <u>not</u> a requirement of special-use valuation?

    a. The decedent must have been a US citizen or resident.

    b. The real property must pass to a qualified heir.

    c. Either the decedent or a family member must have owned and used the property as a farm or business for at least two of the six years immediately prior to the decedent's death.

    d. The combined value of the real and personal property of the farm or closely held business must be at least 50% of the gross estate less certain expenses.

220. If Steve dies and leaves his second wife the right to use their residence for the rest of her life, will it qualify as qualified terminable interest property (QTIP)?

    a. No, because the residence was not left in a trust.

    b. No, because the interest is a terminable interest.

    c. Yes, if the executor makes the QTIP election.

    d. Yes, but only if she has a general power to appoint the residence at her death.

ESTATE TAX REDUCTIONS TECHNIQUES

---

221. Which of the following is/are appropriate estate tax reduction techniques?

1. Overqualifying the estate.

2. Utilizing Totten Trusts.

3. Transferring a client's business to a Grantor Retained Annuity Trust.

4. Transferring a decedent's personal residence to a revocable living trust.

    a. 3 only.

    b. 1 and 3.

    c. 2 and 4.

    d. 1, 2 and 4.

    e. 1, 2, 3 and 4.

222. Which of the following statements concerning estate reduction techniques is (are) correct?

1. An irrevocable trust with Crummey powers may be effective in reducing estate taxes while providing benefits to family members, even if the trust corpus consists of assets other than life insurance.

2. A Qualified Domestic Trust is an appropriate estate planning technique when the decedent has children from a prior marriage.

3. A principal residence transferred to a Qualified Personal Residence trust will be excluded from the grantor's gross estate if the grantor survives the trust term.

4. Gifts of tuition for grandchildren are effective in reducing a grandparent's gross estate and do not reduce the grandparent's available annual exclusions if the tuition payments are made directly to the school.

    a. 3 only.

    b. 1 and 3.

    c. 2 and 4.

    d. 1, 3, and 4.

    e. 1, 2, 3, and 4

COMMON ESTATE PLANNING MISTAKES

223. Which of the following is/are common estate planning mistakes?

    1. Failure to plan for incapacity.

    2. Having an out-of-date Will.

    3. Improper ownership of life insurance policy.

    4. Failure to take advantage of intestacy laws.

        a. 3 only.

        b. 1 and 3.

        c. 2 and 4.

        d. 1, 2, and 3.

        e. 1, 2, 3, and 4.

        f. 1, 2, 3, and 4.

224. Steven is a 64-year-old unmarried individual who is currently employed by ABC Company, a publicly-traded company. He has a son, Robby, and a daughter, Becky. Robby and Becky have different mothers. Steven's most recent Will was created 10 years ago, when he was married to Becky's mother. He has no other estate planning documents.

Steven has the following assets:

— $20,000 savings account, with his daughter Becky named as Pay-on-death beneficiary.

— $250,000 life Insurance policy on his life. Steven's estate is the beneficiary.

— $350,000 personal residence owned as joint tenants with rights of survivorship (JTWROS) with his son Robby.

— $650,000 investment portfolio owned by a revocable living trust. Steven is the trustee and Robby is the beneficiary.

— $800,000 of stock in ABC Company, Steven's employer. The stock is NOT held within a qualified plan.

— $650,000 401(k) plan from ABC Company. Steven's cousin, Bob, is the beneficiary.

Assuming Steven has no desire to leave any assets to his former spouses at his death, which of the following is/are weaknesses of Steven's estate plan?

    1. Failure to avoid probate.

    2. Inappropriate planning for incapacity.

    3. Failure to establish a qualified terminable interest property trust (QTIP) trust upon his death.

    4. Failure to have a buy-sell agreement in place for the sale of the ABC Company stock.

    5. Failure to provide equity of inheritance to his children.

        a. 3 and 4.

        b. 3, 4, and 4.

        c. 1, 2, and 5.

        d. 1, 2, 4, and 5.

        e. 1, 2, 3, 4, and 5.

225. Sonny died with an estate worth $4,000,000. He had a simple Will, which left everything he owned to his wife, Bonny, a US citizen. Which of the following statements is/are correct regarding this arrangement?

    1. At Sonny's death his estate will owe no estate tax.

    2. Bonny must include the entire $4,000,000 (plus appreciation) in her gross estate upon her subsequent death.

    3. Sonny has failed to take advantage of his applicable credit amount

    4. Sonny has underqualified his estate.

        a. 1 and 4.

        b. 1, 2, and 3.

        c. 2, 3, and 4.

        d. 1, 2, 3, and 4.

226. Steven currently has an estate worth $3,000,000. He is concerned about possible underqualification of his estate, and would like to do some estate planning. Which of the following independent strategies would possibly result in the underqualification of Steven's estate?

    a. Bequeath his entire estate to a trust, giving his surviving spouse a general power of appointment.

    b. Bequeath the applicable exclusion amount to his surviving spouse, and the remainder of his estate to a qualified terminable interest property trust.

    c. Bequeath his entire estate to a qualified terminable interest property trust for the benefit of his surviving spouse and his children from a previous marriage.

    d. Bequeath his entire estate to a bypass trust, giving his surviving spouse the right to the income from the trust for the remainder of her life.

227. Which of the following statements is correct regarding estate planning with the marital deduction?

    a. If underqualification occurs, the decedent has wasted some of his or her applicable credit amount.

    b. If overqualification occurs, more property could have been left to the surviving spouse tax free than was actually left to the surviving spouse by the decedent.

    c. A bypass trust could be used to take advantage of the applicable credit at the first death, thereby preventing the overqualification of the estate.

    d. If a bequest to a surviving spouse qualifies for the marital deduction, the bequeathed assets will be excluded from the estate of the surviving spouse upon his or her subsequent death.

ESTATE PLANNING

Solutions

Estate Planning

ANSWER SUMMARY

1. e	26. d	51. b	76. c	101. d	126. c	151. c	176. d	201. c	226. d
2. e	27. b	52. b	77. c	102. b	127. e	152. b	177. d	202. d	227. c
3. c	28. e	53. a	78. d	103. b	128. d	153. c	178. a	203. d	
4. c	29. b	54. c	79. b	104. e	129. c	154. b	179. c	204. c	
5. d	30. e	55. b	80. c	105. b	130. a	155. d	180. b	205. c	
6. e	31. e	56. d	81. b	106. c	131. d	156. b	181. c	206. d	
7. e	32. c	57. c	82. d	107. d	132. b	157. d	182. b	207. d	
8. d	33. d	58. b	83. a	108. e	133. d	158. a	183. b	208. b	
9. d	34. e	59. d	84. b	109. e	134. e	159. c	184. c	209. c	
10. b	35. d	60. b	85. c	110. e	135. a	160. c	185. d	210. c	
11. d	36. e	61. b	86. e	111. c	136. e	161. b	186. c	211. b	
12. e	37. c	62. e	87. a	112. c	137. d	162. c	187. c	212. d	
13. b	38. b	63. e	88. d	113. b	138. d	163. c	188. b	213. d	
14. b	39. a	64. d	89. d	114. c	139. c	164. c	189. d	214. e	
15. e	40. c	65. b	90. b	115. d	140. c	165. e	190. b	215. c	
16. e	41. c	66. d	91. e	116. b	141. a	166. a	191. c	216. b	
17. c	42. a	67. e	92. b	117. b	142. d	167. c	192. c	217. e	
18. b	43. d	68. b	93. e	118. e	143. a	168. c	193. d	218. b	
19. a	44. b	69. c	94. b	119. c	144. b	169. d	194. b	219. c	
20. d	45. c	70. b	95. a	120. a	145. a	170. c	195. b	220. c	
21. b	46. d	71. a	96. b	121. e	146. c	171. c	196. a	221. a	
22. c	47. a	72. b	97. b	122. d	147. a	172. a	197. c	222. d	
23. d	48. e	73. e	98. c	123. d	148. c	173. c	198. e	223. d	
24. b	49. d	74. c	99. d	124. c	149. c	174. b	199. b	224. c	
25. d	50. c	75. b	100. a	125. d	150. a	175. c	200. e	225. b	

BASIC CONCEPTS

Estate Planning

1. e

   All are incorporated in the definition of estate planning.

Estates

2. e

   All of those persons have need for a will, a plan for incapacity, and a need to care for persons or dogs.

Estates

3. c

   The establishment of priorities occurs after the definition of problem areas.

Benefits of Estate Planning

4. c

   The main benefit of estate planning is to insure property passes to intended persons.

BASIC DOCUMENTS INCLUDED IN AN ESTATE PLAN

Incapacity

5. d

All of the arrangements are methods of providing for incapacity.

Estate Pitfalls

6. e

All of the items are potential problems:

Ancillary probate indicates the estate owns property outside the decedent's state of domicile and may cause excessive costs and delays. Joint tenancies with rights of survivorship and trust arrangements are methods used to avoid ancilliary probate.

The rule against perpetuities may void some trust arrangements.

A will that includes funeral instructions may be lost or not reviewed until sometime following the decedent's death, thus resulting in the funeral instructions not being carried out.

Attempts to disinherit spouses and/or minor children are usually limited by state probate statutes. An attorney should be consulted in all such cases.

Estate Planning Documents

7. e

All are important and common provisions in a well-drafted will.

Estate Documents

8. d

Statement 1 is incorrect. A durable power of attorney does not always substitute for a living will because in many states a specific statute governs living wills, and unless the durable power meets that specific language, it will not be a valid living will. The other Statements (2-4) are correct.

Estate Documents

9. d

A durable power of attorney does not survive the death of the principal. The rest of the statements (1, 3, and 4) are correct.

Basic Documents

10. b

She should not gift; she may need the money. She is single and under the applicable exclusion amount, therefore, has no need for an ABC trust arrangement.

General Power of Appointment

11. d

This is a general power of appointment. Statements 1, 2, and 4 are correct. Statement 3 is incorrect; she can appoint for any reason and to any person.

Durable Powers (CFP® Certification Examination, released 12/96)

12. e

Statement 1 is inappropriate, may create other legal problems, and will not accomplish what is intended. Statement 2 is appropriate due to her declining health. Statement 3 is inappropriate due to the irrevocability and her need to have access to the assets during incapacity. Statement 4 is inappropriate because it is unnecessary. She is well below the estate tax applicable exclusion amount of $2,000,000 (for 2007).

Powers of Attorney

13. b

A durable power of attorney for health care appoints a surrogate decision-maker for health care decisions only. It covers more potential situations than a living will. However, a living will is still an important estate planning tool because not all states allow the holder of the power to make a decision to terminate the life of the principal, whereas a living will does cover that situation. It has no effect on gross estate valuation, nor does it provide for management of assets upon incapacity.

OWNERSHIP OF PROPERTY AND HOW IT IS TRANSFERRED

Estate Planning for Nontraditional Relationships

14. **b**

The question asks which is least appropriate. Intestate probate is probate without a will. In instances where the individuals are not blood related, they would be unlikely to receive anything in an intestate probate.

Estate Planning for Nontraditional Relationships

15. **e**

None of the above will accomplish transfers between these parties. Statements 1 and 2 go through probate. Since there is no will, the probate estate will follow intestate distribution rules. Thus it is unlikely either would inherit from the other. Statements 3 and 4 are only available to married spouses. Joint tenancy with the right of survivorship would be a good option.

Estate Planning for Nontraditional Relationships

16. **e**

Statement 1 is incorrect because tenancy by the entirety is only available to married couples. Statements 2, 3, and 4 are all good planning suggestions.

Property

17. **c**

Community property and tenancy by the entirety can only be entered into by spouses. Joint tenancy (JTWROS) is often used by spouses to avoid probate but is not limited to spouses.

Estate Planning for Nontraditional Relationships

18. **b**

Statement 1 is correct because the marital deduction only applies to married couples, not cohabitants. Statement 2 is incorrect because the annual exclusion will be available on gifts from Steve to Susan, provided that the gifts are present-interest gifts. Statement 3 is incorrect because the marital deduction can only be taken if the couple is married. Statement 4 is correct because unmarried cohabitants have little (or no) intestacy rights.

Property

19. **a**

Only Statement 1 is correct. Anyone may establish a joint tenancy. Only <u>half</u> the value in a spousal joint tenancy is deemed included in the estate of the first spouse to die. Community property is not joint property. The first spouse to die can generally transfer his share of community to anyone he selects. Unlike a joint tenancy, in community property there is no survivorship transfer to the surviving spouse although some community property states have modified this rule by statute.

Property

20. d

Statement 3 is incorrect because the property will automatically pass to the surviving tenants by operation of law, regardless of the decedent's will. All other statements are correct.

Property

21. b

Statement 3 is incorrect because community property does not avoid probate. There are no rights of survivorship with community property. Statement 4 is incorrect because assets acquired before marriage remain separate property. Statements 1 and 2 are correct statements.

Property Interest

22. c

Only Tenants by the Entirety is an ownership form exclusive to married couples. Tenants by Marriage is not a form of ownership.

Property Interest

23. d

If a couple moves from a common law state to a community property state, separate property will generally remain separate property. Option (a) is incorrect because there is no such election. Option (b) is incorrect because community property does not have survivorship rights. Option (c) is incorrect because separate property generally retains its character as separate property after a move to a community property state.

Property Interest

24. b

Statement 1 is correct, because property acquired by one spouse as a gift is separate property. Therefore, Statement 2 is incorrect. Statement 3 is correct. Since the property is separate property, the business interest transferred to Chris would be fully includible in his gross estate. Statement 4 is incorrect because the 100% step-up rule only applies to community property.

25. d

The land will be included in Stephen's gross estate based on the percentage-of-contribution rule. Since Stephen contributed the entire purchase price of the land, the entire value of the land will be included in his gross estate at the time of death.

26. d

The land will be included in Stephen's gross estate based on the percentage-of-contribution rule. Since Stephen contributed the entire purchase price of the land, the entire value of the land will be included in his gross estate at the time of death.

Since Stephen must include the entire value of the land in his gross estate, the entire value of the land will receive a step-up in basis. Therefore, the daughter's basis will be equal to the full date of death value.

27. **b**

A is incorrect. The property will not receive a full step-up in basis at the first spouse's death. Only the portion of the property included in the decedent's gross estate will be eligible for a step-up in basis.

C is incorrect. Joint tenants have the right to sever the interest in property without the consent of the joint tenant.

D is correct. When the first spouse dies, the property included in the decedent spouse's gross estate will be eligible for the estate tax marital deduction.

THE PROBATE PROCESS

Probate

28. e

All are examples of property that passes through probate.

Probate

29. b

Only Statement 4 is true.

Probate

30. e

1 is correct. Life insurance with a named beneficiary passes by contract at death, thus avoiding probate.

2 is correct. A payable-on death (P.O.D) bank account passes by contract at death, thus avoiding probate.

3 is correct. Trusts, both revocable and irrevocable, created during life avoid probate because they have a named beneficiary.

4 is correct. Assets titled joint tenancy with rights of survivorship (JTWROS) pass by operation of law, thus avoiding probate.

Probate

31. e

All of the statements are correct.

Probate

32. c

1 is correct. Property held in fee simple is property owned outright by the decedent. This property can be passed by will, or pass via the state's intestate laws. In either case, the property will pass through probate.

2 is incorrect. Life insurance with a named beneficiary passes by contract at death, thus avoiding probate.

3 is correct. Property owned as tenants in common can be passed by will, or pass via the state's intestate laws. In either case, the property will pass through probate.

4 is incorrect. Retirement plans avoid probate because they pass by contract.

Probate

33. d

Clear title to heirs and legatees is not a disadvantage; it is an advantage of probate.

Probate

34. e

All are substitutes for the probate process. Revocable living trusts become irrevocable at death of the grantor.

Probate

35. d

The stamp collection owned joint tenants with rights of survivorship (JTWROS) avoids probate.

Probate

36. e

Payable-on-death (POD) and transfer-on-death (TOD) arrangements pass by contract at death, thus avoiding probate.

Property held JTWROS passes by operation of law, thus avoiding probate.

Life insurance with a named beneficiary passes by contract, thus avoiding probate.

FEDERAL GIFT AND ESTATE TAXATION

Applicable Credit Amount

37. c

The applicable credit amount (previously known as the unified credit) can be used to reduce or eliminate estate or gift tax liability. For 2007, the applicable credit amount is $345,800 for gift tax and $780,800 for estate tax.

Statement 1 is incorrect. A gift to a citizen spouse is eligible for the unlimited marital deduction. Therefore, there will be no estate or gift tax liability.

Statement 2 is correct. Lifetime gifts to children may result in gift tax liability. This liability can be reduced or eliminated by the applicable credit amount.

Statement 3 is correct. Testamentary (after-death) transfers to friends may result in estate tax liability. This liability can be reduced or eliminated by the applicable credit amount.

Statement 4 is incorrect. A gift or testamentary bequest to a public charity is eligible for the unlimited charitable deduction. Therefore, there will be no gift or estate tax liability.

Annual Exclusion

38. b

B is correct. The annual exclusion is allowed for lifetime gifts, but not for bequests.

A is incorrect. A larger applicable credit amount is allowed for estate tax purposes than for gift tax purposes.

C is incorrect. Although the charitable deduction is available for gifts given to a qualified charity, it is also available for bequests to qualified charities. Therefore, it is not an advantage of lifetime gifting over bequests.

D is incorrect. A QDOT can only be used for assets transferred to a non-US citizen spouse at death.

THE FEDERAL GIFT TAX

Gifts

39. a

($205,000 current gifts − 48,000 annual exclusion) ÷ 2 = $78,500 each. When gifts are split, all gifts for that year must be split. "Taxable gifts" is a term of art meaning a gift, net of the annual exclusion, gift splitting, the marital deduction, and the charitable deduction. The two donees allow for $48,000 in annual exclusions (for 2007).

Gifts

40. c

By reserving the right to revoke, the individual has not completed the gift in Statement 3.

Statement 4 does constitute a complete gift under the gift tax statutes. However, taxes would not be payable due to the unlimited gift tax marital deduction.

Gifts

41. c

There is not a gift until the account is drawn on by the donee for donee's own benefit. If Jeff died, Kim would receive the proceeds of the account by operational law, not by gift.

Gifts

42. a

Statement 1 is incorrect because it is not a gift; it is legal support and is not subject to gift tax.

Statement 2 is incorrect. Payment of tuition directly to an educational institution is a qualified transfer that is not subject to gift tax.

Statement 3 is incorrect. Payment of medical expenses directly to the provider is a qualified transfer that is not subject to gift tax.

Gifts

43. d

Payments for medical expenses are qualified transfers only if made directly to the medical provider.

Gifts

44. b

Note that the question asks for gross, not taxable gifts. The interest in Statement 4 is not a gift because the loan is less than $10,000 and, therefore, meets one of the exceptions to the imputed interest rule.

$40,000 + 33,000 + 14,000 = $87,000.

Gifts

45. c

Since gain property was gifted, the gift tax paid is allocated to the recipient's basis.

Rosario's basis	$12,000
FMV at date of gift	$20,000
Donee's basis before gift tax	$12,000 (donor's basis)
Gift tax paid	$5,100
($8,000 ÷ $8,000*) × $5,000 =	$2,000 gift tax allocated to basis
Donee's basis: $12,000 + $5,000 =	$17,000

* $20,000 FMV – $12,000 annual exclusion amount. If the annual exclusion was unavailable, then the calculation would have been $8,000 ÷ $20,000 × $5,000 = $2,000. The Donee's basis would have them been $12,000 + $2,000 = $14,000.

Gifts

46. d

Donee	FMV	Annual Exclusion	Taxable Gifts
Nephew	$12,000	($12,000)	0
Niece	$8,000	($8,000)	0
Friend	$20,000	($12,000)	$8,000
Father	$60,000	($12,000)	$48,000
Niece	$18,000	$0	$18,000
Total	$118,000	($41,000)	$74,000

The gift of a remainder interest in a trust is a future interest gift and is not eligible for the annual exclusion.

Gifts

47. a

1. Payment directly to hospital is a qualified transfer, not a gift.

2. Generally, support payments to a parent are not a legal obligation and, therefore, will be treated as a gift. $19,000 to her mother is reduced by $12,000, therefore, taxable gift, is: $7,000

3. $15,000 to Mike is reduced by $12,000, therefore, taxable gift is: $3,000

4. The loan is less than $100,000; and the borrower's net investment income is less than $1,000, so there is no imputed interest income/expense. Consequently, since there is no imputed interest, there is no taxable gift.

   Taxable Gifts $10,000

Gifts

48. e

The question asks for exclusions and deductions:

	Total		Exclusions/ Deductions		Taxable Gift	Reason
1.	$20,000	–	$12,000	=	$8,000	Annual exclusion for 2007
2.	$60,000	–	$60,000	=	$0	Unlimited gifts to spouse
3.	$15,000	–	$12,000	=	$3,000	Annual exclusion for 2007
4.	$100,000	–	$100,000	=	$0	Charitable gift
	Total		$184,000		$11,000	

Gifts

49. d

The necklace would be a taxable gift. Since John was not married at the time of the gift, he cannot take advantage of the marital deduction on gifts to his fiancée.

Options (a) and (c) are incorrect because payments of tuition or medical expenses directly to a provider are not considered taxable gifts for gift tax purposes.

Option (b) is incorrect because the donation to the church would be eligible for the charitable deduction for gift tax purposes.

Option (e) is incorrect because John could use the annual exclusion on the gift to his friend.

Gifts

50. c

The taxable gift is calculated as follows:

The gift to the United Way is eligible for the charitable deduction.

Description	Total Gift	Reduction/ Exclusion	Taxable Gift
United Way	$22,000	($22,000)	0
Daughter	$26,000	($12,000)	14,000
Political Organization	$18,000	($18,000)	0
Friend	$6,000	($6,000)	0
Total Taxable Gift			$14,000

The donation to the political organization is not a taxable gift for gift tax purposes.

The gifts to the daughter and friend are both eligible for the annual exclusion.

Gifts of Life Insurance

51. b

The annual exclusion is available when a life insurance policy is gifted, as long as it is a present interest gift. All of the other statements are true.

Gifts

52. b

The annual exclusion is taken before the marital deduction, so the correct answer is $45,000 – $12,000 = $33,000.

Gifts

53. a

Statement 1 is a qualified transfer, thus not a taxable gift. Statement 3 is a gift to a spouse, thus qualifying for the unlimited marital deduction. Statement 2 is a completed gift. The annual exclusion will be allowed because the gift is a present interest, thus the portion of the gift that is taxable is $20,000 ($32,000 – $12,000).

Gifts

54. c

Husband and wife do not have to file a joint income tax return to gift split.

Gifts

55. b

	Total Gifts	Exclusions	Taxable Gifts
Son	$60,000	$24,000	$36,000
Wife	$120,000	$120,000	- 0 -
Church	$40,000	$40,000	- 0 -
Nephew	$30,000	$24,000	$6,000
Mother	$30,000	$24,000	$6,000
Total	$280,000	$232,000	$48,000

Ron's taxable gifts will be $24,000 ($48,000 ÷ 2).

Gifts

56. d

Split-gift election requires the filing of a gift tax return, even when there is no tax due.

Gifts

57. c

The interest-free loan is a gift loan of $10,000 or less, therefore, there is no imputed income, and thus, no gift. Gift = ($50,000 + 35,000 + 8,000) = $93,000.

Gifts

58. b

Taxable gifts are the net of $93,000 – $24,000 annual exclusion for 2007 = $69,000.

Gifts

59. d

Option (a) is a nondeductible donation.

Options (b) and (c) are qualified transfers not subject to gift tax.

Option (d) occurs before the marriage; therefore, it is a gift. The marital deduction is not available for gifts before the marriage.

Gifts

60. b

Tom has made a gift to Sue equal to the increase in the value of Sue's stock. Beneficiary designation of life insurance is not a gift. Assets held in a revocable trust are not a completed gift. These are not taxable.

Gifts

61. b

The loan does not meet any of the exceptions, so interest will be imputed (income to Shannon, expense to Sue). Although, Shannon must impute the interest, she receives no deduction. We do not have enough information to determine if Sue has deductible interest (e.g., she used the proceeds to buy a qualified residence). Options (a), (c), and (d) are correct.

Gifts

62. e

All are gifts subject to gift tax. Statement 4 falls under the gift tax statutes, however, the unlimited marital deduction can be utilized to result in no gift tax owed.

Gifts

63. e

A gift does not occur until the withdrawal by Rachel for her own benefit.

Gifts

64. d

Statement 4, a payment made directly to an individual as a reimbursement for medical expenses, is not a qualified transfer. All the other statements are true.

Gifts

65. b

Calculated as follows: $12,000(annual exclusion) × 8(donees) × 10(years) × 2(gift splitting) = $1,920,000.

Each spouse can gift $12,000 (for 2007) per donee without resulting in a taxable gift. Over the ten-year period they are able to gift a total of $1,920,000.

Gifts

66. d

The gift tax return is always due April 15th (excluding extensions); therefore, Statement 1 is incorrect. All of the others (Statements 2, 3 and 4) are correct descriptions of rules regarding the federal gift tax return.

Gifts

67. e

Statements 1, 2, 3, and 4 are all correct descriptions regarding the federal gift tax return.

Gifts

68. b

Statements 3 and 4 are false. Income from gift property generally will be taxed to the donee for income tax purposes. Generation-skipping transfer taxes do apply to "lifetime" gifts. Statements 1 and 2 are true.

Gifts

69. c

$12,000 annual exclusion (for 2007) × 6 donees × 2 for gift splitting = $144,000.

Basis of Gift

70. b

The donee's gain basis for the property received is generally the same as that of the donor. The donee's loss basis is the lower of either the donor's adjusted basis or the fair market value as of the date of the gift.

Basis of Gift

71. a

The basis of property received pursuant to a divorce is carryover basis. Therefore, Jan had a basis in the property of $35,000 when she gifted the property to Jonathan.

On the date of the gift, the fair market value of the property was less than Jan's basis. Therefore, the double basis rule applies.

The son's gain basis is $35,000. His loss basis is $30,000. Since his selling price of $33,000 is between the gain and the loss basis, there is no recognized gain or loss.

Basis of Gift

72. b

On the date of the gift, the fair market value of the property was less than the donor's basis. Therefore, the double basis rule applies. The daughter's gain basis is $1,800. She has a recognized gain of $200, which is calculated as follows:

Amount realized	$2,000
Basis for stock	(1,800)
Realized gain	$200
Recognized gain	$200

If the daughter had sold the bonds for less than $1,000, she would use her loss basis of $1,000.

Basis of Gift

73. e

On the date of the gift, the fair market value of the property was less than the donor's basis. Therefore, the double basis rule applies.

The gain basis for Ana is $80,000, and the loss basis is $55,000. Because the sales price is within this range, no gain or loss is recognized. The gift tax paid is irrelevant, because there was no unrealized appreciation as of the date of the gift. If FMV is less than the adjusted basis at the date of the gift, no basis adjustment is made for gift tax paid.

Basis of Gift

74. c

Since the property was appreciated property as of the date of the gift, the gift tax paid is allocated to the donee's basis in the property.

James' basis is calculated as follows:

Donor's adjusted basis + [(unrealized appreciation ÷ FMV at date of gift) × gift tax paid].

$105,000 + [($70,000 ÷ $163,000*) × $12,000] = $110,153.

$105,000 + $5,153 = $110,153.

* FMV $175,000 – $12,000 annual exclusion = $163,000.

Basis of Gift

75. b

Since the property was appreciated property as of the date of the gift, the gift tax paid is allocated to the donee's basis in the property.

Tom's basis is calculated as follows:

$42,000 + [(18,000 ÷ 60,000) × 4,500] = $43,350.

$42,000 + $1,350 = $43,350.

Gain and loss basis are equal when FMV exceeds the donor's adjusted basis at the time of the gift.

Basis of Gift

76. c

On the date of the gift, the fair market value of the property was less than the donor's basis. Therefore, the double basis rule applies.

The donee's gain basis for the property received is the same as the donor's basis. The donee's loss basis is the lower of the donor's adjusted basis or the fair market value on the date of the gift. If FMV is less than the adjusted basis at date of gift, no basis adjustment is made for gift tax paid.

Basis and Holding Periods

77. c

The holding period associated with the gain basis rule includes the holding period of the donor. The holding period associated with the loss basis rule begins on the date of the gift.

Basis of Gift

78. d

The basis for depreciation is John's gain basis of $4,800. However, Jack cannot depreciate the asset more than $4,500 (the fair market value).

Gift Tax Filing

79. b

Statements 1 and 2 require filing; Statement 3 is not a completed gift; and Statement 4 is a gift of community property and is less than the annual exclusion.

Net Gift

80. c

A net gift is a technique in which the donee agrees to pay the gift tax. Net gifts are considered part sale and part gift. Therefore, the donor will have taxable income to the extent gift tax paid actually exceeds the donor's adjusted basis.

Gifts

81. b

Donor retains power in Statement 1 and life estate in Statement 2. Both situations will cause inclusion. Prior gifts are not included in the gross estate (unless the gift was a life insurance policy); therefore, Statements 3 and 4 do not cause inclusion.

Annual Exclusion

82. d

A transfer to a GRAT will result in a future interest gift that is not eligible for the annual exclusion.

Transfers to an UGMA account, a qualified tuition plan, a (529 plan), and a 2503(c) trust are all eligible for the annual exclusion.

Annual Exclusion

83. a

A transfer to a QPRT will result in a gift that is not eligible for the annual exclusion. The transfer to a QPRT is a future interest gift.

A transfer to a revocable trust will not be eligible for the annual exclusion because the transfer is not a completed gift.

Transfers to a Crummey Trust and a 2503(b) trust are eligible for the annual exclusion.

Gifts

84. b

The basis to the donee is the donor's carryover basis, less depreciation.

$60,000 (cost) − $10,000 (depreciation) = $50,000.

Gifts

85. c

The property was appreciated property as of the date of the gift. Therefore, gift tax paid by the donor is allocated to the donee's basis in the property.

$50,000 + [(90,000 ÷ 140,000) × 30,000] = $69,286.

$50,000 + $19,286 = $69,286.

Gifts

86. e

$24,000 (for 2007) per child (annual exclusion)	=	$48,000
$1,000,000 (for 2007) per parent (applicable exclusion amount)	=	$2,000,000
Total that can be gifted without paying gift tax		$2,048,000

Gifts

87. a

($250,000 – 48,000 annual exclusion) ÷ 2 = $101,000 each.

Basis of Inherited Property

88. d

The basis for inherited property is the fair market value at the date of death (primary valuation date) or the alternate valuation date. The alternate valuation date was not elected, so Robin's basis for the land is $25,000.

Gift Splitting

89. d

All are correct.

Transfers

90. b

Only Statement 2 is correct. A taxable gift has not occurred because of the marital deduction.

Annual Exclusion

91. e

For 2007, the answer is ($1,000,000 applicable exclusion amount × 2 donors) + 12,000 annual exclusion × 2 donors = $2,024,000.

Note: The applicable exclusion amount for gift tax is $1,000,000 and estate tax is $2,000,000 for 2007.

Gifts

92. b

Only Statement 4 is false. Statements 1, 2, and 3 are true.

Basis of Gift

93. e

The gain basis for Donna is $75,000, and the loss basis is $50,000. Because the sales price is within this range, no gain or loss is recognized. The gift tax paid is irrelevant, because there was no unrealized appreciation as of the date of the gift. If FMV is less than the adjusted basis at date of gift, no basis adjustment is made for gift tax paid.

Gifts

94. b

Gift basis to a donee is the basis of the donor ($100,000). Option (a) is incorrect because Paul would get a step up in basis to the fair market value at his father's death because the death occurred greater than one year from the gift. Option (c) is incorrect because it would be a partial gift of $250,000 and a partial sale of $50,000. Option (d) is incorrect because Paul should not gift property that has declined in value.

Gifts

95. a

The savings account would be the most appropriate gift to her son. The basis of cash is always equal to the fair market value of the cash; therefore, Jack would not have any capital gain issues.

The common stock is not the best possible gift in this situation because Jack would receive a carryover basis of $4,000 in the stock, resulting in a sizable capital gain if sold. Robin would be better off leaving the stock in her estate, so Jack can get a step-up in basis at Robin's death.

The mutual fund is also not the best gift, because the property has declined in value. The $5,000 current loss on the property may be lost to Jack forever due to the double basis rule. Robin would be better off selling the mutual fund and recognizing the loss on her income tax return.

A qualified plan such as a 401(k) cannot be gifted.

Gifts

96. b

The common stock would be the best possible gift in this situation because the charity could sell the stock without paying capital gain tax (the charity is a tax-exempt entity). Robin should transfer low-basis assets to charity.

The savings account would not be the most appropriate gift. The basis of cash is always equal to the fair market value of the cash; therefore, Robin would be better off transferring this high-basis property to her heirs.

The mutual fund is also not the best gift, because the property has declined in value. Robin would be better off selling the mutual fund and recognizing the loss on her income tax return.

A qualified plan such as a 401(k) cannot be gifted.

Gifts

97. b

Option (b) provides income to Mom, and if gift splitting is elected, no gift tax would result.

Option (a) is not appropriate since it does not provide Mom with income.

Option (c) is not appropriate since income is the main objective, and it pays only a small dividend.

Option (d) is inappropriate since a zero-coupon bond provides no cash flow, but would trigger taxable income each year.

Crummey Provisions

98. c

All beneficiaries must be notified of the right to withdraw. There are no catch-up provisions for years where no gift is made to the trust. There can be gift tax consequences to the beneficiaries if the right to withdraw lapses and the amount exceeds the 5%/$5,000 amount.

The Federal Estate Tax

Gross Estate—Inclusion

99. d

The dividends declared to the decedent after death are excluded from the gross estate.

Gross Estate—Inclusion

100. a

An annuity that is payable to the decedent for life, then payable to a beneficiary after the annuitant's death, would be included in the annuitant's gross estate.

Gross Estate—Inclusion

101. d

$750,000 will be included in Laura's gross estate. Property held JTWROS is includible in the decedent's gross estate based on the relative contribution of the cost of the property. Since Laura originally contributed 75% of the purchase price of the tract of land, she will be required to include $750,000 ($1,000,000 × 75%) in her gross estate.

Gross Estate—Inclusion

102. b

Statement 2 is not included in the gross estate because gifts made within three years of death are not included in the gross estate (unless the gift was a life insurance policy). Such gifts are added back to the taxable estate in arriving at the tax base, but the question asked for the gross estate.

Gross Estate—Inclusion

103. b

Statement 1 is correct because the policy was transferred to an ILIT more than three years ago. Therefore, the proceeds would not be included in the decedent's gross estate.

Statement 2 is incorrect because the real estate would be included in the decedent's gross estate.

Statement 3 is correct because a limited (or special) power of appointment over property does not cause inclusion in the gross estate. Only a general power of appointment causes inclusion.

Statement 4 is incorrect because the assets would be included in the gross estate, even though the assets qualify for the marital deduction.

Statement 5 is incorrect because gift tax paid on gifts made within three years of death is included in the gross estate.

Gross Estate—Inclusion

104. e

If a holder possesses a general power of appointment over property, the value of the property will be included in the holder's estate at death. However, a power of appointment will not be considered a general power of appointment if the power is exercisable in favor of the holders' HEALTH, EDUCATION, MAINTENANCE, or SUPPORT (HEMS). Therefore, Option (e) is the only power of appointment that will not be considered a general power of appointment.

Gross Estate—Inclusion

105. b

The gross estate includes any gift tax paid on gifts made within three years of death. The value of the gift would not be included in the gross estate, but would be added to the taxable estate as a post 1976 taxable gift.

Gross Estate—Inclusion

106. c

The dividend is not included in the gross estate because it was declared after Omar's death. All other items are included based on their FMV at the date of death.

$180,000 + $50,000 + $2,500 + $42,000 = $274,500.

Gross Income—Inclusions

107. d

Both assets are includible in the gross estate ($825,000). Property held JTWROS is included in the gross estate to the extent of the decedent's contribution percentage. Art contributed 100% of the purchase price, therefore he has 100% inclusion in his gross estate.

Gross Estate—Inclusions

108. e

All assets are includible in the gross estate. Liabilities are irrelevant to the determination of the gross estate ($670,000). The liabilities are deducted from the gross estate in arriving at the adjusted gross estate.

Gross Estate—Inclusions

109. e

Statement 1 is incorrect because the gift would not be included in the gross estate, even if made within three years of death. Note: Any gift tax paid resulting from the gift would have been included in the gross estate.

Statement 2 is correct. If the grantor dies during the trust term, the entire value (as of the date of death) of the GRAT will be included in the grantor's gross estate.

Statement 3 is correct. The holder of a general power of appointment must include the value of the property in his or her gross estate at death.

Statement 4 is correct. The value of the assets will be included in the gross estate because they were not donated until death. The assets will also be eligible for the charitable deduction.

Gross Estate—Inclusions

110. e

The gift of $30,000 cash is not included in the gross estate because only certain gifts (e.g., life insurance) are subject to the 3-year addback rule. The jointly held property is 50% included, based on relative contribution. The last two items are 100% includible due to incidence of ownership and retained interest, respectively.

Estate Tax Deductions

111. c

Statement 1 is correct. Mary Sue retained a life estate in the gifted property. The gift is an incomplete gift; therefore, the full fair market value of the gift would be included in her gross estate upon death.

Statement 2 is correct. When property is held as JTWROS, the estate inclusion is based on relative contributions to the purchase price of the property. Since Mary Sue purchased the residence, she must include the entire value of the residence in her gross estate.

Statement 3 is incorrect because the gift would not be included in the gross estate, even if made within three years of death. Note: any gift tax paid resulting from the gift would have been included in the gross estate.

Statement 4 is correct because the policy was transferred to an ILIT within three years of death. Therefore, the proceeds would be included in the decedent's gross estate.

Estate Tax Deductions

112. c

Penalties are never deductible under administrative expenses.

Estate Tax Deductions

113. b

Funeral costs are deductions from the gross estate in arriving at the adjusted gross estate.

The marital deduction and the charitable deduction are deductions from the adjusted gross estate in arriving at the taxable estate.

Gift tax paid on prior taxable gifts is a credit against the estate tax.

Estate Tax Deductions

114. c

The charitable deduction is a deduction from the adjusted gross estate in arriving at the taxable estate.

Casualty losses, funeral costs, and administrative costs (attorney fees) are deductions from the gross estate in arriving at the adjusted gross estate.

Prior taxable gifts are ADDED to the taxable estate in arriving at the tax base.

Gross Estate and Deductions

115. d

A bequest is not deductible in computing the taxable estate. Funeral expenses, debts (mortgage, etc.), and administrative expenses (attorney fees, etc.) are all deductible.

Gross Estate and Deductions

116. b

($4,500 + 6,000 + 45,000 + 75,000) = $130,500.

The $1,000 is not deductible on the estate tax return (Form 706). However, it is deductible on the fiduciary income tax return (Form 1041).

Gross Estate and Deductions

117. b

The marital deduction is $375,000 (the amount bequeathed to the widow).

Taxable Estate—General

118. e

The applicable exclusion amount (exemption equivalent) for 2007 is $2,000,000 for estate tax.

Note: In 2007, the applicable exclusion amount is $1,000,000 for gift tax and $2,000,000 for estate tax.

Estates—General

119. c

The marital deduction is not a credit. It is a deduction from the gross estate.

Estates—General

120. a

The calculation is $1,230,800 tax from table − $780,800 applicable credit amount for 2007 = $450,000.

Estates—General

121. e

The applicable credit amount for 2007 is $345,800 for gift tax and $780,800 for estate tax. Gifts are added back to the taxable estate, and then the entire applicable credit amount is taken. Thus, the applicable credit amount for estate tax of $780,800 would be used in the calculation of estate tax.

Estates—General

122. d

The value of the gross estate must be over $2,000,000 (the applicable exclusion amount for 2007), not $1,500,000.

Estates—General

123. d

$2,000,000 is the applicable exclusion amount (exemption equivalency) for 2007.

Estates—Filing

124. c

Nine months is correct.

Estate Tax—Extensions

125. d

Statement 4 is incorrect. The estate tax might cause liquidation of assets, but that is not sufficient for extension of time. Statements 1, 2, and 3 are correct.

Estates

126. c

The applicable credit amount for 2007 is $345,800 for gift tax and $780,800 for estate tax. This is the credit equivalent for $1,000,000 of assets for gift tax and $2,000,000 of assets for estate tax, the applicable exclusion.

Gross Estate

127. e

All of the items listed will reduce the gross estate or the taxable estate.

Marital Deduction

128. d

The marital deduction applies in both community property and separate property states. All of the other statements are correct.

Marital Deduction

129. c

A Qualified Domestic Trust (QDOT) is used when the surviving spouse is not a US citizen. When the surviving spouse is not a US citizen, the marital deduction is not available to the decedent. A QDOT is a trust that is used to defer any estate tax until the noncitizen spouse's death.

Marital Deduction

130. a

Since the policy is owned by Bill, the full amount of insurance proceeds ($2,000,000) must be included in his gross estate. Since his wife is not a US citizen, the proceeds will NOT qualify for the marital deduction.

Community Property Basis

131. d

Both decedent's and survivor's shares of the community property receive a basis adjustment to the fair market value on the date of the decedent's death (or alternate valuation date, if properly elected).

Deathbed Gifts

132. b

If a beneficiary receives property from a decedent that the decedent acquired by gift from the beneficiary within one year of the decedent's death, the donor/beneficiary takes the decedent's basis (which will be the donor's basis). No stepped-up basis is received.

Since Junior died within one year of the gift, and bequeathed the property to the original donor (Tom), Tom's basis in the property will not be stepped up. Therefore, Tom's basis will be $30,000, his original basis in the property.

Deathbed Gifts

133. d

If a beneficiary receives property from a decedent that the decedent acquired by gift from the beneficiary within one year of the decedent's death, the donor/beneficiary takes the decedent's basis (which will be the donor's basis). The property does not get a stepped-up basis.

Therefore, Val's basis is $150,000, and his capital gain is $160,000 ($310,000 – $150,000).

Estate Deductions

134. e

All are deductions from the gross estate to arrive at the taxable estate.

Federal Estate Tax

135. a

Funeral expenses are deducted on the estate tax return (Form 706).

Federal Estate Tax

136. e

IRC Section 303—stock redemption taxed as capital gain.

IRC Section 6166—Election to pay estate tax in installments.

IRC Section 2032—Alternate valuation date.

IRC Section 2032A—Special-use valuation of real estate.

Gross Estate

137. d

The proceeds of the life insurance is pulled back into the estate because it was transferred within three years of date of death. Option (b) is not pulled back in because it is not specifically included in the three-year rule. Option (c) is included in the gross estate but the estate will receive an equivalent charitable deduction.

VALUATION OF ASSETS

Valuation
138. d

The value is the mean [(high + low) ÷ 2] on the date of gift. Since Thursday the market was closed, it is the mean average (high and low) selling price for the 2 days. It is not the closing price. (60 + 56 + 62 + 58.5) ÷ 4 = 59.13. We can average the values since the sale date is equidistant from the valuation date. See Volume I for the treatment of valuation where sale dates are not equal.

Valuation of Securities for an Estate
139. c

The value of the stock reported on the Form 706 will be the mean of the high and the low stock price on the date of death. It is not the stock's closing price for stock on the trading day.

(60 + 58) ÷ 2 = 59.

Valuation of Stock
140. c

$$\frac{(1 \times 28) + (2 \times 25)}{3} = \frac{78}{3} = 26$$

According to the IRS Regulations, the next trading price following the death should be multiplied by the number of trading days between the first trade before the date of death and the date of death (in this case, 1 day). Added to this number is the first trading price before the death multiplied by the number of trading days between the date of death and the first trade following the date of death (in this case, 2 days). This sum should be divided by the sum of trading days between trades.

Buy-Sell Agreements
141. a

If properly structured and executed, buy-sell agreements can be used to establish valuation at DOD and can be either entity or cross-purchase agreements. They are useful for both closely held corporations and partnerships. Publicly traded stock already has an established value. Therefore, a buy-sell agreement is not needed.

Buy-Sell Agreements
142. d

John is the owner and the beneficiary. The face value of the policy is $2 million.

Buy-Sell Agreements
143. a

Each partner's interest is worth $300,000, and the surviving partners are each expected to provide one-half of the purchase price of the deceased's interest.

Buy-Sell Agreements

144. b

The partnership would purchase one policy for each partner's life.

Buy-Sell Agreements

145. a

Section 303 stock redemptions only apply to incorporated businesses.

Buy-Sell Agreements

146. c

Option (a) is incorrect, since a buy-sell agreement need not be funded with life insurance. Option (b) is incorrect, because life insurance premiums are not deductible by the corporation. Option (d) is incorrect, because in a cross-purchase agreement, the partners purchase the life insurance on the lives of the other partners (if the agreement is funded with life insurance).

Life Insurance Uses

147. a

It will be the same total amount as a cross-purchase plan. Premiums are not deductible.

Business Application of Life Insurance

148. c

This is a classic cross-purchase life insurance plan $1,200,000 \div 4 = $300,000 per partner. Each partner purchase $100,000 of life insurance on each other partner for a total of three polices totaling $300,000. Upon the death of a partner, each partner uses the death proceeds in combination with the other partners to purchase the $300,000 share of the deceased partner. This effectively increases each surviving partner's equity in the partnership by the $100,000 he or she paid to the heirs or the estate of the deceased partner.

Buy/Sell Agreements

149. c

Four at the entity level. One for each partner

Buy-Sell Agreement

150. a

Statement 2 is incorrect because the entity approach occurs when the business entity purchases life insurance policies on each owner. Statement 3 is incorrect because the life insurance proceeds are tax exempt.

Estate Valuation

151. c

The note should be included in the gross estate at the remaining principal amount plus accrued interest. If the interest rate is below market or the maturity date is quite distant, these factors may affect the valuation. In addition, if the note is worthless because of the financial condition of the borrower, it may be discounted. However, forgiveness of the debt will not affect the valuation.

Estate Valuation

152. b

Statement 1 is incorrect because Mary will not be eligible for a minority discount, since she owns a controlling (70%) interest in the corporation.

Statement 2 is incorrect because a blockage discount only applies to publicly traded stock, not closely held stock.

Statement 3 is correct. Mary is critical to the operation of the business.

Statement 4 is correct.

Family Limited Partnerships

153. c

The parents/grandparents retain general partnership interests while transferring limited partnership interests to children/grandchildren. A discount for minority interest/marketability can be used in valuation purposes. FLP's are particularly useful with assets expected to appreciate since the post-gift appreciation will be removed from the estate, and any appreciation on interests not gifted will generally receive valuation discounts.

THE MARITAL DEDUCTION

Marital Deduction

154. b

If the spouse is a nonresident, noncitizen, a QDOT must be used to qualify for the marital deduction.

Marital Deduction

155. d

Spouse must actually survive the condition. If the spouse does not survive, the property is not qualified. The present value of the annuity or expected unitrust payment will qualify for the marital deduction. The present value of the remainder interest will qualify for the charitable deduction.

Marital Deduction

156. b

1 is incorrect. A QDOT would be appropriate when the surviving spouse is not a US Citizen. A QTIP trust would be appropriate when there has been a second marriage.

2 is correct. At least one trustee of the QDOT must be a US Citizen.

3 is correct. A QDOT is a type of marital trust. All income must be distributed to the surviving non-US-citizen spouse each year.

4 is incorrect. The QDOT treatment can be elected by the executor.

Marital Deduction

157. d

A is incorrect. Overqualification of the estate occurs when the decedent fails to utilize his/her applicable credit amount. A bypass trust (which does not qualify for the marital deduction) allows the decedent to take advantage of the applicable credit amount.

B is incorrect. A bypass trust does not qualify for the marital deduction.

C is incorrect. Although income CAN be paid to the surviving spouse from the bypass trust, there is no requirement.

E is incorrect. A power of appointment trust, not a bypass trust, provides a general power of appointment over trust property to the surviving spouse.

Marital Deduction

158. a

A is correct. Since the disclaimed property will be transferred to the surviving spouse, it will qualify for the marital deduction.

B is incorrect. Since Oscar cannot direct who the property will pass to, he has not made a taxable gift.

C is incorrect. A disclaimant cannot benefit from disclaimed property.

D is incorrect. Since Oscar disclaimed the property, it will not be included in his gross estate upon his death.

Trusts
159. c

A marital power of appointment trust is a trust in which the surviving spouse is given general power and, therefore, automatically qualifies for the marital deduction as an exception to the terminable interest rule.

Powers of Appointment
160. c

Option (c) is the only correct answer. A springing power may also spring on incapacity. A springing power is any power that becomes valid at a certain occurrence.

CRATs v. CRUTs
161. b

Only CRUTs permit additional contributions after inception.

Charitable Remainder Interest
162. c

Pooled income funds are prohibited from investing in tax-exempt securities.

Charitable Remainder Interest
163. c

Pooled income funds do not allow sprinkling provisions.

Charitable Remainder Interest
164. c

Statements 1 and 2 are correct. Pooled income funds do not allow a term other than the actual life of the beneficiary.

Charitable Remainder Interest
165. e

At the creation, the trust is revocable; therefore, it does not qualify as Options (a), (b), or (c).

Charitable Remainder Interest
166. a

The trust is created when funded, but because of the right to revoke, it does not qualify for any charitable deduction.

Trusts

167. c

Statement 1 is incorrect. A trust has at least 3 parties: the grantor, the trustee, and the beneficiary.

Statement 2 is incorrect. A revocable trust becomes irrevocable at death and assets pass according to the trust instrument, thus avoiding probate.

Statement 3 and 4 are both correct.

Guardianship

168. c

Appointments relative to the "person" are usually called guardianships. A ward is deemed by a court to be incapable of managing his/her personal and/or financial affairs in response to a hearing sought by an interested party. A guardian is appointed by the court to protect the ward according to the state's rules for guardianships. The state government must provide ongoing supervision of a guardianship. The federal government is not a party to guardianships that fall exclusively under state laws.

Charitable Remainder Interest

169. d

Statement 1 is correct. The grantor can act as the trustee of the CRAT, controlling the assets within the trust.

Statement 2 is correct. The grantor can act as the trustee of the CRUT, controlling the assets within the trust.

Statement 3 is incorrect. The charity manages the assets in a pooled income fund.

Trusts

170. c

The B trust should be funded with the applicable exclusion amount in the year of death. For 2007, the applicable exclusion amount is $2,000,000 for estate tax.

Troy puts $2,000,000 in the B trust (applicable exclusion amount) and the balance of his assets in the A trust.

GRAT

171. c

Statement 1 is incorrect. A taxable gift will occur when the GRAT is established, not at the end of the GRAT term.

Statement 2 is incorrect. If the grantor dies during the trust term, the entire value of the trust assets is included in the grantor's gross estate, not a pro rata portion.

Statement 3 is correct. The trust is a grantor trust; therefore, all income will be taxed to the grantor.

Statement 4 is correct. If the grantor survives the trust term, none of the trust assets will be included in the grantor's gross estate. However, the taxable gift (that occurs when the trust is established) must be added back to the taxable estate as a prior taxable gift.

GRAT
172. a

Statement 1 is correct. A taxable gift will occur when the GRAT is established.

Statement 2 is incorrect. The gift will not be eligible for the annual exclusion, since it is not a present interest gift.

Statement 3 is incorrect. A GRUT will result in a higher annuity payment to the grantor each year (if the assets are appreciating in value). For estate planning purposes, the grantor would want to remove assets from the estate. Therefore, a GRUT would be inappropriate because it would bring a higher amount into the grantor's estate each year than the GRAT.

Statement 4 is correct. If the grantor survives the trust term, the beneficiaries will not receive a step up in basis of the trust assets. If the grantor died during the trust term, the trust assets would be included in the grantor's gross estate; therefore, the heirs would receive a step up in basis.

QPRT
173. c

Statement 1 is correct. If the grantor dies during the trust term, the entire value of trust property is included in the grantor's gross estate.

Statement 2 is incorrect. At the end of the trust term, ownership of the house will be transferred to the beneficiaries.

Statement 3 is correct. The taxable gift will be based on the fair market value of the house (on the date of transfer) less the present value of the right to live in the house.

Statement 4 is incorrect. Vacation homes are often transferred to QPRTs.

Charitable Remainder Trusts
174. b

Option (b) is correct. The grantor will receive an immediate income tax deduction based on the present value of the remainder interest to charity.

Option (a) is incorrect because the annuity payment received from a CRAT is fixed.

Option (c) is incorrect because the payment received by the grantor will be taxed to the grantor, based on an allocation of trust income and capital gains.

Option (d) is incorrect because a CRAT and CRUT cannot have a trust term longer than 20 years.

Charitable Trusts
175. c

Option (c) is correct. A CLAT provides a fixed annuity to charity for the duration of the trust.

Option (a) is incorrect because a CLUT provides a periodic payment to CHARITY, not the grantor.

Option (b) is incorrect because the trust does not qualify as a CRAT. A valid CRAT must have a payout rate of at least 5%. The payout rate of this trust is only 4% ($40,000 annuity divided by $1,000,000 initial fair market value of property transferred).

Option (d) is incorrect because CRATs and CRUTs are ideal for highly appreciated property. The trust is tax exempt and can sell the property without recognizing capital gain.

Taxable Gift

176. d

A SCIN will not result in a taxable gift, since a SCIN is a sale of property between family members.

Estate Reduction Techniques

177. d

Statement 1 is correct because limited partnership interests are transferred over time to donees to remove the value of the property (typically a closely held business) from the donor's gross estate.

Statement 2 is incorrect because Totten trusts are used to avoid probate, not to lower the gross estate.

Statement 3 is correct, because the value of the residence will be excluded from the gross estate, as long as the grantor survives the trust term.

Statement 4 is correct, because the value of the insurance will be excluded from the gross estate, as long as the transferor survives at least three years.

Estate Reduction Techniques

178. a

Statement 1 is correct, because the value of the GRAT property will be excluded from the gross estate, as long as the grantor survives the trust term.

Statement 2 is incorrect, because a revocable living trust is designed to avoid probate, not to lower the gross estate.

Statement 3 is correct. By gifting during his/her lifetime, a donor removes the property from his or her estate.

Statement 4 is incorrect. POD accounts are designed to avoid probate, not lower the estate.

OTHER LIFETIME TRANSFERS

Installment Notes (SCINS)

179. e

All are correct. The present value of a self-canceling installment note balance is not included in the gross estate of the seller (decedent) since the value at death is zero.

Bargain Sale

180. b

Statement 1 is correct. The difference between the fair market value of the asset and the consideration received is considered a gift.

Statement 2 is incorrect. The gift portion will be eligible for the annual exclusion if it is a completed, present interest gift.

Statement 3 is incorrect, as bargain sale transactions are typically between family members.

Statement 4 is correct.

181. c

A is incorrect. Limited partnership interests are transferred to the junior family members and may qualify for valuation discounts. The general partnership interest, which is retained by the senior family member, is not entitled to a valuation discount.

B is incorrect. The transfer of the limited partnership interests to the junior family members is considered a present interest gift and is eligible for the gift tax annual exclusion.

D is incorrect. One advantage of a family limited partnership is the senior family member's ability to retain control of the business, while removing most of the value of the business from his or her gross estate.

182. b

Stan will have a taxable gain of $40,000 ($90,000 sales price less $50,000 basis).

A is incorrect. A bargain sale is a part sale and part gift. After the transaction has been completed, the property will be removed from the donor/seller's gross estate, regardless of when death occurs.

C is incorrect. The gift portion of the bargain sale is eligible for the gift tax annual exclusion.

D is incorrect. Stan has made a $50,000 gift to Marvin ($140,000 value less $90,000 sales price).

183. b

Rosanne's total gain from the sale is $400,000 ($500,000 – $100,000).

She received a 20% payment this year ($100,000 / $500,000), and therefore must recognize a gain of $80,000, which is 20% of the entire gain.

184. c

A is incorrect. Installment notes can be secured.

B is incorrect. The seller receives payments for the term of the note, not for his or her life expectancy.

D is incorrect. Since the property was sold, the three-year gross estate inclusion rule does not apply.

185. d

Since the annuity payment was determined based upon IRS life expectancy tables and interest rates, there will be no gift tax consequences.

A is incorrect. Under a private annuity, the payments cease after the death of the seller.

B is incorrect. Interest expense relating to the payment of the private annuity payments is non-deductible.

C is incorrect. The annuity payments received are taxed as part capital gain, part ordinary income, and part return of capital.

186. c

A is incorrect. A bargain sale will result in a gift for gift tax purposes.

B is incorrect. If Wendy dies during the note term, the present value of the future note payments will be included in her gross estate.

D is incorrect. A private annuity is an unsecured transaction.

LIFE INSURANCE IN ESTATE PLANNING

Life Insurance

187. c

Always includible in the gross estate.

Life Insurance

188. b

If the insured is permitted to borrow against the policy, the insured will possess "incidents of ownership" in the policy. This will cause inclusion of the policy proceeds in the gross estate of the insured at death.

Life Insurance

189. d

The policy is owned by John and not included in Jack's estate.

Life Insurance

190. b

Statements 1 and 2 are incorrect. John is terminally ill, and as a result, the proceeds from the viatical settlement are excluded from his gross income for income tax purposes regardless of when he actually dies.

Statement 3 is incorrect. The three-year inclusion rule of life insurance policies does not apply to viatical settlements.

Statement 4 is correct.

THE GENERATION-SKIPPING TRANSFER TAX (GSTT)

GSTT

191. c

The GSTT is a separate tax in addition to the gift and estate tax and applies to transferees at least two generations younger than the transferor.

GSTT

192. c

No exception for Option (c) because he died after January 1, 1987. In order to be exempted from GSTT, it must meet one of the following:

1. Trusts that were irrevocable prior to September 25, 1985.

2. Wills that could not be changed after 1987 (capacity).

GSTT

193. d

All are subject to GSTT rules.

GSTT

194. b

There are three younger generations, including the son, granddaughter, and great-grandson.

Main generation—James and Carol (this requires the knowledge that Carol, even though much younger, is placed in the same generation as James because they are married).

1st younger generation—The son, Bill, and nephew, Bob. He is one generation below his father because lineal descendents are placed in the generation that they fall into based on birth and not age. Bob is also a lineal descendent even though he is James' nephew.

2nd younger generation—Allison. Allison is in this generation because she is a lineal descendent (following the same rules as Bill).

3rd younger generation—Michael. Michael is in this generation because he is a lineal descendent (following the same rules as Bill and Allison).

GSTT

195. b

The GSTT is only levied once at Bob's death (taxable termination).

GSTT

196. a

There are no skip persons in this example. In this case, the unrelated person must be 37½ years younger than the transferor to be a skip person.

GSTT

197. c

GSTT aggregate, lifetime exemption for 2007 is $2,000,000.

GSTT

198. e

All are subject to GSTT.

GSTT

199. b

John is not a skip person because of the predeceased parent rule. Hazel is not a skip person because her marriage to Bill's son places her in the son's generation.

GSTT

200. e

All statements are correct. In addition, there is the predeceased parent rule, which allows a generation to be skipped from grandparent to grandchild if the parent is deceased. The exception also extends to collateral heirs if a decedent has no living lineal descendents.

Life Insurance

201. c

The life insurance proceeds would be a gift to Lexie. The donor of a gift is liable for the gift tax. At the death of Connie, Glennon owned the policy and could have named himself the beneficiary. In effect, he gave the insurance proceeds to Lexie.

GSTT

202. d

The grandchild is a minor. Set up an irrevocable trust and use the GSTT lifetime exemption against premiums.

GSTT

203. d

Option (a) is covered by his annual exclusion. Option (b) is not a skip person. Option (c) is an excluded transfer. Option (d) is to a skip person because a nonlineal descendant is a skip person if more than 37½ years younger than the transferor.

SPECIAL PROVISIONS FOR SMALL BUSINESS, FARMS, ILLIQUID ESTATES

Special Use Valuation

204. c

To qualify for special use valuation, the value of the property must be at least 50% of the decedent's adjusted gross estate. Since the adjusted gross estate is $2,000,000, the value of the farm must be at least $1,000,000.

Closely-Held Stock

205. c

The estate does qualify for Section 303 because the value of the closely-held stock exceeds 35% of the adjusted gross estate.

Only redemptions up to $120,000 ($50,000 funeral expenses plus $70,000 estate taxes) will qualify for disposition of an asset (capital gain) treatment, because under Section 303, redemption proceeds can't exceed death taxes plus deductible funeral and administrative expenses.

Section 6166

206. d

If the heirs dispose of the closely-held business interest, the deferred tax will be immediately payable.

A is incorrect. The value of the closely-held business must comprise at least 35% of the decedent's adjusted gross estate.

B is incorrect. The estate tax is delayed for five years, but is then payable in 10 equal annual installments.

C is incorrect. The interest is calculated based on the Federal underpayment rate.

POSTMORTEM PLANNING

Postmortem Planning

207. d

To utilize the alternate valuation date there are two requirements:

1. Must reduce the estate tax liability.
2. Must reduce the gross estate.

Postmortem Planning

208. b

($325,000 + 1,850,000 + 90,000 + 80,000) = $2,345,000.

There are three rules applicable to the valuation of assets assuming that the alternate valuation date is properly elected. Rule 1—generally, all assets are valued on the alternate valuation date. Rule 2—(1st exception) any asset disposed of between the date of death and the alternate valuation date is valued on the date of disposition. Rule 3—(2nd exception) all wasting assets (leases, installment notes, annuities, and patents), which decline in value due to time as opposed to market conditions, are always valued on the date of death.

Postmortem Planning

209. c

Executor elects where to deduct administrative expenses (on estate tax return or estate's income tax return), and no double deduction is allowed.

Postmortem Planning

210. c

Since the trust is revocable, the assets will be included in the grantor's gross estate. This will result in a step to FMV basis and no capital gains tax. The new basis can be greater or less than the decedent's basis depending on the FMV at date of death.

Alternative Valuation Date

211. b

The alternate valuation date is 6 months from the date of death.

Estates—Liquidity

212. d

Statement 4 is wrong because of the less than or equal to 100 shareholders statement. The rule is properly expressed in Statement 3. S corporation can qualify if less than or equal to ≤ 45 shareholders or if value in gross estates is 20% or more of the total value of the voting stock.

Estate Taxation

213. d

The election must be made on Form 706 to be valid. Therefore, Statement 3 is incorrect. Statements 1, 2, and 4 are correct.

Disclaimers

214. e

All are correct.

Installments

215. c

Statements 2 and 3 are correct. Statement 1 is incorrect. (1) The 6166 election permits installment payments of both FET (Federal Estate Tax) and GSTT (Generation-Skipping Transfer Tax) and (2) the installment payment period can be up to 14 years--not 12. Statement 4 is incorrect, because interests in corporations, partnerships, and sole proprietorships may be aggregated in order to arrive at the 35% requirement if the decedent's interest has <u>over 20% of each</u> business.

Postmortem Elections

216. b

The closely held corporation is 38.8% of the AGE. Section 2032A cannot be elected because it requires the value of the closely held corporation to be at least 50% of the AGE. Section 6166 requires the closely held corporation interest to be more than 35% of the AGE, so it is available. Section 303 would not apply since the company is not a corporation. Section 2057 was repealed in 2004.

Income in Respect of a Decedent

217. e

All are correct.

Postmortem Elections

218. b

The farm would be valued at the current-use value of $1,400,000. Recapture will occur if Jeb sells the farm <u>or</u> if the farm discontinues its qualified use, so Option (b) is incorrect. Any additional estate liability because of recapture is a liability of Jeb.

Special-Use Valuation

219. c

Special-use valuation requires that either the decedent or a family member must have owned and used the property as a farm or business for at least FIVE of the EIGHT years immediately prior to the decedent's death.

QTIP

220. c

The residence will qualify as QTIP property if the executor makes the QTIP election on Steve's estate tax return. The surviving spouse does not need to be given a general power of appointment, and the residence does not need to be left a trust.

ESTATE TAX REDUCTIONS TECHNIQUES

Estate Tax Reduction

221. a

1 is incorrect. Over qualifying the estate occurs when a decedent uses too much marital deduction, thus wasting the decedent's applicable credit amount.

2 is incorrect. A totten Trust (POD designation) will be effective in reducing the probate estate, but is not an effective estate tax reduction technique.

3 is correct. A GRAT would be an effective way to reduce a decedent's gross estate. If the grantor survives the trust term, the GRAT assets are excluded from the decedent's gross estate.

4 is incorrect. A revocable living trust will be effective in reducing the probate estate, but is not an effective estate tax reduction technique.

Estate Tax Reduction

222. d

1 is correct. A Crummey trust will allow a future interest gift to qualify for the annual exclusion. The trust assets will be excluded from the grantor's gross estate.

2 is incorrect. A QTIP trust (not a QDOT) would be appropriate when there are children from a previous marriage.

3 is correct. If the grantor survives the trust term, the residence will be excluded from the grantor's estate.

4 is correct. Tuition payments made directly to the institution are not considered gifts for gift tax purposes.

COMMON ESTATE PLANNING MISTAKES

Estate Planning Mistakes
223. d

1 is correct. Many estates fail to have a power of attorney (one for property and one for health care) or living will.

2. is correct. wills should be updated periodically for changing circumstances (marriage, divorce, children, etc.)

3 is correct. If the decedent-insured possesses incidents of ownership in a life insurance policy, the entire death benefit will be included in the gross estate.

4 is incorrect. Intestacy laws pass property of decedents who die without a Will. The intestacy laws often do not pass the property to the desired heirs.

Estate Planning Mistakes
224. c

1 is correct. The ABC Company stock, as well as the life insurance (his estate is beneficiary) will both be included in his probate estate.

2 is correct. Steven has no estate planning documents other than an outdated Will. He should consider a power of attorney and living will.

3 is incorrect. A QTIP trust is used to take advantage of the marital deduction, and provide assets to children of a prior marriage. Steven is not currently married, and therefore could not benefit from a marital deduction. A QTIP trust is not appropriate.

4 is incorrect. A buy-sell agreement is typically used to transfer a closely-held business. ABC Company is a publicly-traded company, and therefore, a buy-sell agreement is probably not necessary.

5 is correct. The only asset left directly to Becky is the $20,000 savings account.

225. b

1 is correct. Since Sonny has left everything to his surviving spouse, the marital deduction will reduce Sonny's taxable estate to zero.

2 is correct. Since Sonny will receive the marital deduction at his death, the assets passed to Bonny must be included in her gross estate upon her subsequent death.

3 is correct. Because Sonny's taxable estate is zero, he will have failed to utilize his applicable credit amount for estate tax purposes.

4 is incorrect. By transferring too much to his surviving spouse, Sonny has failed to utilize his applicable credit amount for estate tax purposes. He has overqualified, not underqualified, his estate.

226. d

The bypass trust will not qualify for the estate tax marital deduction. At Steven's death his estate will owe estate tax because the entire $3,000,000 will be included in his taxable estate. Steven has failed to take advantage of the marital deduction, and has therefore underqualified his estate.

A is incorrect. By bequeathing all of his assets to a general power of appointment trust, he will be qualifying all of his assets for the marital deduction, thereby overqualifying (not underqualifying) his estate.

B is incorrect. By bequeathing all of his assets to his surviving spouse and a QTIP trust, he will be qualifying all of his assets for the marital deduction, thereby overqualifying (not underqualifying) his estate.

C is incorrect. By bequeathing all of his assets to a QTIP trust, he will be qualifying all of his assets for the marital deduction, thereby overqualifying (not underqualifying) his estate.

227. c

A is incorrect. If overqualification occurs, the decedent has wasted some of his or her applicable credit amount.

B is incorrect. If underqualification occurs, more property could have been left to the surviving spouse tax-free than was actually left to the surviving spouse by the decedent.

D is incorrect. If a transfer to a surviving spouse qualifies for the marital deduction, the assets will be included in the surviving spouse's gross estate upon his or her subsequent death.